Welfare Reform

The Next Act

Edited by Alan Weil
and Kenneth Finegold

Also of interest from the Urban Institute Press:

Welfare Reform
The Next Act

THE URBAN INSTITUTE PRESS
Washington, D.C.

THE URBAN INSTITUTE PRESS
2100 M Street, N.W.
Washington, DC 20037

Library of Congress Cataloging in Publication Data

Welfare reform : the next act / Alan Weil and Kenneth Finegold, editors.
    p. cm.
Includes bibliographical references and index.
  ISBN 0-87766-710-1 (pbk. : alk. paper)
   1. Welfare recipients—United States. 2. Welfare recepients—Employment—
United States. 3. Temporary Assistance for Needy Families (Program) 4. Public
welfare administration—United States. I. Weil, Alan. II. Finegold, Kenneth, 1957–
  HV95 .W462 2002
  361.6'8'0973—dc21

2002002495

Printed in the United States of America

THE URBAN INSTITUTE is a nonprofit policy research and educational organization established in Washington, D.C., in 1968. Its staff investigates the social, economic, and governance problems confronting the nation and evaluates the public and private means to alleviate them. The Institute disseminates its research findings through publications, its Web site, the media, seminars, and forums.

Through work that ranges from broad conceptual studies to administrative and technical assistance, Institute researchers contribute to the stock of knowledge available to guide decisionmaking in the public interest.

Conclusions or opinions expressed in Institute publications are those of the authors and do not necessarily reflect the views of officers or trustees of the Institute, advisory groups, or any organizations that provide financial support to the Institute.

Contents

Acknowledgments

This book is a product of the *Assessing the New Federalism* (ANF) project, and would not have been possible without the many foundations supporting ANF. The project has received funding from The Annie E. Casey Foundation, The Robert Wood Johnson Foundation, the W.K. Kellogg Foundation, The Ford Foundation, The Henry J. Kaiser Family Foundation, the David and Lucile Packard Foundation, The John D. and Catherine T. MacArthur Foundation, the Charles Stewart Mott Foundation, The McKnight Foundation, The Commonwealth Fund, the Stuart Foundation, the Weingart Foundation, The Fund for New Jersey, The Lynde and Harry Bradley Foundation, the Joyce Foundation, and the Rockefeller Foundation.

We thank Robert Reischauer, Kathleen Courrier, Harold Leibovitz, and Susan Brown for their comments on the book outline and early drafts of the book. We appreciate the contributions made by the Urban Institute Press, especially Frederick Custer, its director, and Blair Potter and Elizabeth Miranda, who edited the chapters. Olga Popovic, Alyssa Wigton, and Sarah Staveteig, three members of the *Assessing the New Federalism* project staff, helped make sure all the pieces were in place and that the book was always moving forward.

The ANF project has involved more Urban Institute researchers than can be mentioned here. We are grateful for the contributions they have made to the project and to our understanding of social policy. In addition to the authors of the many ANF briefs, papers, and articles cited in the book, we particularly appreciate those who worked on the National Survey of America's Families and the case studies that form the basis for much of our knowledge of welfare reform.

Introduction

Alan Weil and Kenneth Finegold

J ust one year after President Bill Clinton signed sweeping welfare reform legislation into law, he declared, "I think it's fair to say the debate is over. We now know that welfare reform works" (Harris and Havemann 1997). Other public officials quickly joined the chorus, and in their platforms for the 2000 presidential campaign, both major parties heralded welfare reform as a success. Congressional debate over federal welfare policy since reforms were enacted in August 1996 has been limited to discussion of the law's immigrant provisions and the level of funding for the program. Other important features of the law have gone largely unquestioned.

With five years of research on welfare to draw upon, it is time to take a dispassionate look at welfare reform. A determination of success implies well-defined goals and strong evidence that policy is furthering those goals. Given the political compromises that generated the legislation, it is not surprising that the goals expressed in welfare reform are somewhat ambiguous. Progress toward some goals is apparent, but to attribute all good news to welfare policy is to deny the importance of external factors, such as the unprecedented strength of the economy during welfare's early years, or to ignore that one of the central features of reform—time limits—has barely begun to have an effect. A review of the evidence provides a basis for both optimism and concern.

The substantial policy shift embodied in welfare reform followed years of accumulated grievances surrounding the old Aid to Families with Dependent Children (AFDC) program, which was established in 1935 as part of the Social Security Act. Yet, lurking behind broad agreement that the old welfare system had failed were highly divergent views about the reasons for the failure. Had welfare failed because it encouraged births outside of marriage, allowed single mothers to stay at home while most other mothers were out working, and created multiple generations of dependence? Because low benefits and withdrawal of those benefits as soon as recipients started working kept families trapped in poverty? Or because too many decisions best made at the state or local level were centralized in Washington?

Despite numerous perspectives on why the old system failed, early claims of reform's success were based primarily on a single factor: the rapid decline in the number of people receiving assistance. Although this simple metric is appealing, it does not capture the many possible dimensions of welfare's success or failure. Declining caseloads may or may not reflect declining need, hardship, or even eligibility for assistance, if those who are eligible are deterred or discouraged from applying. Caseload statistics say nothing about the long-term employment prospects of those who leave welfare, the well-being of children in the families welfare is intended to assist, or changes in family structure.

Since 1996, the Urban Institute's *Assessing the New Federalism* (ANF) project has gathered and analyzed data on policy choices made by states and on the resulting well-being of children and adults, particularly those in low-income families. The project reaches far beyond welfare policy, but many of the issues it covers speak directly to the future of welfare. This book draws heavily, although not exclusively, upon data sources developed as part of ANF (see appendix).

Congress must reauthorize funding for Temporary Assistance for Needy Families (TANF), child care subsidies, food stamps, and other programs for low-income families before October 1, 2002. Reauthorization offers a focal point for discussing welfare policy. The issues discussed in this book, however, will remain on the national agenda after that debate has come to an end.

This introduction provides an overview of the history of welfare reform, what research has revealed about the welfare system as it exists today, and how families are faring under the new system. It then presents five recommendations for improving welfare policy. Each of the chapters that follows examines an aspect of welfare reform and discusses policy implications in greater detail. Chapter 1 provides an overview of how states and localities have implemented welfare reforms. Chapters 2 and 3, on work and family structure, focus on concerns emphasized in the federal welfare reform legislation; chapters 4 and 5, on income and child well-being, focus on emerging concerns. The next three chapters examine programs to support work. Chapter 6 discusses employment programs, and chapters 7 and 8 discuss child care and health insurance programs. Chapters 9, 10, and 11 look at three particularly vulnerable subgroups: the "hard-to-serve," immigrants, and racial and ethnic minorities. Chapter 12 addresses the fiscal issues in TANF reauthorization and in the larger continuing debates about welfare policy.

A Brief History of Welfare Reform

Throughout the twentieth century, U.S. welfare policy was caught between two competing values: the desire to help those who could not help themselves, and the concern that charity would create dependency. AFDC was an entitlement program—that is, families that met state and federal criteria for cash assistance had a legal right to receive it. Within parameters set by Congress, states administered the program, set eligibility criteria, and shared costs with the federal government.

As more mothers began to work outside the home, AFDC became increasingly unpopular, and was seen as a source of financial support that allowed poor single mothers to stay at home but was not available to middle-class or married mothers. Moreover, some observers suggested that welfare, which was targeted to unmarried mothers, contributed to increases in divorce and in births outside of marriage.

Bipartisan dissatisfaction with AFDC led to periodic efforts to reform welfare by shifting its emphasis toward putting mothers to work. The Family Support Act of 1988 increased the amount of income welfare recipients could earn without losing benefits, provided transitional Medicaid and child care for those who left welfare for work, permitted states to require that teenage mothers live with their parents or other adults, strengthened child support enforcement and establishment of paternity, and expanded AFDC eligibility for two-parent families (Weaver 2000). The act also established a new work program, Job Opportunities and Basic Skills Training (JOBS), and made child care an entitlement for families participating in JOBS. In 1996, 16 percent of adult AFDC recipients were participating in JOBS (Bell with Douglas 2000).

Between 1986 and 1996, many states received waivers from the Reagan, Bush, and Clinton administrations for welfare reform experiments (Zedlewski, Holcomb, and Duke 1998; Office of the Assistant Secretary for Planning and Evaluation 1997; Teles 1998). Waivers expanded earnings disregards, transitional assistance, and two-parent eligibility, but they also included time limits, tougher work requirements, and family caps on benefits (which prohibited families already on cash assistance from receiving increased grants when additional children were born).

Welfare reform, embodied in the Personal Responsibility and Work Opportunity Reconciliation Act of 1996 (PRWORA), represents a major shift in policy in several areas (see box 1 for key provisions of the law).[1] The law abolished open-ended funding of welfare and replaced it with

---

Box 1. Key Provisions of the Personal Responsibility and Work Opportunity Reconciliation Act of 1996 (PRWORA)

Temporary Assistance for Needy Families (TANF)

- *Purposes.* Increase state flexibility; keep children in own homes or homes of other relatives; end parental dependence on government benefits by promoting job preparation, work, and marriage; discourage pregnancies outside of marriage; encourage formation and maintenance of two-parent families.
- *Block grant.* Replaced Aid to Families with Dependent Children (AFDC) entitlement with TANF block grant. Allocation to states based primarily on historic spending levels.
- *Time limits.* Federal lifetime limit of 60 months on cash assistance. Period may be shorter at state option. States may exempt up to 20 percent of recipients, and may continue benefits beyond federal time limits with own funds.
- *Work requirements.* Recipients required to work after two years of cash assistance. States must meet targets for percentage of cases in work activities, or face financial penalties.
- *Family cap.* States may deny additional benefits when children are born to families already receiving cash assistance.

Immigrants

- Restricted eligibility of noncitizen immigrants for Supplemental Security Income, food stamps.
- States may restrict eligibility of noncitizen immigrants for TANF and Medicaid.

Child Care

- Consolidated four existing programs into Child Care and Development Fund block grant.
- Eliminated the entitlements for child care for current and former welfare recipients.
- Allowed states to transfer TANF funds into CCDF, or to spend directly for child care.
- Increased CCDF funding levels.

Medicaid

- Delinked Medicaid eligibility from welfare.
- Froze state eligibility standards as of the date law was enacted.
- States may cover all members of a family using a slingle, higher income eligibility standard.

Child Support

- States required to strengthen child support enforcement.
- Eliminated requirement that states disregard first $50 of monthly child support in calculating TANF eligibility and benefits.

Food Stamps

- Reduced maximum benefit and limited deductions.
- Able-bodied adults without dependents limited to three months of benefits if not working at least 20 hours per week.

Supplemental Security Income

- Narrower standards of disability for children.
- More frequent review of disability status for children and adults.

the TANF block grant, which provides each state with a fixed amount of money as long as the state meets certain conditions. It also restricted eligibility for TANF and other means-tested programs, required states to strengthen child support laws, and delinked Medicaid eligibility from welfare.

The Reformed Welfare System

The most prominent features of the new welfare system are the time limit on benefits and the work activity requirement. An adult cannot receive federal welfare funds for more than five years over the course of his or her lifetime. In addition, federal law requires states to cut off assistance after two years of continuous receipt if the adult is not participating in a work activity. Most states require participation in such an activity in even less time.

States are free to impose additional conditions on receiving assistance. Some states have gone beyond the basic requirement of participation in job search or job training activities to require that children remain in school or that parents take classes in parenting or money management. Federal law requires states to reduce benefits for families that fail to follow program rules, and 31 states impose full family sanctions that eliminate benefits entirely in cases of noncompliance. States may refuse to accept or process a TANF application until the applicant has attempted to secure a job or assistance from another source, or they may offer one-time payments to help the family meet a specific need rather than provide ongoing assistance.

Welfare policy now focuses on work. Whereas states had a mixture of approaches to encouraging or assisting recipients to move to work before PRWORA was enacted, most of them have now adopted some variant of a work-first approach (chapter 1). This move was spurred by increasingly stringent federal standards for the share of a state's welfare recipients that must participate in federally defined work activities. More states are supplementing their work-first requirements with employment and training programs (chapter 6) or with programs to reduce barriers to work among the hard-to-employ (chapter 9). Still, the primary emphasis of welfare policy is moving recipients into paid work as quickly as possible.

Consistent with the focus on work are efforts to make work pay. Employed current and former welfare recipients are typically paid low wages and receive few benefits from their employers. New state and federal policies supplement low wages to such an extent that even a minimum-wage job, worked full-time, can form the foundation for lifting a family of three slightly above the poverty level—if the family receives all the government benefits for which it is eligible. Chief among state efforts to make work pay is the trend toward higher earnings disregards, which allow recipients to keep more of their benefits as they enter the paid labor force. A few states use TANF funds to support state-level earned income tax credits. By far the largest contribution to making work pay is the federal earned income tax credit (EITC). In addition, the federal minimum hourly wage rose from $4.25 to $5.15 in September 1997.

Recent policy changes have recast low-income programs including child care subsidies (chapter 7), health insurance programs (chapter 8), and food stamps as work supports to move and keep people off welfare. Direct federal funding for child care has increased, and states are designating some of their TANF funds for child care, as well as spending their own money on it. Similarly, the new State Children's Health Insurance Program (SCHIP) has expanded federal and state funding for publicly provided health insurance. These newly expanded work support programs combine with older work supports, such as unemployment insurance and family and medical leave.

In conjunction with supporting work, new policies deny assistance to people who do not work. The work requirements in TANF are stricter than those in AFDC, fewer recipients are exempted from them, and failure to comply with them can lead to financial sanctions. In addition, PRWORA limits nonworking able-bodied adults without dependents to three months of food stamps (Bell and Gallagher 2001), and state General Assistance programs have declined (Gallagher et al. 1999; Gallagher 1999).

States have done less to achieve welfare reform's family structure goals—encouraging marriage, reducing the number of births outside of marriage, and keeping children in their own homes or the homes of relatives—than they have to promote work (chapter 3). Many states make TANF available on a fairly equal basis to families with single and with married parents, which reverses a longstanding bias in the welfare system against serving two-parent families and thereby possibly discouraging marriage. Twenty states have adopted family caps that deny additional benefits to adults who have children while they are on welfare. Another PRWORA provision strengthens the child support system, with the federal government developing a data registry to facilitate collections from working noncustodial parents, states being required to adopt new child support enforcement tools, and individual welfare recipients facing sanctions if they fail to cooperate with the child support system.

A New Federalism

Welfare reform changed more than welfare policy; it changed the relationships among national, state, and local governments and among public and private organizations at each of these levels. State flexibility was deliberately expanded under welfare reform. While the size of the cash grant was left to state discretion under AFDC, states may now choose whom they will assist, what requirements they will impose upon those who receive aid, and what non-cash supports those families will receive.

With the expansion of state flexibility to set welfare policy has come greater diversity in state approaches to welfare. States have made different choices about how much to focus on getting welfare recipients into the labor force quickly, helping people overcome barriers to getting a job, or providing postemployment services so people can keep their jobs; who should get child care subsidies and how much they should receive; how to encourage marriage and reduce childbearing outside of marriage; whether to use state funds to replace benefits for noncitizen immigrants rendered ineligible for welfare by PRWORA; and how much of their TANF grants to spend, save, or transfer. States have also made different decisions about which of these choices should be made at the local level and thus about the extent to which flexibility and diversity should be increased within as well as among states.

Despite its stated purpose of increasing state flexibility, PRWORA also imposed new rules on states that reduce flexibility. Most significant are the federal time limits and work participation requirements. These provisions make it more difficult for states to adopt strategies that blend welfare receipt with work, training, or other activities. States also face new requirements with respect to child support enforcement and treatment of noncitizen immigrants.

Encouraging a variety of approaches to welfare has several benefits. It can lead states to experiment with welfare policies to determine what works best. Flexibility also enables states to tailor their policies to the specific needs of their populations. And state-specific welfare policies can better reflect local values and preferences (Weil 2002).

This diversity creates problems as well. Two children in identical situations in different states now live with very different realities. One may have household resources above the poverty level, stable and high-quality child care, and health insurance, while the other may have none of these. Differences in state policies existed before PRWORA, but the potential for extreme variation is now greater.

The end of the AFDC entitlement had important fiscal implications for states. An entitlement program expands or contracts with the number of people on welfare, but a block grant gives each state a fixed annual amount. The abolition of the entitlement may have also curtailed the federal courts' ability to expand benefits and eligibility, as they had done under AFDC and other social programs (U.S. Congress 1996, 267; Melnick 1994).

Evolution, Not Revolution

Some aspects of welfare policy shifted dramatically when PRWORA was enacted, but the underlying structure and administration of the welfare system have changed relatively little since 1996. States and localities quickly implemented the new program rules, especially time limits and work requirements. With their new funds, states expanded existing programs such as welfare-to-work and child care. Some states forged new links to community-based service providers, created "one-stop shops," or changed caseworker roles to emphasize job counseling over application processing. However, every state continues to operate a system of cash assistance with rule-based determination of eligibility as its administrative core. No state has replaced cash assistance with vouchers, a negative income tax, or a program of orphanage construction. Every state continues to operate TANF as if it were an entitlement, without the waiting lists that characterize other assistance programs such as housing and child care. For that matter, no state has declined to accept its federal TANF grant.

Once states implemented time limits and work requirements, they could make as few or as many changes in their welfare policies as they chose, so long as they maintained their own spending at the required levels. States had little difficulty meeting federal work participation targets as caseloads declined and the economy was strong. While Wisconsin and a few other states and localities have attracted media attention for making substantial changes in their welfare systems, most states have taken a decidedly incremental approach.

Most state and local governments have addressed PRWORA's family structure goals only at the margin, making adjustments to reduce marriage penalties or using relatively small, experimental programs to promote marriage, encourage responsible fatherhood, promote sexual abstinence, or discourage childbearing outside of marriage. Child support enforcement has become much tougher, but in this area PRWORA continued a trend well under way before 1996.

How Low-Income Families Are Faring under Welfare Reform

The most widely reported fact of welfare reform is the rapid and large decline in the number of families receiving cash assistance. Figure 1 shows that the number of recipients in 2000 was less than half of what it had been in 1996. Researchers continue to debate how much of this drop

Figure 1. *Total and Child-Only Welfare Cases, 1985–2001*

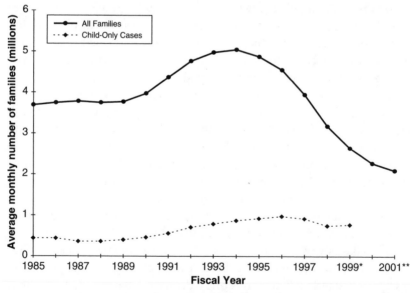

Sources: Administration for Children and Families (1988–1997), Office of Planning, Research, and Evaluation (2000), Farrell et al. (2000), and Administration for Children and Families (2000a, 2000b, 2001a, 20001b).

*Most recent year for which child-only data are available.

**Data for April–September 2001 imputed using FY 2000 data and available FY 2001 data.

should be attributed to welfare reform and how much to low unemployment or to other policies such as the EITC or minimum wage (Bell 2001).

Less widely reported is the fact that child-only cases now account for a larger share of TANF recipients, approaching 30 percent in 1999. Figure 1 shows that while the number of child-only cases has dropped under welfare reform, it has done so less steeply and consistently than the overall caseload; hence the increased percentage of these cases. Child-only cases include children whose parents are ineligible because of sanctions, receipt of Supplemental Security Income (SSI), or immigration status, and children living with nonparent caregivers (Farrell et al. 2000). The time limits and work requirements that are central components of welfare reform do not apply to child-only cases.

Chapter 2 shows that most former welfare recipients, and almost a third of current recipients, are now employed. Both groups typically have jobs that offer low wages and few benefits. Recent data, however, show gains in wages among single mothers, especially high-school dropouts (Lerman 2001a, 2001b). Predictions that employers would be unwilling to hire welfare recipients or that there were not enough jobs in metropolitan labor markets to absorb recipients without displacing other low-skilled workers do not appear to have been borne out (see chapter 6).

Chapter 4 presents evidence that the combination of earnings and work supports has made low-income children and single mothers financially better off, in the aggregate, than they were before welfare reform. This finding stands in contrast to predictions that child poverty would increase if welfare reform were enacted. More troubling findings in chapter 4 indicate that many low-income families do not receive the benefits for which they are eligible and that a higher proportion of persons in independent single-parent families are living in extreme poverty under welfare reform.

Some trends in childbearing among teenagers have also been positive in the early years following welfare reform (chapter 3). The decline in births to teenage mothers that began in the early 1990s has continued under PRWORA, and the birthrate among unmarried teens has declined slightly.

Looking beyond the Averages

Aggregate measures of work and earnings paint a positive picture of the former welfare population. Yet the low-income population has always been heterogeneous, and portions of it are not thriving under welfare reform. Some people face substantial barriers to employment (chapter 2) and remain on welfare or cycle off and back on the rolls. In a work-based system, those who do not make it into employment do not share in the benefits provided through the EITC and the more generous earnings disregards. Cash grants remain insufficient to lift these families out of poverty. In addition, many who do find jobs lose other supports designed to help them, such as food stamps and health insurance, leaving them no better off—and sometimes worse off—than when they were not working.

Chapter 10 describes the provisions of PRWORA that explicitly restrict the access of noncitizen immigrants. These restrictions have contributed to the racial and ethnic patterns of program participation and overall well-being explored in chapter 11. Although some of the findings in this book apply across racial and ethnic groups, there are important ways in which black and Hispanic low-income families have fared differently under welfare reform than white low-income families or the low-income population as a whole.

The Well-Being of Children

Welfare is intended to benefit children, but most welfare policy is directed at the behavior of parents. Welfare reform is based on the premise that working parents provide a better environment for raising children than do parents who depend upon public assistance, yet early experimental and survey evidence suggests that the dynamics of welfare, work, and child well-being are more complicated than that (chapter 5). Parental work appears to yield better outcomes for children only when it results in additional financial resources for the family—and then only for some subgroups. Early data show that children in welfare families and in families that have left welfare are at similar risk for poor developmental outcomes, and that there have been no major shifts in well-being for either group. More time is needed to determine whether significant positive or negative changes will occur.

A Virtuous Cycle—So Far

Welfare policy has been in a virtuous cycle in the years since its enactment. The combination of work-oriented welfare policies, an exceptionally strong economy, healthy state budgets, the requirement that states maintain their spending levels, and the block grant structure that has kept the federal contribution constant even as the number of people on welfare has fallen has created a self-reinforcing system. All of the pieces work together, and they all benefit from the same set of dynamics.

Each state's TANF grant was set to cover the costs of the largest caseload that the state had had in the last few years of AFDC. Falling caseloads have resulted in more resources per person remaining on welfare and more resources to fund work supports for low-income families at risk of requiring cash assistance. Chapter 12 shows that combined state and federal spending on welfare-related programs has actually been higher under welfare reform than it would have been under AFDC, and that the federal government is picking up a larger share of the tab than it did before. This combination of circumstances has yielded large new pots of flexible funds. It would be an overstatement to say that welfare reform has accomplished what it has because policymakers threw money at the problem, but it would be naive to deny the role that extra funds have played in promoting the welfare reform agenda.

Yet this virtuous cycle could just as easily become vicious. Low unemployment and sustained economic growth have contributed to the recent decline in welfare caseloads. A recession will reverse these trends while straining state budgets. If the number of people on welfare rises, funds that would have been used to help people find work, support work, or make work pay will be needed to provide cash assistance to the neediest welfare families. Federal work participation requirements could become harder to meet, further reducing state resources. Many of the families most affected by a recession will not be eligible for unemployment insurance, and some will have already used up their lifetime limit of five years on TANF cash assistance. Federal and state contingency mechanisms for funding TANF programs during recessions or other emergencies, chapter 12 suggests, are inadequate.

The new structure of welfare may make the highs and lows of policy more extreme than they were in the past. The United States has been living through the highs; it has yet to experience the lows.

Policy Implications

Each chapter in this book describes policy implications stemming from findings in the area it covers. As the editors, we have identified five overarching recommendations that emerge from the research presented here.[2]

Keep Federal Policy Stable

One of the most encouraging aspects of the current welfare system is that states and localities have begun to move from relatively narrow work-first policies to more complex ways of identifying and overcoming barriers to work, providing financial and in-kind support for work, and promoting job retention and advancement. This evolution has taken time, and it has depended upon the existence of sufficient federal resources and a stable federal funding commitment.

At least as important as these state policies are local developments. In some localities, public agencies have developed new relationships with each other and with the private for-profit and nonprofit sectors. These relationships enable welfare recipients and former recipients to obtain a constellation of services and supports to assist them in their economic progress. As with evolving state policy, these relationships take time to build, and arise only when local leaders have resources, commitment, and focus.

These positive aspects of welfare reform took time to develop, even in the most forward-looking states. They will evolve more slowly in other locations. Moreover, they are sufficiently fragile that they must be nurtured everywhere if they are to become a permanent part of social welfare policy.

Major shifts in the federal welfare environment, whether in the form of budget cuts or substantial new statutory or regulatory provisions, threaten the best aspects of existing welfare policy. If states are forced to shift their attention to new topics, the creative aspects of welfare policy are the ones most likely to suffer. Therefore, *the overall structure and design of federal welfare policy should remain stable for at least the next few years to enable states and localities to continue developing systems that support welfare families making the transition to work.*

Retain Core Funding and Expand Funding for Work Supports

Most TANF funds are being spent in three areas: cash support for the neediest families, transfers to existing or new job search and work support programs that often serve a broader low-income population, and new services to help those who face barriers to work. Most states waited a couple of years to be sure that the number of welfare recipients would continue to decline before they began shifting funds into the second category, and spending in the third remains relatively low.

It is difficult to determine what it will cost to continue to meet needs in these areas. The number of people receiving cash assistance is no longer declining rapidly, suggesting that future needs will be equal to or higher than today's. States are continuing to identify new needs for their work support programs, reaching beyond child care to areas such as transportation. The need for intensive services designed to overcome substantial barriers such as illiteracy, substance abuse, or poor mental health is even harder to determine, as most of these programs are relatively new and their effectiveness and long-term costs and benefits are not known. Given that states are now generally spending their entire block grant to meet these varied needs, even in the context of record low welfare caseloads, *the federal government should maintain existing overall funding for the TANF block grant—both the federal and the state shares—adjusted upward to account for the effects of inflation.*

Combining spending on these three areas of need into a single block grant gives states the flexibility to allocate resources to their highest priority. Unfortunately, the relative costs of these endeavors vary substantially, and they vary across states because they depend upon the composition of the welfare caseload and the characteristics and strength of local labor markets. Placing funding for all three areas into a single grant forces them to compete against each other, with results that may impede the overall goals of welfare reform.

Funding for child care is simply too low to meet the needs of low-income families in a work-oriented welfare system. Almost all states have elected to spend some of their TANF money on child care, whether directly, indirectly through transfers to the Child Care and Development Fund (CCDF), or both. Yet waiting lists and other methods of rationing are widespread, suggesting that many families who meet federal eligibility standards and want child care subsidies are not getting them. In addition, funding child care out of TANF is inequitable because the block grant is based upon factors that have little to do with the demand for or cost of child care assistance. While it is appropriate that states retain the option of shifting TANF funds into the CCDF, *the federal government should increase direct funding for child care.*

Increase States' Flexibility to Support Working Families

Despite welfare reform's stated goal of increasing state and local flexibility, several aspects of the law constrain states' flexibility. Two prime examples are the five-year lifetime limit on benefits and the work participation requirements states must meet in order to obtain their block grant without penalty. Both provisions support the federal goals of promoting work and ensuring that cash assistance is temporary.

Unfortunately, these constraints may prevent states from adopting policies that support working families. Specifically, states that use expansive income disregards, thereby allowing welfare recipients who work to keep a larger share of their cash assistance, may find a larger share of their recipients hitting the time limit. The work participation requirements negatively affect states that impose substantial nonwork requirements on some of their welfare recipients, whether to expand recipients' earning capacity through education, to provide them with intensive services such as language skills, or to meet other requirements, such as those imposed by the child welfare system.

Research demonstrating that increased family income is good for children suggests that states wishing to provide work supports that also increase income should be permitted to do so. Therefore, *federal policies with respect to time limits and work participation requirements should be modified so they do not discourage states from adopting policies that enable families to combine cash assistance with work or other activities designed to improve the likelihood the family will become economically self-sufficient.*

Respond to a Weaker Economy

All of the good news about welfare reform came during an unprecedented period of sustained economic growth. It is clear now that the economic sands have shifted. When setting public policies that affect the most vulnerable families, federal and state policymakers cannot risk waiting too long to respond to an economic downturn.

In most means-tested programs, the obvious response to economic weakness is to expand appropriations to meet the needs of a larger population. For TANF, this response may be necessary, but it is not sufficient. Existing program rules, including the "Temporary" in TANF, are based on the premise that needy parents can and should move into jobs. If the pace of this movement falls, the effects will ripple throughout the program. Program costs and administrative burdens will increase, families will become more likely to exhaust their lifetime benefits, and states will find it harder to meet federal welfare participation and maintenance of effort requirements.

As an entitlement program, AFDC ensured that appropriations would automatically increase during economic downturns and that families would receive benefits as long as they needed them. TANF's block grant funding does not have these features. *States and the federal government should ensure that program rules and funding respond to the many different challenges TANF will face in worse economic times. These provisions include a more effective mechanism for increasing funding when needs increase and an approach that ties individual work requirements and state performance measures to labor market conditions.*

Solidify the New Federal Role

Under PRWORA, states take the lead in setting welfare policy, leaving the federal government fewer options for affecting the policies it is funding. Yet federal dominance in financing TANF, and the important national goals stated in the welfare reform legislation, suggest that a federal role remains. The government must adjust to its new role in a manner that encourages continuous improvement in welfare policy.

The federal government exercises complete or primary control over many aspects of the safety net other than TANF, through programs such as the EITC, the Food Stamp program, SSI, and Medicaid. In order for these programs to meet the needs of families, they must work together, despite the variability in TANF across states. Therefore, *the federal government must ensure that the safety net programs it controls operate effectively, reach eligible populations, and are coordinated with TANF as it exists in the states.*

Experimentation—as distinct from simple variation in welfare policies—can benefit the federal government as well as the states. Experimentation entails the use of analytic tools to evaluate the effects of different policies. Under AFDC, when a state wanted to try an innovative policy, one of the conditions for receiving a waiver was an evaluation of the initiative. TANF has eliminated the need for waivers, and with it the requirement for evaluation. While states conduct some evaluations on their own, their incentives to do so under PRWORA are weak, since they bear the full costs. *The federal government should explicitly fund more welfare policy experiments to determine the effects of different program designs and interventions.*

With better knowledge, states can make better policy—and so can the federal government. If the evidence shows that objectives such as reducing poverty or improving the well-being of children can be achieved through specific policies, the federal government may want to create incentives for states to adopt programs that further these goals. If most states use their block grants for a particular purpose, such as child care, the federal government may determine that this action reflects a need that should be protected from competition within the TANF grant and therefore funded directly. Block grants are easy to cut in tight fiscal times because they do not have a well-defined constituency. They are particularly vulnerable if spending does not conform closely with federal goals. Therefore, *the federal government should monitor state policy choices and research evidence so that devolution does not result in abandonment of the federal role in achieving the national objectives of welfare policy.*

The Next Act

There are reasons to be optimistic about the future of welfare, even if no federal policy changes are made. First, PRWORA has tapped into a tremendous reservoir of creativity. The combination of state and local control, new policy objectives, and, in some areas, new funding has brought new actors and ideas into the arena of welfare policy. The sense of possibility is palpable, suggesting that the entire welfare system is better situated to respond to change than the more rigid system of the past.

Second, welfare reform has transformed the central question of American welfare policy, from how much to give single mothers who do not work, to how to support work among low-income families with children. The new frame has different implications than the old one for the politics of welfare and for resource allocation decisions.

Third, dramatic increases in work among current and former welfare recipients may provide lasting benefits that are not yet visible. One premise of welfare reform was that working parents are inherently good for families, providing children with role models and parents with routines and links to the outside world, greater self-esteem, a more optimistic sense of their future, and the possibility of higher income. To the extent that this is true, welfare reform will have substantial long-term benefits for children. In addition, a period of successful employment may provide parents with a sense of hope and potential that will benefit them even in more difficult economic times.

Yet we refuse to join the bandwagon declaring welfare reform an unqualified success. The strong economy has played an indispensable role in the encouraging data on work, earnings, and poverty. Most data showing improvements in the circumstances of low-income families represent averages, while some subgroups fare worse. Welfare recipients are only starting to reach the five-year lifetime limit on benefits, which is one of the central provisions of the federal reform law. Some of welfare's most important outcomes are long-term ones that may not be observable for decades or even generations. In many respects, welfare reform simply has not yet been tested.

The first act of welfare reform demonstrated recipients' capacity for work and the value of supporting all low-income working families, regardless of whether they are receiving welfare. The next act should make this new, work-based welfare system adequate to meet the needs of a diverse group of vulnerable families through all phases of the economic cycle.

NOTES

The editors thank Matthew Stagner and Sheila Zedlewski for their review of an earlier draft of this introduction; Sarah Staveteig for her help with research; and Gina Adams, Martha Burt, Kathleen Courrier, Frederick Custer, Pamela Holcomb, Harold Leibovitz, Robert Lerman, Robert Reischauer, and Martha Zaslow for their suggestions.

1. See Urban Institute (1996) for a more detailed summary of PRWORA and a comparison with the laws in effect at the time of its passage.

2. We do not purport to speak for all book authors when presenting these recommendations.

REFERENCES

Administration for Children and Families. See U.S. Department of Health and Human Services, Administration for Children and Families.

Bell, Stephen H. 2001. *Why Are Welfare Caseloads Falling?* Washington, D.C.: Urban Institute. *Assessing the New Federalism* Discussion Paper 01-02.

Bell, Stephen H., with Toby Douglas. 2000. *Making Sure of Where We Started: State Employment and Training Systems for Welfare Recipients on the Eve of Federal Reform.* Washington, D.C.: Urban Institute. *Assessing the New Federalism* Occasional Paper 37.

Bell, Stephen H., and L. Jerome Gallagher. 2001. "Prime-Age Adults without Children or Disabilities: The 'Least Deserving of the Poor'—or Are They?" Washington, D.C.: Urban Institute. *Assessing the New Federalism* Brief B-26.

Farrell, Mary, Michael Fishman, Stephanie Laud, and Vincena Allen. 2000. *Understanding the AFDC/TANF Child-Only Caseload: Policies, Composition, and Characteristics in Three States.* Report prepared for U.S. Department of Health and Human Services, Assistant Secretary for Planning and Evaluation. http://aspe.hhs.gov/hsp/child-only-caseload00/index.htm.

Gallagher, L. Jerome. 1999. "A Shrinking Portion of the Safety Net: General Assistance from 1989 to 1998." Washington, D.C.: Urban Institute. *Assessing the New Federalism* Brief A-36.

Gallagher, L. Jerome, Cori E. Uccello, Alicia B. Pierce, and Erin B. Reidy. 1999. *State General Assistance Programs 1998.* Washington, D.C.: Urban Institute. *Assessing the New Federalism* Discussion Paper 99-01.

Harris, John F., and Judith Havemann. 1997. "Welfare Rolls Continue Sharp Decline; Percentage on Assistance Is Lowest Since 1970; Many Factors are Cited." *Washington Post,* August 13. A-1.

Lerman, Robert I. 2001a. "Jobs and Wages Up Sharply for Single Moms, Gains Especially High after Welfare Reform." *Single Parents' Earnings Monitor.* July 25.

———. 2001b. "Less Educated Single Mothers Achieved High Wage and Employment Gains in the Mid-1990s." *Single Parents' Earnings Monitor.* October 26.

Melnick, R. Shep. 1994. *Between the Lines: Interpreting Welfare Rights.* Washington, D.C.: Brookings Institution.

Office of the Assistant Secretary for Planning and Evaluation. 1997. *Setting the Baseline: A Report on State Welfare Waivers.* June. http://aspe.hhs.gov/hsp/isp/waiver2/title.htm.

Office of Planning, Research, and Evaluation. 2000. *Characteristics and Financial Circumstances of TANF Recipients, FY 1999.* http://www.acf.dhhs.gov/programs/opre/characteristics/fy99/analysis.htm (accessed November 15, 2001).

Teles, Steven M. 1998. *Whose Welfare? AFDC and Elite Politics.* Lawrence, Kans.: University Press of Kansas.

Urban Institute. 1996. *A Comparison of Selected Key Provisions of the Welfare Reform Reconciliation Act of 1996 with Current Law.* Washington, D.C.: Urban Institute. http://www.urban.org/welfare/WRCA96.htm.

U.S. Congress. 1996. House of Representatives. *Personal Responsibility and Work Opportunity Reconciliation Act of 1996: Conference Report to Accompany H.R. 3734.* Report 104-725. 104th cong., 2d sess., July 30. http://frwebgate.access.gpo.gov/cgi-bin/getdoc.cgi?dbname=104_cong_reports&docid=f:hr725.104.pdf.

U.S. Department of Health and Human Services, Administration for Children and Families. 1988–1997. *Characteristics and Financial Circumstances of AFDC Recipients.* 10 vols. Washington, D.C.: U.S. Government Printing Office.

———. 2000a. *TANF 1936–1999 Statistics.* http://www.acf.dhhs.gov/news/stats/3697.htm (accessed November 15, 2001).

———. 2000b. *TANF Total Number of Families, January–June 2000.* http://www.acf.dhhs.gov/news/stats/families.htm (accessed November 15, 2001).

————. 2001a. *TANF Total Number of Families and Recipients, July–September 2000.* http://www.acf.dhhs.gov/news/stats/welfare.htm (accessed November 15, 2001).

————. 2001b. *TANF Total Number of Families and Recipients, September 2000–March 2001.* http://www.acf.dhhs.gov/news/tables.htm (accessed November 15, 2001).

Weaver, R. Kent. 2000. *Ending Welfare as We Know It.* Washington, D.C.: Brookings Institution Press.

Weil, Alan. 2002. "Program Redesign by States in the Wake of Welfare Reform: Making Sense of the Effects of Devolution." In *For Better and For Worse: Welfare Reform and the Well-Being of Children and Families,* edited by Greg Duncan and P. Lindsay Chase-Lansdale (63–80). New York: Russell Sage Foundation Press.

Zedlewski, Sheila R., Pamela A. Holcomb, and Amy-Ellen Duke. 1998. *Cash Assistance in Transition: The Story of 13 States.* Washington, D.C.: Urban Institute. *Assessing the New Federalism* Occasional Paper No. 16.

1

Putting Policy into Practice
Five Years of Welfare Reform

Pamela A. Holcomb and Karin Martinson

Sweeping changes in the welfare system were legislated in 1996, but welfare reform did not really take hold until these changes were implemented locally, where families come into contact with the system, goals and policies are translated into practice, rules are applied, and services are delivered. The new legislation set the course for a work-oriented welfare system designed to provide temporary financial support for needy families, and it gave the states unprecedented fiscal and policy authority to carry out its goals. The states responded by devising various policies to promote and reinforce employment, including stricter work requirements for welfare recipients, narrower criteria for exemptions, more severe sanctions for noncompliance with welfare rules and regulations, and more generous treatment of recipients' earned income.

The timing, pace, and intensity of these changes varied within and across states. Although many states had already initiated some work-focused programs under federal waivers, the new law's mix of mandates and incentives motivated all states to adopt or advance a "work-first" approach to welfare. This approach emphasizes engaging recipients in a job search to provide quick exposure to and entry into employment (Holcomb 1999; Zedlewski, Holcomb, and Duke 1998).

Even in the short space of five years, the focus of initial work-related welfare reform efforts has changed and broadened. Welfare agencies have increasingly begun to explore how a work-first strategy can be enhanced to better meet the needs of TANF recipients. These enhancements are typically focused on two areas: developing a wider range of services for hard-to-employ welfare recipients, who face significant barriers to employment; and providing employment retention and advancement services for recipients who do find jobs. Neither type of service is provided in a simple work-first program.

Generalizations about "what is really happening" under welfare reform are risky because variation across and within states is tremendous. In addition, the research microscope and media reports have focused a disproportionate share of attention on states and localities that have made the most significant reforms, potentially skewing public perceptions of the extent and types of change thus far. This chapter draws upon the ANF case studies to describe how 17 localities in 13 states, representing a broad cross-section of the national experience, have addressed the challenge of moving welfare recipients into work. It looks at similarities and variations in their work-first programs, sanctions and time limits, and organization and delivery of services—and particularly at how these responses to welfare reform have changed over time. (See the appendix for more detail on the ANF case studies.)

Work-First Programs and Their Evolution

From the outset, states and localities combined the elements commonly found in work-first programs in different ways and put them into operation differently. In addition, states and localities typically narrowed the previously existing criteria for exempting welfare recipients from work requirements.[1] Three basic welfare-to-work approaches emerge from the 17 ANF sites.

STRICTLY WORK FIRST
This approach aims to move welfare recipients into unsubsidized employment as quickly as possible. Recipients are required to use short-term job-search assistance, typically as their first work-related activity. The job search component often provides some instruction in job readiness skills. A strictly work-first approach generally contains little or no assessment of recipients' needs or barriers to employment, education or training, or services to address barriers facing the hard-to-employ.

MIXED SERVICES (WORK FIRST SUPPLEMENTED WITH EDUCATION AND TRAINING)

This approach also emphasizes immediate employment, but it blends strictly work-first elements with the kind of investment in human capital common to pre-TANF welfare-to-work programs. Job search is generally required as an initial activity, but recipients who do not find jobs right away may participate in education and training activities. Efforts to identify and assess barriers are typically reserved for those who cannot find employment after completing a job search. In addition, recipients in mixed services programs may engage in a broader range of activities than can be counted toward federally mandated participation rates under PRWORA.

ENHANCED MIXED SERVICES (WORK FIRST WITH A FOCUS ON REDUCING BARRIERS)

This approach typically maintains an immediate work requirement for most recipients, but it allows recipients to meet the requirement through a broad range of activities, particularly if a job search proves unsuccessful. In addition, it offers a more diverse mix of services, including specialized services for people identified as hard to employ. The focus on reducing barriers to employment includes in-depth assessment of recipients' barriers at some point in the program.

Serving the Hard-to-Employ

In the period immediately after welfare reform was enacted (1996 to 1997), most of the ANF study sites relied on a strictly work-first model, although the sites in California, Minnesota, and New York chose the mixed services approach (table 1-1)[2] (Holcomb 1999; Zedlewski et al. 1998). Only one site—Denver—formally incorporated barrier reduction into its work-first program.[3]

In the ensuing years, many states and localities modified their work-first approach to include a stronger program focus on serving hard-to-employ welfare recipients and their families. As shown in table 1-1, ANF sites in Alabama, Florida, New Jersey, Washington, and Wisconsin have shifted from a strictly work-first program to an enhanced mixed services program with a focus on barrier reduction, albeit to varying degrees. Three other sites in California and New York have moved from a mixed

Table 1-1. *Shifts in Service Strategies*

Strategy	Initial TANF Program, by County[a]	2000 Program, by County
Strictly work-first	Dade/Miami	
	El Paso	El Paso
	Harris/Houston	Harris/Houston
	Hillsborough/Tampa	
	Hinds/Jackson	Hinds/Jackson
	Hudson/Jersey City	
	Jefferson/Birmingham	
	King/Seattle	
	Milwaukee	
	Suffolk/Boston	Suffolk/Boston
	Wayne/Detroit	Wayne/Detroit
Mixed services	Alameda/Oakland	Alameda/Oakland
	Erie/Buffalo	
	Hennepin/Minneapolis	Hennepin/Minneapolis
	Los Angeles	
	San Diego	
Enhanced mixed services	Denver	Dade/Miami
		Denver
		Erie/Buffalo
		Hillsborough/Tampa
		Hudson/Jersey City
		Jefferson/Birmingham
		King/Seattle
		Los Angeles
		Milwaukee
		San Diego

Source: ANF case studies.

[a] Most states implemented their TANF programs in 1996 or early 1997. Washington implemented its program in late 1997, and California did so in early 1998.

services approach to one focused more sharply on barrier reduction for the hard-to-employ. During site visits in 2000, program administrators and staff typically reported that while the strong economy and the emphasis on immediate employment appear to have helped the most job-ready recipients leave welfare, a greater challenge remains: serving the less employable clients with multiple barriers who were left behind.[4]

These clients face an array of diverse and complex barriers to employment, including physical disabilities, mental health or substance abuse issues, limited English proficiency, learning disabilities, and domestic violence (see chapter 9).

The TANF programs that focus on barrier reduction usually added or redirected staff to specialize in addressing the needs of the hard-to-employ, or contracted with organizations that had expertise in addressing specific barriers such as substance abuse or domestic violence. The following examples illustrate the types of services and strategies being used to help reduce barriers to employment:

- In Dade/Miami and Hillsborough/Tampa, substance abuse and mental health services outreach, assessment, and treatment are provided by alcohol, drug, and mental health specialists located in local TANF offices.
- In Hudson/Jersey City, job coaches were added to the staff to work intensively with long-term TANF recipients, and an outside health services provider was hired under contract to provide assessments and referrals at the TANF office for recipients with substance abuse problems.
- In King/Seattle, case managers could request that specialized staff provide additional assessments of hard-to-employ recipients and help the case managers with service planning and referrals.
- In Milwaukee, expanded efforts to address the mental health, physical health, and family problems of hard-to-employ recipients and their families included adding or redirecting staff to conduct in-depth assessments and make appropriate referrals.
- In Erie/Buffalo, case management teams provide services to welfare recipients identified as having substance abuse problems.

Providing Post-Employment Services

Initially, most ANF study sites focused on getting individuals into jobs, not helping them maintain or advance in them. By 2000, however, some sites' programs were expanding beyond traditional supports, such as child care subsidies and medical assistance, to include post-employment services for recipients who had found jobs.

In general, development and implementation of career advancement services for TANF recipients are a lower priority than job retention services, and both retention and advancement services lag behind efforts to reduce job barriers for hard-to-employ recipients. Several ANF sites do have systematic services in place for the vast majority of recipients who find jobs. In these sites, post-employment services, like pre-employment services, are generally provided through workforce development agencies or community-based organizations hired under contract.

Sites that have fairly comprehensive post-employment services often target them to recipients who are combining work and cash assistance. These services consist primarily of making regular contact with recipients to identify and resolve work or support service problems. A few sites include more innovative or comprehensive approaches. Denver, for example, provides financial incentives for finding and keeping a job. As part of a statewide effort, Suffolk/Boston received substantial resources to provide a comprehensive set of post-employment services, including transition support, job retention, skills and educational advancement, and reemployment and job upgrade services. Given the generally limited nature of job retention and career advancement services across sites, TANF administrators and staff typically consider this an area that needs more attention and resources (see chapter 6).[5]

Sanctions and Time Limits

Under TANF, states also use sanctions and time limits to encourage work. Recipients who fail to comply with program rules and requirements are subject to sanctions that generally take the form of monetary penalties that reduce or eliminate TANF benefits for recipients and their families. In contrast, time limits set a deadline on the cumulative length of time recipients may receive cash assistance.

Imposing Sanctions

Before welfare reform, penalties for noncompliance applied only to adult recipients, resulting in a partial reduction in benefits for their families. Under TANF, states have considerable discretion over sanction policies, and many have opted for more stringent sanctions. Over half of the states (31) impose full-family sanctions for noncompliance. In 18 of these states, the grant is initially reduced but is terminated if there are additional instances of noncompliance. In the remaining 13, the full-family sanction is immediate (Rowe 2000). Among the ANF sites, only the two in Florida have immediate full-family sanctions. The rest are split fairly evenly between partial reductions in benefits and graduated full-family sanctions.

Despite the overall movement toward stiffer sanctions, there appears to be significant variation in how these policies are enforced. Even in sites with relatively strict policies regarding sanctions, there is generally some caseworker discretion for determining when to sanction a client. Some staff may be more flexible and lenient than others in terms of giving clients additional chances to comply before imposing a sanction. Enforcement of sanctions can also vary, because the process is complex, often necessitating multiple steps, extensive tracking and reporting, and the involvement of multiple workers within and across agencies.

One interesting sanction-related development is the growing interest in bringing sanctioned families back into compliance. For example, Dade/Miami, Hennepin/Minneapolis, and Alameda/Oakland are contracting with community-based organizations to visit sanctioned families in their homes in order to identify and resolve outstanding barriers to compliance. These efforts, which were just getting off the ground, indicate a willingness to consider that noncompliance may be a red flag for hard-to-employ recipients whose barriers to employment have yet to be identified.

Applying Time Limits

Most of the ANF sites have no experience with what happens when welfare recipients reach their time limits. Only three states—Florida, Massachusetts, and Wisconsin—have established time limits of less than five years and thus have experienced families exhausting the limits. Program administrators in these states note the importance of providing clear criteria for exemptions from or extensions of time limits, particularly for families that are otherwise in compliance with TANF rules and regulations.

To ensure that time limits are applied properly, cases are reviewed by local or state authorities before benefits are terminated. Reviews can be intensive and time-consuming. For example, the process in Suffolk/Boston includes interviews with workers, supervisors, and vendors. In addition, the welfare and health departments have a collaborative program for people dropped from TANF because of time limits; it includes continued follow-up, a home visit and in-depth family assessment, and referrals to agencies that can help families find food, housing, employment, transportation, and child care.

Organization and Delivery of Services

A paramount challenge facing those charged with implementing welfare reform has been to build an institutional infrastructure and service delivery system that can meet the demands arising from new goals and policies. To this end, significant efforts have been made to change the institutional structures, processes, and relationships for providing cash assistance, work services, and supportive services to families. Institutional change has taken different forms across states and localities, but it has included one or more of the following elements: changing aspects of the front door of welfare agencies, altering staff functions and responsibilities, shifting some or all of TANF's employment responsibilities to different agencies, and forging new organizational links with outside service providers.

Changing How Welfare Looks at the Front Door

As one step toward instilling the goals of work and self-reliance into welfare recipients, many states and localities changed their application process—the initial point of contact between the welfare system and potential recipients. Under welfare reform, states could establish new requirements for applicants and divert individuals from ongoing cash assistance by providing short-term assistance or referring them to alternative sources of assistance. Most of the ANF sites implemented at least one of four new elements in their application process: required attendance at a program orientation before TANF benefits can be approved; lump-sum payment programs (one-time or short-term cash or in-kind payments in lieu of receiving TANF); job search requirements that must be fulfilled before TANF benefits can be approved; or formal referrals to programs other than TANF (table 1-2).

Most sites require that applicants for cash assistance attend an orientation on the TANF program before they can receive benefits. These orientations typically convey a strong message that work is expected, emphasizing TANF's work requirements, work-related support services (such as child care), and policies on time limits, sanctions, and other issues. In Hennepin/Minneapolis, Alameda/Oakland, and San Diego, such orientations are part of the initial application process and generally take place at the TANF office on the same day a person applies for benefits. In other localities, mandatory orientation may take place on a different day and at a different location (e.g., a workforce development

Table 1-2. *Pre-Application Requirements and Diversion Programs*

Site	Required Orientation	Lump-Sum Payments	Required Job Search	Formal Referrals
Alameda/Oakland	*	*		
Dade/Miami	*	*		
Denver	*	*	*	
El Paso	*	*		
Erie/Buffalo	*	*		*
Harris/Houston	*	*		
Hennepin/Minneapolis	*	*		
Hillsborough/Tampa	*	*		
Hinds/Jackson				
Hudson/Jersey City				
Jefferson/Birmingham			*	
King/Seattle		*		
Los Angeles	*	*		
Milwaukee				*
San Diego	*	*		
Suffolk/Boston				
Wayne/Detroit	*		*	
Total	11	11	3	2

Source: ANF case studies.

agency), requiring the applicant to make separate trips and generally making the application process more burdensome.

In the interest of providing alternatives to welfare to people who may need only short-term assistance, many states provide one-time lump-sum payments in lieu of ongoing cash assistance. Eleven of the ANF sites have formal financial diversion components in their TANF programs; however, staff consistently report that very few people apply for such payments, because of stringent eligibility requirements, poor marketing, or both.

Three ANF sites have implemented job search requirements that applicants must meet before they can receive TANF. In Denver, for example, applicants are given 10 days to complete 22 to 24 hours of work-related activities before their otherwise-eligible families can be approved to receive benefits. In Jefferson/Birmingham, applicants must register at the employment service office and make two job contacts before benefits can be approved.

Finally, two sites, Erie/Buffalo and Milwaukee, routinely encourage applicants to seek assistance from other sources rather than applying for TANF. Applicants are assessed and provided information about community agencies that might address some of the family's needs, such as housing or other emergency assistance.

While these types of changes have altered the front-door experience of TANF applicants, traditional matters concerning eligibility (such as processing applications and verifying information) nevertheless continue to receive very high priority within local welfare offices, and dominate much of the application process.

Concerns have been raised that changes in the application process may deter eligible families from seeking assistance or completing the application process. Visits to the ANF sites indicate that agencies typically place less emphasis on attempting to divert applicants than on letting them know that the terms and conditions of welfare receipt have changed. Changes at the front door are designed to deliver the message that work is required, an idea conveyed primarily through program orientations and the posting of information on work requirements, time limits, and sanctions. While these and other aspects of the TANF application process may discourage families from initiating or completing applications for cash assistance or other forms of assistance, this critical issue lies beyond what could be observed in the case studies.

Changing Welfare Staff Responsibilities

Changing the focus from income maintenance to helping families become employed has required welfare agencies to reexamine how they do business and to consider new ways of structuring responsibilities across organizations and staff.

Integrating responsibility for determining TANF eligibility and administering TANF's work program into a single staff position is one means by which welfare agencies have sought to instill a strong work message in all aspects of the welfare experience (table 1-3). Although it has generated much interest, this type of staffing change is by no means a universal trend. In fact, only three study sites have completely integrated the eligibility-determination and employment functions of welfare agency staff. Employment services at these sites are still provided by outside service providers.

Welfare staff administer at least some portion of the TANF work program at eight ANF study sites. These sites are more likely to observe the

Table 1-3. *Staffing Strategies*

Strategy	Sites
Welfare agency has integrated eligibility and employment staff[a]	King/Seattle Suffolk/Boston Wayne/Detroit
Welfare agency has separate eligibility and employment staffs[a]	Alameda/Oakland Birmingham Denver Erie/Buffalo Hinds/Jackson Hudson/Jersey City Los Angeles San Diego
Welfare agency responsible for eligibility, other providers responsible for employment services	Dade/Miami El Paso Harris/Houston Hennepin/Minneapolis Hillsborough/Tampa Milwaukee

[a] With reliance on outside contractors to provide employment services in most sites.
Source: ANF case studies.

traditional division of responsibility between staff who handle eligibility and staff who handle employment-related services, including monitoring of work participation. Services are often provided by outside contractors at these sites. Since the skills and knowledge required to perform these two types of work are quite different, this approach provides the advantage of allowing staff to develop expertise in one area.

Another variation, found in six sites, places responsibility for eligibility-related matters within the welfare agency, but transfers all staff responsibilities related to employment (including monitoring client participation and provision of services) to outside providers that possess greater expertise in employment assistance.

Establishing Links with Employment Programs

In the past, welfare agencies assumed primary responsibility for administering benefits and employment-related services for recipients, typically with little or no involvement from the workforce development system. However, to make cash assistance programs more employment-oriented and to gain access to employment expertise, welfare departments are becoming increasingly involved with workforce development agencies (which are responsible for WIA, and, formerly, the Job Training Partnership Act) and other employment-related programs.

By 2000, local workforce development agencies were playing an important role in TANF programs in more than half of the ANF case study sites. Most of the other sites had relatively little integration of or coordination between the welfare and workforce development systems. The increased local involvement began prior to the enactment of welfare reform in some cases and after it in others, and sometimes reflected increased interaction at the state level. The degree and nature of involvement with workforce development agencies varies. Some sites, including Hennepin/Minneapolis, Denver, Wayne/Detroit, and King/Seattle, lodge administrative responsibility for TANF employment services within the workforce development agency. Others, such as Suffolk/Boston, have significantly increased their connections with and reliance on the workforce development agency as part of welfare reform implementation. Only one of the case study sites, Milwaukee, has gone so far as to transfer both eligibility and work components of cash assistance into a reconstituted Department of Workforce Development.

Even in sites where workforce development agencies play a small role, the increased amount of contracting with outside organizations to provide employment services is a notable characteristic of welfare reform implementation. For example, in Erie/Buffalo, the welfare department contracts with over 20 different providers, including community-based organizations and community colleges, to provide employment and training programs.

Developing New Institutional Relationships

Because welfare agency staff traditionally lacked experience in assessing and dealing with the many difficult issues facing hard-to-employ welfare recipients, states and localities have created or expanded organizational links to specialized service providers trained to meet the needs of these recipients. This means not only that welfare agencies have increased their involvement with workforce development agencies, but also that they have entered into contracts and other types of agreements and partnerships with a variety of social service and behavioral health service providers, including organizations specializing in domestic violence, mental health, and substance abuse treatment.

Many community-based organizations had little to no involvement with welfare agencies before the implementation of reform. Today, these organizations are playing an increasingly important role in the delivery of welfare services. In some ANF sites, welfare agencies contract with for-profit organizations, but contracts with nonprofit community-based organizations are far more prevalent.

Policy Implications

Five years into the implementation of welfare reform, states and localities are continuing to develop new programs. The strictly work-first approach that predominated during the initial years of TANF has subsequently given way in many ANF sites to variants that include a broader program focus. A more comprehensive welfare system is evolving, one with new institutional partners and a greater focus on services rather than cash assistance.

The evolution that has occurred thus far has taken tremendous effort. The move beyond the basic work-first model has been into new and largely uncharted territory for TANF agencies. Implementation of such systems presents ongoing challenges, and states and localities must continually confront and work to improve the factors that hold such systems together: strong, diverse, and coordinated interorganizational linkages; the ability to track and share information across agency and program staff; sufficient staff capacity and capability; accountability through monitoring and performance-based measures; and a comprehensive mix of services. Program staff and clients have had to navigate a much more complicated system that transcends traditional program boundary lines.

During TANF reauthorization and into the future, federal policy-makers will have an opportunity to either promote or hinder state and local efforts to develop the comprehensive services and supports needed by welfare recipients and other low-income working families. Expanding the definition of allowable work activities to include some activities that might be suitable for the hard-to-employ could motivate states to pursue more creative strategies for moving these welfare recipients into work. Broadening the activities that count toward TANF's work participation requirement should not diminish the focus on employment;

rather, it should encourage states to expand beyond a strictly work-focused approach.

States and localities could not have made the progress they have without the increased flexibility and resources afforded under PRWORA. Helping hard-to-employ recipients reduce the multiple barriers to employment they face and helping former recipients and their families stay off welfare once they have found jobs requires more resources than the simpler work-first programs that predominated during the early years of TANF implementation. If federal resources are scaled back or flexibility is greatly diminished, particularly during a new era when caseloads are level or beginning to rise, states and localities may retrench from the progress they have made. Those TANF systems in the earlier phases of moving beyond a narrow work-first focus may be stopped in their tracks. The momentum in welfare policy is currently toward greater experimentation and building upon lessons learned to date. A reduction in resources would stop this positive momentum.

NOTES

The authors are indebted to the large team of researchers, too numerous to list here, who conducted the ANF site visits on which this paper is based. We also want to extend deep appreciation to all the individuals—state and local agency staff, service providers, community advocates, and others—who so generously gave their time to be interviewed for these case studies.

1. Most states now require TANF mothers with children age 1 or even younger to participate in work activities for 35 or more hours a week. In addition, some states narrowed or eliminated exemptions stemming from disability.

2. When a county and its core city have the same name—as Los Angeles, San Diego, Denver, El Paso, and Milwaukee do—the site name refers to the county. In each of these sites except Denver, the county encompasses a larger area than the core city. All other site names refer to the county and are listed along with the more widely recognized name of the core city.

3. Denver's TANF program included a family counseling program, staffed by several vendors, that provided services to recipients needing mental health, substance abuse, and domestic violence services.

4. Loprest (see chapter 2) finds that the characteristics of the welfare caseload have not changed significantly over time. From the perspective of program administrators and staff, however, the caseload seems to have become more disadvantaged. In part, this is because staff end up spending more time and resources on hard-to-employ recipients, who remain on welfare longer. Moreover, in the pre-TANF era, hard-to-employ recipients were more likely to have been exempt or simply not to have worked.

5. Several studies have shown that job loss and return to cash assistance is common among welfare recipients. Loprest (chapter 2) finds that over one-fifth of those who left TANF between 1997 and 1999 were back on the rolls when they were interviewed in 1999. A study of welfare recipients in the National Evaluation of Welfare-to-Work Strategies (NEWWS) found that whereas 80 percent had worked in a given four-year period, only one-fourth had worked steadily, one-fourth had worked very little, and the rest had worked intermittently (Martinson 2000). Studies using data from national longitudinal surveys have identified very similar employment patterns (e.g., Rangarajan, Schochet, and Chu 1998).

REFERENCES

Holcomb, Pamela A. 1999. "State Welfare-to-Work Demonstrations." In *Families, Poverty and Welfare Reform: Confronting a New Policy Era,* edited by Lawrence B. Joseph. Chicago: University of Illinois Press.

Martinson, Karin. 2000. *The Experiences of Welfare Recipients Who Find Jobs: Findings from the National Evaluation of Welfare-to-Work Strategies.* New York: Manpower Demonstration Research Corporation.

Rangarajan, Anu, Peter Schochet, and Dexter Chu. 1998. *Employment Experiences of Welfare Recipients Who Find Jobs: Is Targeting Possible?* Princeton, N.J.: Mathematica Policy Research, Inc.

Rowe, Gretchen. 2000. "State TANF Policies as of July 1999." *Welfare Rules Databook.* Washington, D.C.: The Urban Institute.

Zedlewski, Sheila, Pamela A. Holcomb, and Amy-Ellen Duke. 1998. *Cash Assistance in Transition: The Story of 13 States.* Washington, D.C.: The Urban Institute. *Assessing the New Federalism* Occasional Paper No. 16.

2

Making the Transition from Welfare to Work

Successes but Continuing Concerns

Pamela J. Loprest

Welfare reform is intended to end dependence on government assistance, by promoting job preparation and work. The dramatic decline in AFDC and TANF caseloads since the mid-1990s shows that dependence on cash assistance has indeed fallen. In the face of welfare program work requirements and a robust economy, many recipients left welfare and went to work. But behind this simple picture of a downward trend in caseloads is a more complex reality that includes families struggling with the transition from welfare to work.

Many former recipients who have gone to work are having difficulty making ends meet, faced with low wages and few benefits. Others returned to the welfare rolls quickly after losing a job or having child care arrangements fall through. Still other recipients have not yet joined the workforce because of multiple serious barriers that impede the transition. Some of these recipients continue to rely on welfare, and face time limits on benefits. Finally, some former welfare recipients no longer collect benefits because they failed to comply with program rules, but have few alternative sources of income.

This chapter describes the relative size and circumstances of each of these groups at the time they were interviewed in 1999 for the NSAF. For those who left welfare for work or who are combining welfare with paid work, the chapter describes their earnings and the benefits they receive.

For those who left welfare but subsequently returned, it examines the barriers to work that might have led to their return. For those who are not working, the chapter describes their barriers to work and examines evidence of hardship.

Many Recipients Have Found Work

At the time of reform, many observers questioned whether welfare recipients would be able to find jobs.[1] The limited skills and lack of prior work experience of many recipients, coupled with perceived employer bias, led to predictions that work-oriented policies would fail. However, the economic boom and low unemployment rates of the past half-decade created favorable employment conditions. These conditions, combined with the increased federal and state emphasis on work under welfare reform, boosted employment among current and former recipients.

Federal welfare reform required that work activity begin within two years of recipients' entrance to welfare, mandated reductions in benefits for those who failed to comply with work requirements, and created work participation quotas for states. Many states required welfare recipients to participate in work activities soon after beginning to receive assistance (or, in some cases, at the point of applying for assistance) and decreased the number of recipients who were exempted from these requirements. Most states either had or adopted work-first policies, which emphasized finding paid work over education or job training programs.[2] A number of states also increased the incentive to work by allowing recipients to keep more of their earnings, a policy referred to as "increasing earnings disregards." State and federal policies that set a limit on how long people could receive benefits also served to encourage employment.

These policies had the potential both to enable more people to leave welfare with a job and to increase employment of current welfare recipients. In states with expanded earnings disregards as well as higher benefits, workers could combine work and welfare, which resulted in increased employment rates of current recipients.

Data from the NSAF provide a national picture of employment among former and current welfare recipients in 1999. These data show that a large number of those who left welfare between 1997 and 1999, as well as many who were still on welfare in 1999, are working.

About 50 percent of people who left welfare between 1997 and 1999 were working at the time they were interviewed in 1999. Excluding those who were back on welfare, 64 percent were working. Of former recipients who had not returned to welfare, 71 percent in single-parent families were employed in 1999, while 54 percent in two-parent families were employed. (The percentage of employed former recipients is lower in two-parent families largely because a spouse or partner was often employed.)

These national rates of employment are fairly consistent with rates in a wide variety of states and local areas. A synthesis of 15 state and local studies of former welfare recipients finds that in most areas employment in the three months after leaving welfare was between 55 and 65 percent (Acs and Loprest 2001). Most studies find that at least 70 percent worked at some point during the year they left welfare. These findings hold for such demographically disparate states as New York, Iowa, and Georgia.

The employment rates of former welfare recipients are also similar to those of other groups in the U.S. economy. For instance, employment among all single women with children has been increasing rapidly over the last decade. In 1999, about three-quarters of single women with children under 18 were employed.[3] The rate is similar among single mothers who left welfare.

Similarly, former welfare recipients worked at about the same rates as low-income mothers who had never received welfare or who had left welfare before 1997. Fifty-five percent of non-welfare women with a family income below 200 percent of the federal poverty level were working, compared to 64 percent of former welfare recipients. Limiting the comparison to single-parent families, 69 percent of women who had not received welfare were working, as were 71 percent of former recipients who had left welfare between 1997 and 1999.

Work has also increased dramatically among current welfare recipients. According to the NSAF, 32 percent of recipients reported doing some amount of paid work in 1999, compared to 22 percent in 1997. Likewise, administrative data collected by the U.S. Department of Health and Human Services indicate that the percentage of welfare recipients who are working has increased steadily, from around 7 percent in the early 1990s to 33 percent in 1999 (U.S. Department of Health and Human Services 2000).

Low Wages and Benefits

Although finding a job is an important step in the transition off welfare, many recipients have relatively little education or work experience, limiting their prospects to jobs at the low end of the labor market. Thus, even though many current and former recipients are working, they are in low-wage jobs with few benefits. The nature of these jobs has implications for family well-being and stability.

The median hourly wage of employed former welfare recipients in 1999 was $7.15. At the 25th percentile the hourly wage was $6.05, and at the 75th percentile, $9.00.[4] More than two-thirds of these workers are employed full-time; that is, 35 hours or more a week. About a quarter regularly work night shifts or have irregular schedules, which can make securing child care difficult. Most of the jobs held by former recipients have limited benefits. For instance, about a third of employers offer health insurance, and only one-third to one-half provide paid sick leave (Acs and Loprest 2001). Half of former recipients' jobs are in the service sector, historically the lowest-paying sector of the labor market, whereas only 10 percent are in the manufacturing sector, which tends to have higher-paying jobs for workers without a college education.

There is no simple way to characterize the sufficiency of former recipients' wages. The majority of former recipients earn more than the minimum wage of $5.15. Their median wage of $7.15 is approximately equal to the 25th percentile of wages for all female workers in 1999.[5] Whether this wage is adequate depends on what resources are counted as income and what measure is used to estimate the cost of a family's basic needs.

A former recipient's own earnings may not be the only source of family income. Therefore, any conclusions about the economic well-being of families must also take into account such sources of income as other government benefits and earnings of other family members. For example, 64 percent of former recipients are working, but 79 percent of former recipient families have income from earnings. When the EITC is included in income, full-time, full-year work at the median wage for former recipients provides an income of almost $17,000, which is above the poverty level for a family of three.

Food stamps and Medicaid benefits, for which many low-income former recipients remain eligible, can provide important additional economic support. However, only 27 percent of such workers receive food stamps, suggesting that many eligible people are not applying for them. Similarly, only 34 percent of former welfare recipients and 53 percent of their children have Medicaid coverage (Loprest 2001).

A substantial number of former recipients and their families remain in poverty after going off welfare.[6] Among those working full-time, 35 percent have a monthly income under the poverty level, assuming they work full-time the entire year. Even after estimated EITC, payroll taxes, and food stamps (for those who report receiving them) are included, fully 25 percent of former recipients who work full-time have incomes below the poverty level. (Chapter 4 provides a detailed examination of the income sources of families with children.)

A number of attempts have been made to go beyond traditional measures of poverty in calculating the income or wage levels necessary to meet basic needs. These efforts vary in which needs are considered basic and how they are measured.[7] Moreover, discussions of wage or income sufficiency are complicated by differences in state and local standards of living and resources for low-income families. Most such discussions arrive at totals exceeding the traditional poverty measure.

The quality of current welfare recipients' jobs is generally given less attention than the quality of former recipients' jobs, in part because current recipients have income from TANF. But since many current recipients will move off welfare with these jobs, the characteristics of their jobs should also be considered.

As mentioned above, a growing percentage of current welfare recipients are working. Over half of those working work 35 hours or more a week. These families are able to combine work and welfare in part because they have not yet exceeded their state's earnings limits, a reflection of current recipients' lower median wage ($6.65 per hour, compared to former recipients' $7.15). Many fewer current recipients receive health insurance through their employer—16 percent, as opposed to one-third to one-half of former recipients. This reflects fewer hours worked per week, and possibly less take-up of health benefits because of current recipients' easier access to Medicaid.

As with former recipients, these workers are primarily in the service sector. Moreover, despite some welfare agencies' use of paid government jobs for work experience, only 11 percent of working welfare recipients are employed by the government, a percentage similar to that of former recipients.

Returning to Welfare after Having Left for Work

Leaving welfare, even with a job, is not a permanent transition for a significant number of families. Of those who left welfare between 1997 and 1999, 22 percent were back on welfare when interviewed for NSAF in 1999. These findings are corroborated by many state and local studies across the country. Analysis of a set of these studies shows that one-quarter to one-third of those leaving welfare in a given three-month period were receiving benefits again within the next year (Acs and Loprest 2001).[8]

Past studies show that a significant portion of recipients moved on and off welfare even before welfare reform in 1996. This cycling reflects the fact that the transition to work requires several tries for some recipients. In addition, movement on and off welfare mirrors the general instability of employment patterns among low-wage workers (Pavetti and Acs 1997).

Returns to welfare are of greater concern in the post-reform era because lifetime benefits are limited and recipients are using up those benefits when they return to welfare. Yet those who leave welfare and return generally have more barriers to work than those who leave welfare and continue working. Data from the NSAF have been used to analyze six potential barriers to work: poor physical or mental health, less than high school education, child under age 1, child on SSI, low proficiency in English (NSAF interviews conducted in Spanish served as a proxy for this measure), and lack of work experience. In 1999, of those who had returned to welfare, 46 percent were in poor mental or physical health (compared to 30 percent of working former recipients), and 19 percent had a child under age 1 (compared to 11 percent of working former recipients) (figure 2-1). Another 26 percent of those who returned to welfare had not worked in the past three years (not shown).

Returns to welfare highlight the difficulties some recipients experience in making a stable transition into the labor market. Almost half of those who eventually return to welfare report that they left because they had found a job or had increased hours or wages in an existing job. For these families, simply finding a job did not translate into a permanent exit from welfare.

Barriers to Work among Long-Term Recipients

Many welfare recipients have not moved from welfare to work because they face barriers to the transition. The list of problems that may inhibit working is long, including lack of a high school degree, low functional literacy, lack of work experience, and limited "soft" work skills. It also includes serious physical and mental health problems, substance abuse,

Figure 2-1. *Potential Barriers to Work among Recipients Who Left TANF between 1997 and 1999*

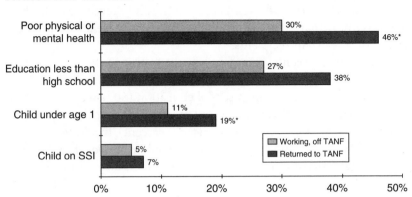

Source: National Survey of America's Families, 1999.

*The two groups are significantly different at the 90 percent confidence level.

a child with serious health problems, and experience of domestic violence. Lack of access to transportation and child care are common barriers as well.[9] These barriers are all associated with a lower probability of work (Danziger et al. 2000).

Data from the NSAF show that, in the 1999 welfare caseload, 40 percent of recipients faced two or more of the six specific barriers to work discussed earlier. Not surprisingly, work activity varied greatly with the number of barriers: 56 percent of recipients with no barriers were working, whereas only 20 percent of those with two or more barriers were working (Zedlewski and Alderson 2001). At the same time, more recipients with multiple barriers were working in 1999 than in 1997, when only 5 percent were employed.

Another matter of concern is the percentage of current welfare recipients who have received benefits continuously over a long period. These families are at greatest risk of hitting the five-year lifetime limit on benefits. Information from the NSAF indicates that, in 1999, 47 percent of welfare recipients nationwide had received benefits continuously for two or more years. Administrative data for 1997 show that 25 percent had received benefits continuously for five years or more (U.S. Department of Health and Human Services 2000).

Some long-term recipients are making the transition into work, however. The NSAF shows that 37 percent of those receiving benefits continuously for two or more years are working. Moreover, several studies show that the welfare caseload is not becoming more disadvantaged over time (Zedlewski and Alderson 2001; Moffitt and Stevens 2001). These findings imply that long-term recipients are leaving welfare at the same rate as other current recipients.

Long-term recipients are more likely than other welfare recipients to face barriers to work. Figure 2-2 shows that, in 1999, more long-term recipients had less than a high school education (50 percent, compared to 38 percent of other recipients), and more had last worked more than three years ago (34 percent, compared to 20 percent). In addition, 39 percent of long-term recipients have poor mental or physical health. These results suggest that a subset of long-term recipients faces serious barriers to work.

Off Welfare but Not Working

Some people are no longer receiving welfare benefits even though they have not made the transition to work. A small number of those who left

Figure 2-2. *Potential Barriers to Work among Current TANF Recipients, 1999*

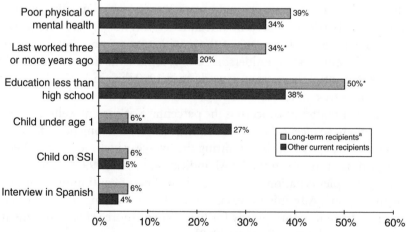

Source: National Survey of America's Families, 1999

[a] Those who have received TANF continuously for two or more years.

* The two groups are significantly different at the 90 percent confidence level.

welfare (2 percent) have moved onto disability benefit programs, and others (16 percent) are temporarily between jobs or have a working spouse. But a significant number of families receive no welfare benefits and have no connection to the labor market, either through recent work or a working spouse, and many are experiencing serious economic hardship. Of the families who left welfare between 1997 and 1999, 12 percent fell into this category in 1999, according to NSAF data.

Some of these families disconnected from work and TANF may have had their benefits terminated because of failure to meet program requirements, such as carrying out required work preparation activities. In fact, the number of families losing benefits because of official sanctions is on the rise (U.S. General Accounting Office 2000). The number losing benefits because of general administrative problems is probably much larger (Cherlin et al. 2001). In 1999, 32 percent of former recipients disconnected from work and TANF who were interviewed for the NSAF said they had left welfare because they did not follow program rules. Only 7 percent of working former recipients gave this reason for leaving.

Some sanctioned recipients choose not to comply with rules because they decide they no longer need or want benefits or any other connection to the welfare system, because, for example, requirements are too much trouble or other sources of income are available. Others fail to follow rules because they do not understand the requirements or because they have health or other problems that make compliance difficult. Because such families no longer receive cash benefits, it is difficult for agencies to maintain contact with them and, therefore, to assess hardship and their need for help. A number of states, including Utah and Tennessee, are working to help sanctioned families understand program requirements in an attempt to bring the families back into compliance and reinstate benefits.

The disconnected face as many or more potential barriers to work as long-term recipients or returning former recipients. Figure 2-3 shows that more than a third have less than a high school education, and almost half had not worked in the three years prior to their interview in 1999. Perhaps of greatest concern, 50 percent of disconnected former recipients report being in poor physical or mental health. Another cause for concern is the relatively large number (19 percent) who have a child with a substantial disability, as measured by the child's receipt of SSI in the year before the NSAF interview. By contrast, only 6 to 8 percent of long-term and returning former recipients have a child receiving SSI. While the

Figure 2-3. *Potential Barriers to Work among Current and Former TANF Recipients Having Difficulties Transitioning to Work*

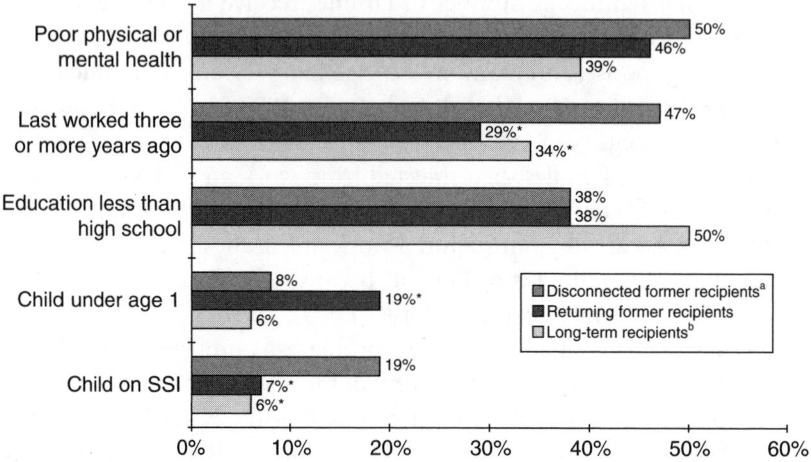

Source: National Survey of America's Families, 1999.

[a] Disconnected former recipients include those who left TANF between 1997 and 1999, no longer receive TANF, are not working, do not have a working spouse or partner and are not receiving public disability benefits.

[b] Long-term recipients are current recipients who have received TANF continuously for two or more years.

* Difference relative to disconnected former recipients is significant at the 90 percent confidence level.

child's SSI benefit is a source of income for the family, special medical and child care needs can make working more difficult for these parents.

Economic hardship among disconnected families is acute. They are not receiving cash assistance from TANF, and they have no earnings from work. The median monthly income for these families in 1999 is estimated from NSAF data at about $210, compared to $1,390 for former welfare families with some earnings. While these estimates probably miss some sources of income, including financial help from families and friends, the contrast in income is nonetheless stark. Even when an estimate of the dollar value of food stamps is included for those families who report receiving them, median monthly income increases to only around $530. Moreover, income estimates for working families would be higher if the value of the EITC were included.

How long disconnected families remain in this state of hardship is unclear. Some may return to welfare in the future.

Policy Implications

Decreases in the welfare caseload and increases in work among current and former recipients have far exceeded the expectations of most people involved in the original debate surrounding welfare reform. Yet reform remains incomplete. Many recipients who are working have trouble making ends meet. Many others have had great difficulties making the transition from welfare to work.

If welfare reform is to succeed in helping families become financially self-sufficient, policies must be tailored to their heterogeneous needs. Therefore, the next steps for policymakers to consider are the following:

- How to enhance the well-being of former recipients who have gone to work. Many of these workers have low-wage jobs and few or no benefits from their employer.
- How to help recipients who leave for work remain employed. Job retention policies should reduce the number of families returning to welfare.
- How to help recipients who face multiple barriers get and keep jobs. Policy interventions for long-term recipients are the most critical, given looming time limits on benefits.
- How to help families who have left welfare and are not working—and who therefore experience severe hardship. Following up with sanctioned families may be a first step to limiting the size of this group.

What policy changes could improve the well-being of former welfare recipients who are working? One possibility is additional programs that provide continuing work supports even after a family has stopped receiving TANF benefits. Most states and localities offer child care subsidies to working former recipients, and some offer assistance paying for transportation costs. Some localities also offer post-employment services, including assistance obtaining food stamps and Medicaid or SCHIP, and short-term supports to deal with transportation, child care, or family emergencies that might threaten job retention. More such programs may follow. An evaluation of one set of programs indicates that they show promise (Rangarajan and Novak 1999). Expanded efforts in this area could help workers keep jobs and could reduce returns to welfare.

Education and training activities that lead to higher-paying jobs or advancement on the job are another way to increase the wages of welfare recipients who go to work. The work-first strategies of many states have focused on welfare recipients' obtaining a job, any job, as a means of "getting a foot in the door." Many state and local governments are now combining work-focused strategies with education and training to help recipients move into higher-paying jobs and jobs with more potential for advancement. In light of TANF's work requirements and time limits on benefits for current welfare recipients, attaining these goals means designing programs that combine work with training and education activities. Some agencies work with employers to place recipients in entry-level jobs that are the first rung of a defined career ladder (with the potential for raises and promotions) or directly in higher-paying jobs with benefits. There is some evidence that employment-focused programs help long-term recipients the most, but that a mix of activities tends to help the broadest range of recipients (Michalopoulos and Schwartz 2000).

Another means of helping current recipients move off welfare is to supplement low wages. Some states have done this through TANF by increasing earnings disregards. Yet recipients who are combining work and welfare continue to use up their lifetime allotment of benefits. Allowing workers to "stop the clock" until their wages increase is one way to support their transition into the labor market. Supplementing low wages through expansion of non-TANF programs, such as the EITC, should also be considered.

For the most part, states have the flexibility to implement the kinds of programs described above. However, PRWORA does restrict the duration of education and training activities for welfare recipients to 12 months. This and other such limitations could be removed or reduced, especially when education and training are conducted in combination with part-time work.

Another change in federal policy might be to hold states directly accountable for the job placement, retention, wage levels, and wage growth of TANF recipients. Similar performance measures are used for programs under the Workforce Investment Act. Currently, one portion of TANF's high-performance bonus is based on job entry, retention, and earnings gains, but since it entails a relatively small amount of money, states may essentially choose not to compete for it.

Policy should also focus on recipients who have not succeeded in moving into the workforce and whose five-year limit on benefits is imminent. Many of these long-term recipients face multiple barriers to work, and it is unlikely that all of them will fall within the 20 percent of state caseloads that can be exempted from the time limit. States therefore need to concentrate their efforts on programs for these recipients, and many are beginning to do so. (See chapter 9 for a more detailed description.)

True to the goal of reducing welfare dependency through work, many states have moved from permanently exempting some recipients from work requirements and time limits to temporarily exempting them. This shift recognizes that some people need additional time to deal with circumstances that pose barriers to work, but can eventually move to work (Thompson et al. 1998). Federal law could embrace this strategy yet maintain a lifetime limit on benefits by linking specific time extensions to various work-preparation activities. The current exemption from time limits for 20 percent of a state's caseload, regardless of the characteristics of that caseload, can result in uneven application of who gets exemptions across and within states at different times. Exemptions or extensions based directly on individual needs and work activity are more likely to accomplish the goal of moving recipients into the workforce.

Finally, former TANF recipients who are not on welfare and not working are at risk of falling beneath the policy radar screen. A few states have organized efforts to get in touch with sanctioned families to make sure they understand the rules and to offer help in coming back into compliance. However, the law provides no incentive for such activity or for efforts to limit situations in which extreme hardship results from loss of welfare benefits.

Balancing the desire for strong sanctions to back up program requirements against the harm caused when families and children lose benefits is a tough problem. It is imperative that more be learned about the extent to which sanctioned recipients misunderstand rules or have problems (e.g., mental illness) that keep them from meeting requirements. In addition, continuing efforts to increase access to food stamps and Medicaid benefits for all eligible former recipients, whether working or not, are critical to supporting the families who leave welfare, including the sanctioned ones.

NOTES

The author would like to acknowledge both the key input of Sheila Zedlewski on this chapter and the research assistance of Donald Alderson.

1. Chapter 5 discusses the evidence regarding absorption of welfare recipients into labor markets from an aggregate perspective. This chapter focuses on evidence regarding employment outcomes for individual recipients.

2. Chapter 1 describes state work policies in more detail.

3. Based on Urban Institute calculations from the monthly Current Population Survey outgoing rotation group.

4. Results regarding jobs of former recipients are from NSAF data. For more detail, see Loprest (2001).

5. Data from the Current Population Survey.

6. This income estimate is based on NSAF data and includes earnings of the former recipient, spouse, or partner at the time of the interview in 1999, plus average monthly receipt from the prior year (1998) of child support payments, SSI, social security, and pension and investment income.

7. Alternative measures to the traditional poverty measure abound, including those of Boushey et al. (2001), who calculate minimum income needs, called "basic family budgets." Alternatives to existing minimum wage legislation, often called "living wages" and set at levels several times higher than the current minimum wage, are also being debated in communities around the country.

8. These studies include only those who had left welfare for at least two months.

9. See Zedlewski and Loprest (2001) for a review of studies that address the prevalence of these barriers.

REFERENCES

Acs, Gregory, and Pamela Loprest. 2001. "Synthesis Report of the Findings from ASPE's 'Leavers' Grants." Washington, D.C.: U.S. Department of Health and Human Services.

Boushey, Heather, Chauna Brocht, Bethney Gundersen, and Jared Bernstein. 2001. *Hardships in America: The Real Story of Working Families.* Washington, D.C.: Economic Policy Institute.

Cherlin, Andrew, Linda Burton, Judith Francis, Jane Henrici, Laura Lein, James Quane, and Karen Bogen. 2001. "Sanctions and Case Closing for Noncompliance: Who Is Affected and Why." Welfare, Children, and Families Policy Brief 01-1. Baltimore, Md.: Johns Hopkins University.

Danziger, Sandra, Mary Corcoran, Sheldon Danziger, Colleen Heflin, Ariel Kalil, Judith Levine, Daniel Rosen, Kristin Seefeldt, Kristine Siefert, and Richard Tolman. 2000. "Barriers to the Employment of Welfare Recipients." Ann Arbor, Mich.: Poverty Research and Training Center, University of Michigan.

Loprest, Pamela. 2001. "How Are Families Who Left Welfare Doing over Time? A Comparison of Two Cohorts of Welfare Leavers." *FRBNY Economic Policy Review.* New York: Federal Reserve Bank of New York.

Michalopoulos, Charles, and Christine Schwartz. 2000. "What Works Best for Whom: Impacts of 20 Welfare-to-Work Programs by Subgroup." Washington, D.C.: U.S. Department of Health and Human Services.

Moffitt, Robert, and David Stevens. 2001. "Changing Caseloads: Macro Influences and Micro Composition." *FRBNY Economic Policy Review.* New York: Federal Reserve Bank of New York.

Pavetti, LaDonna, and Gregory Acs. 1997. "Moving Up, Moving Out, or Going Nowhere? A Study of the Employment Patterns of Young Women." Washington, D.C.: The Urban Institute.

Rangarajan, Anu, and Tim Novak. 1999. "The Struggle to Sustain Employment: The Effectiveness of the Postemployment Services Demonstration. Final Report." Princeton, N.J.: Mathematica Policy Research, Inc.

Thompson, Terri, Pamela Holcomb, Pamela Loprest, and Kathleen Brennan. 1998. *State Welfare-to-Work Policies for People with Disabilities: Changes since Welfare Reform.* Washington, D.C.: U.S. Department of Health and Human Services.

U.S. General Accounting Office. 2000. *Welfare Reform: State Sanction Policies and Number of Families Affected.* FAO-HEHS-00-44. Washington, D.C.: U.S. General Accounting Office.

U.S. Department of Health and Human Services, Administration for Children and Families. 2000. "Temporary Assistance to Needy Families (TANF) Program: Third Annual Report to Congress." Washington, D.C.: U.S. Government Printing Office.

Zedlewski, Sheila, and Donald Alderson. 2001. "Do Families on Welfare in the Post-TANF Era Differ from Their Pre-TANF Counterparts?" Washington, D.C.: The Urban Institute. *Assessing the New Federalism* Discussion Paper 01-03.

Zedlewski, Sheila, and Pamela Loprest. 2001. "How Well Does TANF Work for the Most Disadvantaged Families?" In *The New World of Welfare,* edited by Rebecca M. Blank and Ron Haskins (311–34). Washington, D.C.: Brookings Institution.

3

Family Structure and Childbearing before and after Welfare Reform

Robert I. Lerman

Two of the most important objectives of welfare reform are encouraging two-parent families and stemming the growth in nonmarital births. To achieve these objectives, PRWORA and other welfare policy changes of the 1990s altered benefits and eligibility to promote work and marriage, strengthened procedures for establishing paternity, and improved the enforcement of child support obligations. PRWORA also gave states discretion in disbursing federal grants and allowed them to establish their own programs to encourage dual parenting and marriage.

This chapter describes the family composition trends that preceded PRWORA and contributed to the passage of reforms that are designed to influence individuals' marriage, childbearing, and divorce decisions. It then looks at shifts in family structure since 1996 relative to welfare reform's family structure objectives. Finally, it describes further actions policymakers and researchers can take to ensure that welfare programs achieve these objectives.

Welfare Reform and Family Structure before PRWORA

Concerns over rising levels of divorce, nonmarital births, and single parenthood and over welfare's role in promoting these outcomes are hardly new. Worries over the breakdown of the American family jumped to the center of policy debates with the publication of the Moynihan report in 1965.[1] The report highlighted the sharp rise in female headship among black families, including the jump in the proportion of black children born outside marriage, and called for national action to expand employment opportunities for black men. Although the report elicited criticism, the social problems it highlighted have become increasingly important over the last three decades. Child poverty has become increasingly associated with single-parent families. In addition, a large body of research has found that growing up in a single-parent family has detrimental long-term effects on children beyond those that stem from its connections with poverty.

Policymakers and commentators have often blamed the welfare system for promoting divorce, nonmarital births, and single parenthood, especially among low-income parents.[2] In response, successive administrations and Congresses came to view strengthening families as a primary goal of any reform of the welfare system.[3] Unfortunately, it has never been clear which welfare reforms would effectively promote stable and thriving two-parent, married-couple families without inflicting harm on children in single-parent families.

The trends that prompted calls for reform had been gathering momentum over several decades. The annual number of divorces between couples caring for children doubled between 1950 and 1972, from 6.3 to 12.5 per 1,000 children. That number peaked in 1981 at 18.7, then fell to 16.8 in 1990. The sharp rise in nonmarital births as a percentage of all births began around 1970. Between 1920 and 1968, the nonmarital birth ratio rose only 7 percentage points, from 3 percent to nearly 10 percent (Cutright 1973). In contrast, between 1968 and 2000, the nonmarital birth ratio jumped more than 20 percentage points, from 10 percent to 33 percent. A decline in widowhood and an increase in remarriage partly offset the increase in divorce and nonmarital births. Still, the share of children under age 18 living outside two-parent families rose from 12 percent in 1960 to 32 percent in 1996. Figure 3-1 shows the steady increase in children living outside two-parent families along with the steady rise in the nonmarital birth ratio.

The disturbing trends toward a greater number of children living outside two-parent families occurred among both black and white families. Blacks, however, have historically experienced higher rates of single-

Figure 3-1. *Trends in the Nonmarital Birth Ratio and Share of Children Not Living in Two-Parent Families, 1968–99*

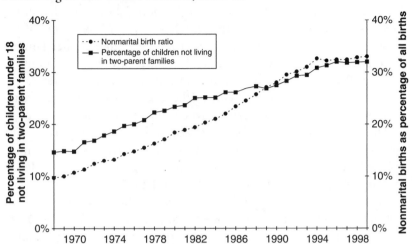

Source: U.S. Bureau of the Census (2000), table CH-1; and National Center for Health Statistics (1999), table 4.

parent households, and the gap increased between 1960 and 1996. In 1960, 9 percent of white children and 33 percent of black children lived outside two-parent families. By 1996, 25 percent of white children and 66 percent of black children lived outside two-parent families. The racial gap in the nonmarital birth ratio widened from 30 percentage points in 1968 to 44 in 1996.

For all families, an increase in the number of children living with never-married parents accounted for about half the rise in the number of children living with single parents during the years between 1960 and 1996. The percentage of children living with a never-married parent rose from only 0.3 percent of all children in 1960 to 10 percent in 1996. This increase is of particular concern because children living with a single, never-married parent often face more serious economic and social disadvantages than do children raised in other single-parent homes. Unlike children of divorced parents, the majority of children born to never-married parents never reside with both of their biological parents. These children are also much less likely to receive child support payments than are children of divorced parents (Sorensen and Halpern 1999).

An increase in the share of children living with a divorced parent accounted for most of the remaining growth in the proportion of children living with single parents. By 1996, about 10 percent of children lived with a divorced parent, up from 2 percent in 1960. Most of the growth occurred among single-mother families; single-father families increased sharply in percentage terms, but started from a very low initial level. In 1960, 8 percent of children lived with unmarried mothers, compared with 24 percent in 1996. During the same period, the share of children living with unmarried fathers rose from 1 percent to 4 percent.

The increase in the number of children living with never-married parents partly reflected changes in marriage patterns among non-married parents. In the past, nonmarital pregnancies more often led to marriage before the birth of a child (Bachu 1999). Between 1950 and 1954, about 5 million women age 15 to 29 gave birth for the first time. About 83 percent of these children were conceived after marriage. Of the 17 percent of children conceived outside of marriage, more than half of the children were born to couples who opted to marry before their child's birth. In 1994, about 6.3 million first births occurred, with 47 percent of those children conceived after marriage. But only 23 percent of the parents who conceived a child before marriage married before the child's birth. Between 1990 and 1994, 40.5 percent of first births among 15- to 29-year-old mothers were nonmarital births.

Decisions by married couples to have fewer children also contributed to the rising share of births to unmarried parents. However, declining marital fertility accounted for only about 20 percent of the increased nonmarital birth ratio between 1960 and 1999 (Offner 2001).

The data on birth rates and on children living in one-parent or two-parent families leave out important details about the living arrangements of children. First, in both 1980 and 1999, about 10 percent of children lived in a family with two parents but only one biological parent (Miller and Moorman 1989; Acs and Nelson 2001a). This group of children is worth noting, since some of the gains for children from living with both parents do not extend to step-parent families. Second, about 3 percent of children live with two biological parents who are not married to each other. These relationships are more often temporary than those between married parents. Third, among children in single-mother families, about a third live in households with other adult relatives or adult non-relatives. These mothers have access to resources drawn from the extended family unit.

Changes in Benefits and Eligibility under PRWORA

Over the past 30 years, virtually all advocates of welfare reform have emphasized the need to raise benefits for two-parent families, both to remedy the system's inequities and to lessen incentives that favor one-parent over two-parent families. Unfortunately, these measures contain inevitable trade-offs between improving family incentives and providing adequate income to the poorest families.

Maintaining benefit policies that are neutral to family structure or that reward two-parent families is difficult under a need-based system. Welfare's primary purpose is to help poor families meet basic expenses. Welfare benefits have traditionally made it easier for single mothers, a group at high risk of poverty, to live independently, without the aid of their children's fathers or their families. This "independence effect" is often reinforced by the structure of benefit eligibility.[4] To target benefits on the poorest families, welfare payments phase out sharply with income. As an unintended consequence, added income from a husband lowers welfare benefits, thereby reducing the economic gain from marriage. Before PRWORA, many poor single parents qualified not only for AFDC, but also for a package of in-kind benefits (including food stamps, Medicaid, child care, and housing assistance). The structure of the benefit package discouraged marriage both because it helped mothers live independently and because added income contributed by a potential spouse would be largely offset by reduced welfare benefits.

In the 1990s, federal and state welfare policy changes significantly altered eligibility requirements to encourage marriage and the formation of two-parent families. In replacing AFDC with TANF, legislators introduced time limits and strict work requirements that could reduce the ability of jobless single parents to make ends meet without the help of work and/or other adults. In addition, under TANF, states have used their discretion to increase the amount of earnings not subject to benefit reductions, thereby allowing single parents more independence while reducing recipients' disincentive to marry a low-wage worker. PRWORA also allowed states to eliminate rules that have long restricted the ability of two-parent families to obtain AFDC benefits. As of 1999, only six states retained the discriminatory AFDC rules, 33 eliminated all restrictions on two-parent families, and the remaining 12 retained only some of the former AFDC restrictions (Rowe 2000).

Other reforms have increased the access that low-income, two-parent families have to in-kind benefits. Changes in Medicaid and the creation of the State Children's Health Insurance Program (SCHIP) raised income eligibility levels and weakened the link between cash welfare assistance and Medicaid.[5] These expansions have provided an additional benefit to working single parents, but have also allowed more poor single mothers who marry a low-wage worker to retain health insurance coverage (Kenney and Haley 2001). Despite these changes, eligible two-parent families are less likely than eligible one-parent families to enroll in Medicaid (Davidoff et al. 2000). Thus, broadening health insurance coverage could have positive or negative effects on marriage incentives.

Before welfare reform, the Food Stamp program applied the same benefit schedules to one-parent and two-parent families. Changes to the program under PRWORA have reduced benefit levels for some families, but they have widened access among families with earnings. PRWORA, by lowering the standard deduction, effectively reduced food stamp benefits for individuals with earnings. Recent changes in regulations, however, have allowed states to raise asset limits, making more working families, including some two-parent families, eligible to receive food stamps (Horng and Dean 2001). PRWORA and state TANF programs contain additional money for child care subsidies, which help mainly low-income single parents. In some cases, these subsidies enhance the independence effect and may discourage single parents from marrying.[6] In other cases, however, the subsidies raise the net income of two-earner married couples.

The major expansions of the EITC that took place in the mid-1990s strengthened marriage incentives for some groups, but weakened such incentives for others. The expanded EITC raises income the most for families with earnings of about $12,000 or less. For each $100 increase in income above that level, the EITC declines by $21. Because EITC payments first increase and then decrease with earnings, the EITC can promote marriage between a low-income working and a nonworking spouse, but can discourage marriage between two low-income workers. For example, as of the 2000 tax year, the EITC provided about $3,607 per year to a one-earner married couple with two children and earnings of $14,000 per year. On the other hand, a mother of two earning $10,000 per year who married a man earning $14,000 per year reduced her family's annual EITC by $2,105. EITC levels are highest for single parents in the kinds of jobs those who leave welfare often obtain and for married couples with very low earnings, usually because only one adult is working.

Despite efforts to increase help for low-income, married-couple families, marital disincentives (and occasional bonuses) remain part of the nation's income transfer system. A recent study of family structure and income and benefits (TANF, food stamps, EITC, Medicaid, and child care) among mothers in Oklahoma shows that marriage often leads to benefit decreases (Hepner and Reed 2000). The study looks at household income for mothers earning various wage rates whose partners are working full-time and earning $8 per hour. It finds that if a nonworking mother marries her partner, her household income rises 30 percent. However, a mother working full-time and earning the minimum wage who chooses to marry her low-wage partner reduces her household income by 19 percent. The reduction in income is much more dramatic if two low-wage working parents living together on an unreported basis decide to marry: Total household income falls by more than half, from $2,418 per month to $1,194.

Detailed tabulations on California reveal continued marriage disincentives, though the size of the effects varies with the earnings of the single mother and her potential husband or partner, and other income sources.[7] For example, the net income of a single mother earning $10,000 per year with no housing benefits or child support would be 134 percent of the federal poverty level; if she married a man earning $14,000 per year, the family's living standard would actually decline to 128 percent of the federal poverty level. On the other hand, family income would reach 170 per cent of the federal poverty level if the couple cohabited on an unreported basis, and 159 percent if the couple reported cohabiting. Marriage ends up raising the income of the former single parent's family by only 35 percent (or about $4,950) of the husband's $14,000 in annual earnings.

Little evidence from state and national programs links reductions in marriage penalties to increases in marriage. However, according to one experimental study, more generous policies for two-parent families significantly increased the level and stability of marriage (Gennetian and Miller 2000). Of married couples in the experimental group receiving more generous benefits, 67 percent were still married three years later, compared with only 48 percent of the couples in the study's control group. These results show that improving the financial incentives to marry (or remain married) could reduce divorces and separations significantly.

Direct Interventions to Encourage Marriage and Discourage Nonmarital Births

States use TANF funds to administer teen pregnancy prevention programs (including abstinence and family planning initiatives), improve incentives for married-couple families, promote responsible fatherhood programs, and run marriage-strengthening programs. Activities aimed at promoting and strengthening marriage include launching publicity campaigns, counseling married and cohabiting couples, and encouraging religious leaders and faith-based programs to offer marriage preparation courses and mentoring.[8]

Since PRWORA, many states have substantially expanded their budgets for teen pregnancy prevention and family planning programs, and 30 states report using TANF money for such programs.[9] Most states (36) are conducting media campaigns to discourage teen pregnancy, and 37 have formed coalitions with nongovernmental organizations to prevent teen pregnancy. Studies reveal that some teen pregnancy prevention programs delay pregnancies and reduce teen childbearing. The most effective are intensive, comprehensive interventions that combine youth development and reproductive health components (Kirby 2001). However, since most state-funded programs are not intensive and long-term, their overall impact on pregnancy and childbearing is still unclear.

Few states are directly involved in promoting marriage or trying to prevent adult nonmarital childbearing. As of 1999, 14 states had programs to encourage sexual abstinence before marriage, but only 3 offered formal programs to encourage marriage among unmarried couples expecting a child. To discourage additional nonmarital childbearing among welfare recipients, some states have imposed family caps that prevent mothers who have another child while on welfare from receiving additional TANF payments. As of 2000, 23 states had imposed such caps, up from 14 states in 1996; so far, existing studies have not convincingly demonstrated that family caps reduce nonmarital births (U.S. General Accounting Office 2001). About half of all southern states—but only about one-quarter of other states—conducted media campaigns discouraging nonmarital pregnancies.

Paternity Establishment and Child Support Enforcement

The Child Support Enforcement (CSE) and welfare systems interact in a manner that makes informal sharing of resources between the custodial and noncustodial parents more advantageous than relying on formal support systems. CSE enforces laws requiring noncustodial parents to help support their children. But these support payments, which lower the noncustodial parent's net income, typically make the custodial parent ineligible for most welfare benefits. Thus, the net income of the custodial parent on welfare largely stays the same.

Although child support does little to help raise the income of most single mothers on welfare, support obligations reduce men's incentive to father nonmarital children or to live separately from a child's mother. Research shows that effective enforcement of paternity and support obligations restrains growth in nonmarital births, divorce, and families headed by single mothers (Nixon 1997; Huang 2001). Support obligations, however, may discourage some divorced fathers from remarrying (Bloom, Conrad, and Miller 1999).

States have stepped up efforts to establish paternity. The sharp increases in legally established paternity rates since 1990 have raised the cost of nonmarital childbearing, because more men are required to pay support. Forty-two states report expanding paternity establishment programs in an effort to reduce nonmarital childbearing (Wertheimer, Jager, and Moore 2000). Some studies suggest that states' efforts to improve their paternity establishment programs are working; states with such programs have seen reductions in the rate of nonmarital births (Plotnick et al. 2000; Nixon 1997). The high paternity rates should lead to increased support awards and payments, especially given the expanded powers and tools granted by Congress under PRWORA. Higher award and payment levels raise the costs of divorce and separation to the noncustodial parent but, in many cases, reduce these costs for the custodial parent. While states with effective child support enforcement have achieved lower divorce rates than other states, the impact on the nation is uncertain, since national increases in child support collections have been modest (Lerman and Sorensen 2001). The disappointing growth in collections stems in part from the weak earnings capacities of noncustodial fathers. Recognizing the problems of collecting child support from unemployed or marginally employed men, policymakers are supporting programs to assist low-income, noncustodial fathers to find jobs and raise their earnings.

Effects of PRWORA on Marriage and Nonmarital Childbearing

Overall, reforms to the nation's welfare benefit structure during the 1990s have

- Reduced the financial incentives for single parents to remain on welfare for several years or to stay on welfare without formal employment;
- Increased work-related benefits to help single parents escape poverty, even in low-wage jobs;
- Raised the costs of unwed parenthood, divorce, and separation for noncustodial parents;
- Eliminated program rules that explicitly discriminated against two-parent, married-couple families;
- Provided additional help to low-income, two-parent families; and
- Added disincentives for individuals who benefit most from PRWORA's progressivity to marry and, in some cases, to share households.

In addition to these reforms, policymakers are increasingly speaking out about the advantages of marriage and the stability of two-parent families. They also emphasize the disadvantages of out-of-wedlock childbearing. Even if new policies offer only modest financial incentives to marry, potential parents and spouses may respond to the moral messages policymakers are trying to convey.

The full effects of program changes and public messages will not emerge for several years.[10] Although it is too early to tie PRWORA to any observed changes in family structure, a review of recent developments reveals how family structure trends are progressing relative to the major objectives of welfare reform.

One positive trend is that fewer teenagers are having children. Nearly all births to teenage mothers occur outside of marriage (Wertheimer and Moore 1998). The number of births per 1,000 women among 18- to 19-year-olds peaked in 1992, at about 94.5, but declined to 79.5 in 2000. An even sharper decline occurred among 15- to 17-year-olds, with births among this group falling from 38.7 in 1991 to 27.5 in 2000. The birth rates of black 18- to 19-year-olds increased rapidly in the late 1980s, peaked in 1990, and declined throughout the 1990s. Although encouraging, much of the reduction occurred between 1991 and 1996, before

PRWORA likely affected behavior. Trends among women age 18 to 29 were less positive. The number of nonmarital births per 100 women in that age group rose from 4.0 in 1995 to 4.3 in 1999.[11] Some of this rise may reflect the increasing rate of cohabitation among couples having children together.

Another positive trend is that the decline in married couples as a share of all couples with children leveled off in the mid-1990s. As figure 3-2 shows, black married-couple families as a percentage of all black families with children hit a low of 36 percent around 1994, then turned upward in 1998, rising to about 38 percent by 2000. The proportion of white children in married-couple families hit a low of 74 percent in 1998 and rose slightly to 75 percent in 2000.[12]

Two recent studies examining less traditional, more complex living arrangements also reveal positive trends in family structure. Dupree and Primus (2001), relying on tabulations of Census data, find that the share of children living with a noncohabiting single mother declined from 19.9 percent in 1995 to 18.4 percent in 2000. The 1.5 percentage point decline pushed up the percentage of children living with married-couple families (by 0.6 percentage points), with a cohabiting or single father (by

Figure 3-2. *Percentage of All Families with Children that Are Married-Couple Families, by Race: 1970–2000*

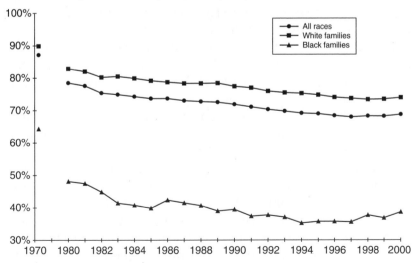

Source: U.S. Bureau of the Census (2000), table FM-2.

0.6 percentage points), and with cohabiting single mothers (by 0.3 percentage points). Among black families, Dupree and Primus find that the share of children living with single mothers fell from 47.1 to 43.1 percent, leading to a 4 percentage point rise in the number of children living with married couple families (from 34.8 percent to 38.9 percent). Hispanic children experienced a comparable, though smaller, shift toward living with married-couple families, while the share of white children living with married couples barely changed.

Using more detailed NSAF data, Acs and Nelson (2001a) find a steeper decline in the overall share of children living with single mothers between 1997 and 1999. According to their study, the share declined 2.1 percentage points, while the share of children living with married parents rose 0.4 percentage points. Interestingly, they observed a sizable increase of 1.4 percentage points in the share of children living with cohabiting parents, with about half of the couples raising children they had in common.

Another study of NSAF data finds that the decline in the proportion of single-parent families did not extend to non-Hispanic black families (Lerman 2001). Black single-parent families made up 51.5 percent of all families with children in 1997 and 51.6 percent in 1999. Cohabiting couples increased sharply among blacks, from 5.0 percent to 7.8 percent of families, while the share of black married-couple families declined from 34.5 percent to 31.5 percent. Between 1997 and 1999, the share of black children living with two biological parents remained steady at 31 percent.

One way to assess whether welfare reform has affected family structure is to simulate future birth rates and marriage patterns based on trends before PRWORA. Would the trends toward higher nonmarital births and single-parent families have continued, or were these shifts already reaching threshold levels? Did strong economic growth help limit the rise in single-parent families?

Acs and Nelson (2001b) deal with these questions by assuming that the *changes* in family structure that low-income families would have experienced without welfare reform can be reasonably projected as equal to the actual changes experienced by moderate-income and moderately educated families. If their assumption is valid, then comparing what happened to low-income and moderate-income families provides a plausible estimate of the effects of welfare policy. Such comparisons show larger drops in single parenthood for low-income than for moderate-income groups, especially in the shift from single-parent families to cohabitating couple families. The proportion of single mother families declined by 2.9 percentage points among those with high school educations or less, but only 0.8 points among those with some college. Almost all of the decline in single parenthood among both groups was offset by increases in cohabitation. These and other differences suggest a role for welfare policy, though subject to an important caveat. The assumption that changes other than welfare policy affected low-income and moderate-income individuals in similar ways is probably untrue since the economic gains were larger among low-income individuals than among moderate-income individuals.

In his analysis of welfare reform's role in affecting family structure, Murray (2001) looks for any departures from long-term trends in marriage, nonmarital childbearing, and teen births. Although some of the post-1960 trends away from marriage and toward nonmarital births became more favorable in the early 1990s, the white nonmarital birth ratios were higher than would have been predicted from extrapolations of past trends. Moreover, black marriage rates continued to decline through the 1990s, and the black nonmarital birth ratio leveled off at extremely high rates. Murray concludes that welfare reform did little to reduce nonmarital births or increase marriage.

Welfare reform might be expected to immediately affect parents about to have, or who have recently had, a baby. Around the time of a child's birth, relationships among the parents tend to be close, and marriage is often a serious option. With welfare's new incentives, single parenting among this segment of the population might be expected to fall sharply. Unfortunately, the decline in single parenting among families with newborns was more modest than for all families between 1997 and 1999. The single-parent share of families with a child age 1 or younger declined from 21.2 percent to 20.0 percent, while the single-parent share for all families fell from 29.3 percent to 27.3 percent. During this time, married couples comprising two biological or adoptive parents became a smaller share of families with children age 1 or younger (falling from 69.8 percent to 68.6 percent). However, cohabiting two-parent families with a child age 1 or younger jumped from 6.8 to 8.6 percent of all families in this group.

The trends among black families with newborns were particularly negative. Among these families, the share of married two-parent couples fell substantially, from 35.8 percent to 25.8 percent of black families with newborns. A rise in cohabiting two-parent families partly offset this drop, jumping from 4.1 to 9.8 percent of black families with newborns. The share of single-parent black families with newborns rose from 55.8 to

59.6 percent. In contrast, whites and Hispanics saw a decline in the share of single-parent families with newborns.

Although the evidence shows mixed progress on family structure objectives, paternity establishment programs have had measurable success. In 1989, when nonmarital births totaled 1.1 million, the CSE system reported only 339,000 established paternities, leaving about 750,000 children with no legal father on record. By 1997, the number of established paternities, including those for children born in earlier years, was equal to the number of nonmarital births (about 1.25 million). As of 2000, CSE established about 200,000 more paternities than nonmarital births. Because research indicates that programs legally establishing paternity lower births conceived outside of marriage (Plotnick et al. 2000), states' emphasis on paternity establishment programs during the 1990s likely played a role in slowing the growth rate of nonmarital births. However, since states embarked on these efforts well before 1996, the recent increases in established paternities may have little to do with PRWORA or other policies implemented in the late 1990s.

Although child support collections rose only modestly in the 1980s and 1990s (Lerman and Sorensen 2001), policymakers continue to emphasize child support enforcement. As noted earlier, welfare recipients gain little from child support, because most payments cut into welfare benefits. However, with more than a million families leaving welfare in recent years, more low-income single parents stand to benefit from support payments. Since 1996, child support collections have risen among low-income custodial parents. Among custodial mothers with a high school education or less, child support receipts increased by 23 percent from 1996 to 1998 (Sorensen 2001). The gains for less-educated single mothers were higher than for more-educated single mothers, suggesting that recent changes in social policy are reaching the right constituents. Also encouraging is the rise in the share of poor children eligible for child support who received payments, up from 29 percent in 1996 to 32 percent in 1998.

Welfare reform might also be expected to affect people's decision to marry. Did the reforms, along with the thriving economy, stimulate an increase in the proportion of young people marrying? The answer, at least in the short term, is no. The proportion of married women continued to decline throughout the 1990s. Between 1995 and 2000, the share of never-married women in the 25 to 29 age group rose from 35 to 38 percent. The already high proportion of never-married black women increased further, from 59 to 62 percent. Marriage rates among younger and older women also declined.

Policy Implications

The central objectives of welfare policies enacted in the 1990s were twofold: to encourage marriage and two-parent families, and to increase the share of single mothers who are employed and thus less reliant on welfare assistance. In some cases, policies implemented to support welfare reform's employment goals conflict with the goal of reducing single parenthood. For example, expanding benefits to low-income, employed single mothers and providing these women with welfare-to-work programs could make them more independent and less likely to marry. In other cases, schedules that phase out benefits quickly once a welfare recipient gains additional income might discourage work and marriage.

An important step toward making marriage an attractive option for low-income families is to reduce or eliminate the financial disincentives remaining in the system. Under existing tax and transfer programs, marriage between a low-earning man and a single mother often does little to increase a family's living standards. In many cases, living standards decline when a cohabiting couple marries. One way to reduce such disincentives is to restructure the EITC, an important source of income for low-wage families. Introducing a tax schedule that grants married-couple families more generous credits than single-parent families would make marriage more attractive. A second option is to use a household definition, rather than marital status, to determine eligibility for benefits other than the EITC. This change would make cohabiting couples entitled to the same benefits as married couples and thus improve the financial status of many families. However, defining recipients by household composition might make single parenting more attractive than cohabitation, since counting the partner's income would lower government benefits. In addition, enforcing valid reporting practices among beneficiaries could cause government agencies to become intrusive, reducing their effectiveness.

A second approach to increasing marriage and family stability is to create programs specifically geared to unmarried new parents. Helping unmarried, low-income parents establish stable families before mother-father and father-child relationships have the chance to erode can have lifelong benefits. Training, family and career counseling, and mentoring would likely prevent some new parents from separating. Even if parents ultimately part, programs that establish clear, fair support obligations could reduce nonpayment. Noncustodial fathers who take an important caretaking role early on may be more likely to meet support obligations and spend time with their children. Shouldering the role of parent might also increase custodial and noncustodial fathers' motivation to succeed in the job market.

A third recommendation for promoting family stability is to develop strategies that discourage nonmarital childbearing and promote married, two-parent families. Many state and federal programs aim to prevent teen pregnancy and teen childbearing through family planning, media campaigns, and partnerships with local organizations. Policymakers and researchers, however, must develop measures to determine whether these approaches are effective. Policymakers should also consider indirect ways to encourage childbearing within marriage, such as improving career outcomes for low-income and minority men and women through educational programs and training development. One reason for the low rate of married-couple minority families is that the unstable employment and inadequate wages of many low-income minority males reduce their marriageability (Edin 2000). With few marriageable men available, minority women have less incentive to delay childbearing or to marry the father of their child.

Intervening early is likely to yield the highest payoff. But while education reforms are necessary, they are not sufficient. Additional steps are necessary to widen the routes to quality careers beyond the four-year college. Doing so should involve expanding access to career internships, apprenticeships, and other well-designed career-oriented programs (Lerman 1999).

Finally, the research and policy community should develop and test major initiatives aimed at improving parenting and preventing nonmarital childbearing. We have learned from an earlier demonstration, Parents' Fair Share, that achieving success with noncustodial fathers of children on welfare is difficult. The program's impacts on their earnings, child support payments, and involvement with their children were disappointing (Knox and Redcross 2000). Yet even this program provides useful lessons. The intervention helped some groups of fathers, and it suggested the importance of early intervention. One of the next steps should be to examine the impact of combining the service orientation embedded in the Fragile Families Demonstration Project with financial incentives more favorable to marriage. Another should be to evaluate the nonmarital childbearing, marriage, and family formation impacts of youth development and career programs.

NOTES

The author wishes to thank Elaine Sorensen, Alan Weil, and Kenneth Finegold for useful comments.

1. See Rainwater and Yancey (1967) for the full report and responses to the report.

2. Murray (1984), for example, argued that welfare benefits helped stimulate single parenthood and its attendant problems by favoring one-parent over two-parent families, reducing the economic incentives to marry or remain married. Research findings, however, have documented only modest impacts of taxes and transfers on the share of single mother families (Moffitt 1998; Hoynes 1997; Alm, Dickert-Conlin, and Whittington 1999). Some recent studies suggest that welfare increases nonmarital childbearing, speeds up second births, and delays remarriage.

3. In 1977, Moynihan, who had been elected to the Senate in 1976, criticized the Carter administration's welfare reform proposal for resembling a negative income tax of the type that, according to a recent experiment, had apparently increased the share of female-headed families and that certainly had not raised the share of two-parent families.

4. An early use of this term came from the conclusions of Hannan, Tuma, and Groeneveld (1977, 1978) that benefits in the form of a negative income tax (NIT) reduced marriage and cohabitation by allowing mothers to live independently. Cain and Wissoker (1990) challenge the findings that the NIT induced lower rates of marriage, but not the conclusion that added income may have an independence effect in other contexts. Lerman (1973) found that as much as one-third of the growth in mother-headed families between 1950 and 1972 resulted from mothers forming separate households instead of living in the households of other relatives.

5. See, for example, Ellwood's 1999 report on five states. In four of the five states examined, all children in families with incomes between 185 and 200 percent of the poverty level qualify for Medicaid or SCHIP; in one of the five (Minnesota), eligibility for children extends to 275 percent of the poverty level.

6. See Long and Clark (1997) for a discussion of the PRWORA changes in child care outlays.

7. Urban Institute calculations from "Expansion of Healthy Families: Design Issues and Marginal Tax Rates" model, supported by a grant from the Medi-Cal Policy Institute. The Medi-Cal Policy Institute's mission is to provide clear and concise data and analysis of the Medi-Cal program. The Medi-Cal Policy Institute is a project of the California HealthCare Foundation, based in Oakland, California.

8. See Wertheimer, Jager, and Moore (2000) and Ooms (2001) for additional details on state activities aimed at curtailing nonmarital births and promoting marriage in an effort to fulfill the family structure objectives of the TANF program.

9. The information in this paragraph comes from Wertheimer, Jager, and Moore (2000).

10. One reason may be that it is more difficult to move women from single motherhood to a stable two-parent situation than to prevent nonmarital childbearing and other routes to single parenthood.

11. These figures are based on the author's tabulations using data from Ventura and Bachrach (2000) and the March 1990, 1995, and 1999 Current Population Surveys.

12. Calculating trends on the basis of the share of children (as opposed to the share of families) in various living arrangements yields similar results.

REFERENCES

Acs, Gregory, and Sandi Nelson. 2001a. " 'Honey, I'm Home.' Changes in Living Arrangements in the Late 1990s." Washington, D.C.: The Urban Institute. *Assessing the New Federalism* Brief B-38.

———. 2001b. "Assessing the Relationship between Welfare Policies and Changes in Living Arrangements of Low-Income Families and Children in the Late 1990s." Unpublished manuscript. Washington, D.C.: The Urban Institute.

Alm, J., S. Dickert-Conlin, and L. A. Whittington. 1999. "Policy Watch: The Marriage Penalty." *Journal of Economic Perspectives* 13 (3): 193–204.

Bachu, Amara. 1999. "Trends in Premarital Childbearing: 1930–1994." Special Studies. Current Population Reports. P23-197. Washington, D.C.: U.S. Census Bureau.

Bloom, David, Cecilia Conrad, and Cynthia Miller. 1999. "Child Support and Fathers' Remarriage and Fertility." In *Fathers under Fire: The Revolution in Child Support Enforcement,* edited by I. Garfinkel, S. McLanahan, D. Meyer, and J. Seltzer (128–56). New York: Russell Sage Foundation.

Cain, Glen G., and Douglas A. Wissoker. 1990. "A Reanalysis of Marital Stability in the Seattle-Denver Income-Maintenance Experiment." *American Journal of Sociology* 95 (5): 1235–69.

Cutright, Phillips. 1973. "Illegitimacy and Income Supplementation." In *Studies in Welfare: The Family, Poverty, and Welfare Programs: Factors Influencing Family Stability,* edited by Robert I. Lerman, vol. 12 (I: 90–138). Washington, D.C.: U.S. Government Printing Office.

Davidoff, Amy J., Bowen Garrett, Diane M. Makuc, and Matthew Schirmer. 2000. "Children Eligible for Medicaid but Not Enrolled: How Great a Policy Concern?" Washington, D.C.: The Urban Institute. *Assessing the New Federalism* Brief A-41.

Dupree, Allen, and Wendell Primus. 2001. "Declining Share of Children Lived with Single Mothers in the Late 1990s." Washington, D.C.: Center on Budget and Policy Priorities.

Edin, Kathryn. 2000. "Few Good Men: Why Poor Mothers Don't Marry or Remarry." *American Prospect* 11 (4): 26–31.

Ellwood, Marilyn. 1999. *The Medicaid Eligibility Maze: Coverage Expands, but Enrollment Problems Persist—Findings from a Five-State Study.* Washington, D.C.: The Urban Institute. *Assessing the New Federalism* Occasional Paper No. 30.

Gennetian, L. A., and C. Miller. 2000. *Encouraging the Formation and Maintenance of Two-Parent Families: Experimental Evidence on Welfare Reform.* Unpublished paper. New York: Manpower Demonstration Research Corporation.

Hannan, Michael T., Nancy Brandon Tuma, and Lyle P. Groeneveld. 1977. "Income and Marital Events: Evidence from an Income-Maintenance Experiment." *American Journal of Sociology* 82: 1186–211.

———. 1978. "Income and Independence Effects on Marital Dissolution: Results from the Seattle and Denver Income-Maintenance Experiments." *American Journal of Sociology* 84: 611–33.

Hepner, Mickey, and W. Robert Reed. 2000. "An Analysis of Work and Marriage Incentives for Welfare Recipients: A State-Level Approach." Norman, Okla.: Department of Economics, University of Oklahoma.

Horng, Ray, and Stacy Dean. 2001. "States' Vehicle Asset Policies in the Food Stamp Program." Washington, D.C.: Center on Budget and Policy Priorities.

Hoynes, Hillary. 1997. "Does Welfare Play Any Role in Female Headship Decisions?" *Journal of Public Economics* 65 (2): 89–117.

Huang, Chien Chung. 2001. "Impacts of Child Support Enforcement on Non-Marital and Marital Births: Is It Different by Racial and Age Groups?" Presented at Joint Center for Poverty Research Conference. Washington, D.C., September.

Kenney, Genevieve, and Jennifer Haley. 2001. "Why Aren't More Uninsured Children Enrolled in Medicaid or SCHIP?" Washington, D.C.: The Urban Institute. *Assessing the New Federalism* Brief B-35.

Kirby, Douglas. 2001. *Emerging Answers: Research Findings on Programs to Reduce Teen Pregnancy.* Washington, D.C.: National Campaign to Prevent Teen Pregnancy.

Knox, Virginia, and Cindy Redcross. 2000. *Parenting and Providing: The Impact of Parents' Fair Share on Parental Involvement.* New York: Manpower Development Research Corporation.

Lerman, Robert I. 1973. "The Family, Poverty, and Welfare Programs: An Introductory Essay on Problems of Analysis and Policy." In *Studies in Public Welfare, The Family, Poverty and Welfare Programs: Factors Influencing Family Instability,* edited by Robert I. Lerman, vol. 12 (I: 1–36). Washington, D.C.: U.S. Government Printing Office.

———. 1999. "Helping Disconnected Youth by Improving Linkages between High Schools and Careers." In *America's Disconnected Youth: Toward a Preventative Strategy,* edited by Douglas Besharov (185–212). Washington, D.C.: American Enterprise Institute and Child Welfare League of American.

———. 2001. "Marriage as a Protective Device Against Economic Hardship." Unpublished manuscript. Washington, D.C.: The Urban Institute.

Lerman, Robert I., and Elaine Sorensen. 2001. "Child Support: Interactions between Private and Public Transfers." NBER Working Paper 8199. Cambridge, Mass.: National Bureau of Economic Research.

Long, Sharon, and Sandra Clark. 1997. "The New Child Care Block Grant: State Funding Choices and Their Implications." Washington, D.C.: The Urban Institute. *Assessing the New Federalism* Brief A-12.

Miller, Louisa F., and Jeanne E. Moorman. 1989. "Married-Couple Families with Children." Studies in Marriage and the Family, P-23, No. 162, 27-36. Washington, D.C.: U.S. Government Printing Office.

Moffitt, Robert. 1998. "The Effect of Welfare on Marriage and Fertility." In *Welfare, the Family, and Reproductive Behavior,* edited by Robert Moffitt (50–97). Washington, D.C.: National Academy Press.

Murray, Charles. 1984. *Losing Ground.* New York: Basic Books.

———. 2001. "Family Formation." In *The New World of Welfare: An Agenda for Reauthorization and Beyond,* edited by Rebecca M. Black and Ron Haskins (137–68). Washington, D.C.: Brookings Institution.

National Center for Health Statistics. 1999. *National Vital Statistics Reports* 48 (16).

Nixon, L. A. 1997. "The Effect of Child Support Enforcement on Marital Dissolution." *Journal of Human Resources* 32 (1): 159–81.

Offner, Paul. 2001. "Reducing Non-Marital Births." Washington, D.C.: Brookings Institution. *Welfare Reform and Beyond* Brief 5.

Ooms, Theodora. 2001. Testimony before the House Ways and Means Committee, Subcommittee on Human Resources. May 22.

Plotnick, R. D., I. Ku, I. Garfinkel, and S. S. McLanahan. 2000. "The Impact of Child Support Enforcement Policy on Nonmarital Childbearing." Paper presented at the Association for Public Policy Analysis and Management's Research Conference. Seattle, Washington.

Rainwater, Lee and William Yancey. 1967. *The Moynihan Report and the Politics of Controversy.* Cambridge, Mass.: MIT Press.

Rowe, Gretchen. 2000. "State TANF Policies as of July 1999." *Welfare Rules Databook.* Washington, D.C.: The Urban Institute.

Sorensen, Elaine. 2001. "Child Support Reforms: Have They Made a Difference for Low-Income Families?" Paper presented at the American Economic Association Meetings. New Orleans, Louisiana, January 5–7.

Sorensen, Elaine, and Ariel Halpern. 1999. "Child Support Enforcement: How Is it Doing?" Washington, D.C.: The Urban Institute. *Assessing the New Federalism* Discussion Paper 99-11.

U.S. Bureau of the Census. 2000. *Families and Living Arrangements: Historical Time Series.* http://www.census.gov/population/www/socdemo/hh-fam.html.

U.S. General Accounting Office. 2001. "Welfare Reform: More Research Needed on TANF Family Caps and Other Policies for Reducing Out-of-Wedlock Births." Washington, D.C. http://www.gao.gov/new.items/d01924.pdf.

Ventura, Stephanie, and Christine Bachrach. 2000. "Nonmarital Childbearing in the United States, 1940–99." *National Vital Statistics Reports* 18 (16).

Wertheimer, Richard, and Kristin Moore. 1998. "Childbearing by Teens: Links to Welfare Reform." Washington, D.C.: The Urban Institute. *Assessing the New Federalism* Brief A-24.

Wertheimer, Richard, Justin Jager, and Kristin Anderson Moore. 2000. "State Policy Initiatives for Reducing Teen and Adult Nonmarital Childbearing: Family Planning to Family Caps." Washington, D.C.: The Urban Institute. *Assessing the New Federalism* Brief A-43.

4

Family Incomes: Rising, Falling, or Holding Steady?

Sheila R. Zedlewski

The dire consequences that many people predicted would flow from enactment of welfare reform legislation in 1996 have not materialized to date. Some predicted that the five-year time limit on welfare benefits and cuts in Supplemental Security Income (SSI), food stamps, and other benefits would lead to greater poverty among families with children (U.S. Department of Health and Human Services 1996; Zedlewski et al. 1996). Others expected hunger and homelessness to soar. Instead, family incomes have risen since welfare reform, and poverty rates have dropped—with one important exception. The disposable income of independent single-parent families in the bottom income quintile, the group most likely to go on welfare, has declined since the passage of PRWORA.

Many factors have contributed to the divergence between the predictions and the experience so far. First, no one anticipated the unprecedented strength of the U.S. economy in the late 1990s. Unemployment rates fell to less than 5 percent in 1998 and then to 4 percent in 2000, the lowest rate since the late 1960s. Second, Congress restored some of the benefit cuts affecting legal immigrants. It reinstated SSI benefits in 1997 and restored some of the food stamp cuts in 1998.[1] Congress also gave states more TANF dollars than originally proposed, and plummeting caseloads freed the states to use block grant funds to provide new supports—

especially child care—for the working poor.[2] Finally, time limits on welfare benefits, included in the original studies of income effects, only began to take effect in most states in the fall of 2001.[3]

This chapter examines how safety net supports affected income and poverty among families with children in 1996 and 1998. It adjusts NSAF data for underreporting of government benefits, includes the value of food stamps and the Earned Income Tax Credit (EITC), and deducts federal income and payroll taxes and out-of-pocket child care expenses.[4] These adjusted data provide estimates of families' disposable income—that is, all sources of cash income, plus the value of food stamps and the EITC, minus federal taxes and out-of-pocket child care expenses.[5] The data also show how the composition of income has changed for families with children, particularly for independent single-parent families (households in which single parents live with their dependent children under age 18 but without other adults).

The results presented here are generally consistent with and expand upon those found by other researchers. While increases in earned income account for most of the improvement in disposable income since 1996, many families also benefited from refundable tax credits, policies that help pay for child care expenses, and increases in child support payments. At the same time, far fewer families received traditional income supports, such as cash welfare and food stamps, in 1998 than in 1996. Independent single parents who fell into the bottom income quintile (below 70 percent of the federal poverty level) suffered an 8 percent drop in real income between 1996 and 1998. The number of persons in independent single-parent families who live in extreme poverty (below 50 percent of the federal poverty level) increased significantly between 1996 and 1998. For these persons, increases in earnings, child support, tax credits, and child care subsidies were not sufficient to offset the loss of benefits from traditional government supports.

This chapter begins with an overview and summary of recent changes in income support policies in the United States. It then examines the change in composition of income and the change in poverty rates for families with children. The final section discusses how the system of income supports might be modified to serve all types of low-income families more effectively. For this to happen, Congress will have to consider not just TANF, but also the broad set of policies known as the safety net.

Government Policies That Affect Family Incomes

During the early 1990s, U.S. income support policy began to focus more attention on families with parents who work yet remain below or near the poverty line. In 1993, Congress expanded the EITC from a maximum payment of $1,511 for workers with two or more children to $3,656 in 1996, a 123 percent increase after adjusting for inflation. Congress also increased the federal minimum wage from $4.25 per hour to $4.75 in 1996 and to $5.15 in 1997. During this same period, many states obtained waivers from federal AFDC policy to increase work incentives for families on welfare. Some states expanded the amount of earnings welfare recipients could keep and still receive cash assistance. Spurred by the new policies and the strong economy, labor force participation rates of single mothers age 16 to 45, which had been essentially flat for many years, rose from about 76 percent in 1993 to over 84 percent in 1997 (*Economic Report of the President* 1999, 112).

Changes in Income Support Policies, 1996 to 1998

Welfare reform moved states further in the direction of supporting work. As noted in the introduction to this book, PRWORA required states to meet strict work participation targets for their welfare caseloads, but it left the means of increasing work up to the states. The law also recognized the importance of supporting families that were moving from welfare to work. It consolidated federal child care dollars into a single grant, the Child Care and Development Fund, and allowed states to shift some of their TANF funds into the child care fund. TANF dollars could be used to pay for work supports as defined by the states, so long as federal dollars were spent on behalf of low-income families. The law also strengthened child support enforcement.

The new legislation narrowed government support for certain groups, however. Most noncitizens were no longer eligible for SSI or food stamps. Disabled children who did not meet a new standard of severe functional limitation were restricted in their eligibility for SSI benefits. The law cut food stamp benefits by moving to a lower payment standard, freezing the standard deduction from income at 1996 levels, and increasing the amount of income counted against benefits. Food stamp eligibility was limited to three months for able-bodied adults who were working fewer than 20 hours per week and who did not have children.

The Balanced Budget Act of 1997 enhanced support for families in several significant ways. It restored SSI eligibility to immigrants living in the United States at the time the welfare reform law was passed, permitted states to cover the cost of food stamp benefits for some or all noncitizens and able-bodied adults who had lost eligibility as a result of PRWORA, and expanded health insurance coverage for children in low-income families outside the welfare system. The new State Children's Health Insurance Program (SCHIP) gave states grants to cover children with family incomes up to 200 percent of the federal poverty level (with an enhanced federal match to cover these costs), or 50 percentage points above existing eligibility, whichever was higher. In 1997, Congress passed the Taxpayer Relief Act, which provided a nonrefundable tax credit worth $400 per child in 1997 and $500 per child thereafter.[6] In 1998, the federal government restored food stamp eligibility to legal immigrant children under age 18, the elderly, and disabled persons living in the United States at the time PRWORA was passed.

Safety Net or Patchwork Quilt?

The system of income support for low-income families falls far short of a tightly woven safety net. Different sets of rules and regulations govern benefit eligibility across the seven major programs that serve low-income families with children (table 4-1).[7] Some programs, such as Medicaid, are entitlements that guarantee benefits to all eligible families, while others, such as child care and housing, operate with discretionary funds that are sufficient to cover only some qualifying families. The maximum income a family can have to qualify for benefits ranges from a low of 18 percent of the federal poverty level in some state TANF programs to more than 300 percent of the federal poverty level in some SCHIP programs. All programs include income from assets in their income eligibility tests, but some programs impose an additional restriction on the amount of assets a family may have, including the fair market value of a car, while other programs have no asset tests. Some income support programs restrict the hours of work individuals can engage in and still be eligible for benefits; some require work as a condition for obtaining benefits; and others have no work-related rules.

Access to services depends largely on the door through which a family enters the support system.[8] Families entering through the welfare cash assistance door have the smoothest access to other safety net programs

(*text continues on page 60*)

Table 4-1. *Major Income Support Programs Serving Families with Children, 1999*

Program	Funding and Governance	Categorical Eligibility	Role of Work and Earnings[a]	Maximum Income[b]	Asset Tests	Maximum Benefit
SSI[c]	Federal entitlement	Severely disabled	Must have limited ability to work	70 percent of FPL	$3,000 per family	70 percent of FPL
TANF[d]	Federal grant to states; states determine eligibility standards within federal guidelines	Families with children	Some states limit work hours and/or require work history for two-parent families	Between 18 and 144 percent of FPL, depending upon state	Financial asset limit set by state. Vehicle value limited to $5,000 in 15 states and D.C.; 24 states have no limit on at least one vehicle	15 to 66 percent of FPL
Food Stamps	Federal government funds and defines eligibility	All households	Eligibility limited to three months for nonworking able-bodied adults without dependents (ABAWDs)	130 percent of FPL	Financial assets <$2,000. Vehicle value limited[e]	29 percent of FPL

(*continued*)

Table 4-1. *Major Income Support Programs Serving Families with Children, 1999 (Continued)*

Program	Funding and Governance	Categorical Eligibility	Role of Work and Earnings[a]	Maximum Income[b]	Asset Tests	Maximum Benefit
Child care	See TANF	Families with children	Must be working, in training, or in job search	Income at or below 85 percent of State Median Income (SMI), or lower at state discretion	—	Up to full cost of care
Housing	See Food Stamps	Renters	—	—	—	Rent limited to maximum of 30 percent of income
EITC	Federal entitlement	Primarily workers with children	Must have earned income	230 percent of FPL	Investment income limited to $2,400 per year	29 percent of FPL (at earnings of 72 percent of FPL)

Health Insurance	Medicaid: Federal- and state-funded entitlement; states determine eligibility standards within federal guidelines. SCHIP: See TANF[e]	Pregnant women, families on and recently off TANF, and low-income children	—	All on SSI All who meet AFDC eligibility as of 1996 Children between 133 percent and 350 percent of FPL, depending upon state	Asset limits eliminated in most states (42) for children's eligibility[h]	Health insurance

FPL = Federal poverty level. All calculations of income and benefits relative to poverty are based on a family with one adult and two children.

[a] Some programs require participation in work activities that are not discussed here.

[b] Level of income (after deductions or disregards, which may be substantial) at which benefits phase down to zero.

[c] Eligibility for elders is not discussed here.

[d] Intermittent supports to low-income families provided using TANF funds may not be considered "assistance," and may have different eligibility rules.

[e] The limit on the fair market value of a vehicle in 1999 was $4,650. However, since TANF recipients are presumptively eligible, the TANF vehicle limits apply in these cases.

[f] Disability-related eligibility other than SSI (e.g., medically needy) is not discussed here.

[g] States may operate SCHIP as a Medicaid expansion, in which case Medicaid rules apply.

[h] See Ross and Cox (2000).

because the programs are often integrated, located together, or form part of a coordinated referral network. Alternative entry points, such as child support or subsidized child care, are considerably less well connected to other programs. Finding a way through this maze of noncash programs has become more important as more low-income families have left the welfare rolls.

How Have Family Incomes and Resources Changed since 1996?

This patchwork of income support policies can have a major effect on family income. An examination of the safety net in 12 states in 1997 revealed that income for a family with one parent and two children could increase dramatically when the parent moved from welfare to work—if the family received all available benefits (Acs et al. 1998). With the move to part-time work at the minimum wage, family income (including cash welfare, earnings, food stamps, and EITC) would increase by 51 percent, on average. With the move to full-time work, total income would grow by another 20 percent. However, the effect of moving from no work to work varies considerably across states because of wide variations in their TANF policies. In general, families realized greater increases in states with particularly low welfare benefits and lower increases in states with more generous welfare benefits.

Sources of Income Support, 1996 to 1998

The picture is less rosy for families that do not receive these supports. Overall, the use of government supports by families with children declined between 1996 and 1998 (table 4-2). A significantly smaller share received TANF, food stamps, and Medicaid or SCHIP benefits in 1998 than in 1996. The EITC continued to play a prominent role in family income, however, with about one-third of families benefiting from the tax credit in each year.

Not surprisingly, these supports matter most to families with incomes in the bottom quintile.[9] Despite significant declines in receipt of assistance after 1996, over half of these families received food stamps, about one-third received TANF, and more than one-half had some Medicaid coverage in 1998. Some families in the second income quintile also received support from TANF and food stamps in 1998, although the rates of receipt declined significantly from 1996. Over one-quarter of families

Table 4-2. *Percentage of Families with Various Sources of Income and Expenses*

Source	All Families with Children (%)			Independent Single-Parent Families (%)		
	1996	1998	Change	1996	1998	Change
All incomes						
Earnings[a]	95	97	2*	83	88	5*
Social insurance[b]	17	16	(1)	16	16	—
Child support receipt	15	15	—	34	35	1
TANF[c]	16	11	(5)*	34	24	(10)*
Food Stamps	21	16	(5)*	48	40	(8)*
Medicaid/SCHIP	22	20	(2)*	43	41	(2)
EITC	35	34	(1)	55	61	6*
SSI	5	5	—	9	7	(2)
Federal taxes	94	95	1*	78	83	5*
Child care expenses[d]	30	30	—	32	34	2
Bottom income quintile[e]						
Earnings[a]	78	85	7*	51	55	4
Social insurance[b]	18	20	2	12	12	—
Child support receipt	17	19	2	26	26	—
TANF[c]	47	32	(15)*	69	52	(17)*
Food Stamps	68	55	(13)*	87	78	(9)*
Medicaid/SCHIP	62	57	(5)*	78	76	(2)
EITC	68	74	6*	37	43	6
SSI	13	13	—	7	9	2
Federal taxes	72	81	9*	39	44	5
Child care expenses[d]	23	25	2	17	20	3
Second income quintile[f]						
Earnings[a]	99	99	—	63	82	19
Social insurance[b]	19	20	1	17	19	2
Child support receipt	16	17	1	25	31	6*
TANF[c]	16	12	(4)*	65	45	(20)*
Food Stamps	23	15	(7)*	88	71	(17)*
Medicaid/SCHIP	28	26	(2)	76	67	(9)*
EITC	69	63	(5)*	54	75	21*
SSI	9	9	1	21	19	(2)

(continued)

Table 4-2. *Percentage of Families with Various Sources of Income and Expenses (Continued)*

Source	All Families with Children (%)			Independent Single-Parent Families (%)		
	1996	1998	Change	1996	1998	Change
Federal taxes	98	97	(1)	56	76	20*
Child care expenses[d]	30	30	—	25	33	8*
Total number (thousands)	37,460	39,310	1,850	7,150	6,600	(550)

Source: The Urban Institute's National Survey of America's Families for 1997 and 1999, representing income years 1996 and 1998, respectively, augmented by the Transfer Income Model, version 3 (TRIM3). TRIM3 corrects for underreporting of government benefits and estimates the value of food stamps and federal taxes (including the EITC).

[a] Includes income from earnings, self-employment, and assets.

[b] Includes income from social security, workers' compensation, and unemployment insurance.

[c] TANF also includes general assistance, although this source of income is rare for families with children.

[d] Families that report out-of-pocket child care expenses.

[e] In 1996, the bottom income quintile of all families with children had incomes below 120 percent of the federal poverty level; for independent single-parent families, it was 70 percent. In 1998, the figures were 130 percent and 70 percent, respectively.

[f] In 1996, the second income quintile of all families with children had incomes between 120 and 180 percent of the federal poverty level; for independent single-parent families, it was 70 to 100 percent. In 1998, the figures were 130 to 190 percent and 70 to 110 percent, respectively.

* Difference from 1996 to 1998 is significant at the 90 percent confidence level or higher. Standard error calculations take into account the NSAF sample design but not error due to microsimulation estimates.

in the second income quintile received some assistance through Medicaid or SCHIP in 1998.

The percentage of all families with children in the bottom income quintile that incurred out-of-pocket expenses for child care rose only slightly in 1998, despite a significant increase in the percentage with earnings. This slight rise probably reflects the availability of child care subsidies for these low-income families.

Table 4-2 also shows receipt of government supports by independent single parents, the group most likely to receive TANF. The number of independent single parents decreased between 1996 and 1998, in part because more unmarried parents, especially those in low-income families, lived with partners (who are often the parents of children in the family) (Acs and Nelson 2001).[10] While 88 percent of all independent single parents had earnings in 1998 (up from 83 percent in 1996), many also received food stamps, the EITC, and Medicaid. A little over one-third received child support, about the same as in 1996.

Independent single-parent families in the bottom income quintile continued to depend heavily on government supports in 1998, although the proportion of these families receiving cash assistance fell significantly, from 69 percent in 1996 to 52 percent in 1998. Three-quarters of these families received food stamps and Medicaid or SCHIP, with much smaller declines in health coverage than in food stamps between 1996 and 1998.[11] More families received assistance from the EITC in 1998 than in 1996, but more also paid taxes and incurred out-of-pocket child care expenses.

Independent single parents in the second income quintile had higher earnings, child support, EITC, tax liabilities, and out-of-pocket child care expenses in 1998 than they did in 1996. At the same time, their receipt of TANF, food stamps, and Medicaid declined significantly.

Amounts of Income Support

Changes in the sources of family income by 1998 were accompanied by changes on the amounts of income (table 4-3).[12] In general, families with children derived considerably more income from nongovernmental

Table 4-3. *Average Annual Income and Expenses for All Families with Children and Independent Single-Parent Families, 1996–1998 (in 1999 dollars)*

Source	All Families with Children ($)			Independent Single-Parent Families ($)		
	1996	1998	Change	1996	1998	Change
All incomes						
Earnings[a]	49,360	52,730	3,370*	18,760	19,730	970
Social insurance[b]	950	860	(90)	860	870	10
Child support receipt	530	560	30*	1,250	1,280	30
TANF[c]	570	360	(210)	1,320	770	(540)*
Food Stamps	520	360	(160)*	1,180	910	(270)*
SSI	300	330	30*	510	460	(50)
EITC	620	620	—	1,000	1,130	130
Federal taxes	(9,360)	(9,570)	(210)	3,020	2,660	(360)
Child care expenses[d]	(1,020)	(1,050)	(30)	950	920	(30)
Total disposable income	**42,470**	**45,200**	**2,730***	**20,910**	**21,570**	**660**

(continued)

Table 4-3. *Average Annual Income and Expenses for All Families with Children and Independent Single-Parent Families, 1996–1998 (in 1999 dollars) (Continued)*

Source	All Families with Children ($)			Independent Single-Parent Families ($)		
	1996	1998	Change	1996	1998	Change
Bottom income quintile[e]						
Earnings[a]	8,280	11,400	3,120*	1,040	1,430	390
Social insurance[b]	840	900	60	510	380	(130)
Child support receipt	350	440	90*	390	490	100
TANF[c]	2,000	1,180	(820)*	2,640	2,000	(640)*
Food Stamps	2,030	1,440	(590)*	3,130	2,680	(450)*
SSI	740	800	60	320	430	110
EITC	1,420	1,600	180	320	430	110
Federal taxes	(790)	(1,570)	(780)*	80	120	40
Child care expenses[d]	(550)	(710)	(160)	290	370	80
Total disposable income	**14,320**	**15,480**	**1,160***	**7,980**	**7,350**	**(630)***
Second income quintile[f]						
Earnings[a]	25,040	27,450	2,410*	3,570	6,690	3,120
Social insurance[b]	960	1,110	150	850	920	70*
Child support receipt	460	500	40	630	780	150
TANF[c]	450	300	(150)*	3,250	1,590	(1,660)*
Food Stamps	330	220	(110)*	2,190	1,440	(750)*
SSI	510	560	50	1,130	1,170	40
EITC	1,130	1,010	(120)	1,050	1,720	670
Federal taxes	(2,960)	(2,930)	30	270	530	260
Child care expenses[d]	(740)	(760)	(20)	510	880	370*
Total disposable income	**25,180**	**27,460**	**2,280***	**11,890**	**12,900**	**1,010***
Total number (thousands)	37,460	39,310	1,850	7,150	6,600	(550)

Source: The Urban Institute's National Survey of America's Families for 1997 and 1999, representing income years 1996 and 1998, respectively, augmented by the Transfer Income Model, version 3 (TRIM3). TRIM3 corrects for underreporting of government benefits and estimates the value of food stamps and federal taxes (including the EITC).

[a] Includes income from earnings, self-employment, and assets.

[b] Includes income from social security, workers' compensation, and unemployment insurance.

[c] TANF also includes general assistance, although this source of income is rare for families with children.

[d] Families' self-reported out-of-pocket child care expenses.

[e] In 1996, the bottom income quintile of all families with children had incomes below 120 percent of the federal poverty level; for independent single-parent families, it was 70 percent. In 1998, the figures were 130 percent and 70 percent, respectively.

[f] In 1996, the second income quintile of all families with children had incomes between 120 and 180 percent of the federal poverty level; for independent single-parent families, it was 70 to 100 percent. In 1998, the figures were 130 to 190 percent and 70 to 110 percent, respectively.

*Difference from 1996 to 1998 is significant at the 90 percent confidence level or higher. Standard error calculations take into account the NSAF sample design but not error due to microsimulation estimates.

sources in 1998 than in 1996: On average, their earnings increased by almost 7 percent. Meanwhile, income from social insurance decreased by 9 percent for these families (social insurance includes unemployment compensation, which probably accounts for the decline). Child support payments increased only slightly.

On average, families with children in the bottom income quintile received less in TANF and food stamp benefits in 1998 than they did two years earlier. These benefits accounted for 17 percent of their disposable income in 1998, down from 28 percent in 1996. Total pre-tax cash income (including earnings, social insurance, child support, TANF, and SSI) rose by 19 percent between 1996 and 1998, but disposable income increased by 8 percent. Child care expenses were greater in 1998, and increased federal tax liabilities more than offset the increase in the refundable EITC for families in the bottom quintile.

The picture for all families with children in the second income quintile is different. Both EITC and tax liabilities declined somewhat between 1996 and 1998, reflecting higher average incomes in this quintile and a reduction in tax liabilities, from the new child tax credit passed in 1997. Average annual disposable income increased by 9 percent for this group.

Independent single-parent families in the bottom income quintile experienced a sizeable decline (19 percent) in TANF and food stamp benefits between 1996 and 1998, and increases in other sources of support fell far short of offsetting it. On average, these families received only $390 more in earnings each year, and income from social insurance dropped by $130.[13] Although child support went up, it still provided only 7 percent of disposable income for families in this income group in 1998. These families also reported paying more out-of-pocket for child care. The net result was an 8 percent decline in disposable income for the 1.3 million independent single-parent families in the bottom income quintile.

The income picture differs considerably for independent single-parent families in the second quintile. Income from TANF and food stamps declined even more dramatically (45 percent), but income from earnings increased by 87 percent. The value of the EITC also rose 64 percent from 1996. Even though other taxes and child care expenses increased, disposable income for this group increased by 9 percent.

In sum, disposable income rose for families with children in all income quintiles between 1996 and 1998 (figure 4-1). Moreover, disposable income increased for independent single-parent families except those in the

Figure 4-1. *Change in Disposable Income of All Families with Children and Independent Single-Parent Families, 1996–1998*

All families with children

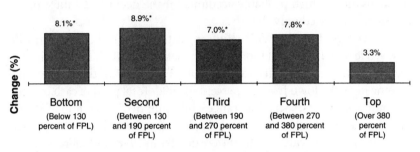

Disposable Income Quintile[1]

Independent single-parent families

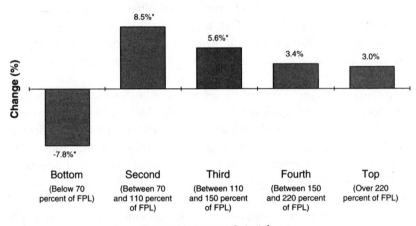

Disposable Income Quintile[1]

Source: The Urban Institute's National Survey of America's Families for 1997 and 1999, representing income years 1996 and 1998, respectively, augmented by the Transfer Income Model, version 3 (TRIM3). TRIM3 corrects for underreporting of government benefits and estimates the value of food stamps and federal taxes (including the EITC).

FPL = federal poverty level.

*Difference from 1996 to 1998 is significant at the 90 percent confidence level or higher. Standard error calculations take into account the NSAF sample design but not error due to microsimulation estimates.

[1]Income quintile definitions show 1998 disposable income relative to FPL.

bottom income quintile. The decline in income for these families stands in marked contrast to the results for the average family with children.

These results are generally consistent with findings from other studies. One study determined from Census data that disposable income for the poorest fifth of single-mother families fell by 7 percent between 1995 and 1997 (Primus et al. 1999). This study included adjustments for under-reporting of benefits in the Census data and the net effect of taxes. (It was not able to include out-of-pocket child care costs, but it did include housing assistance.) Another study reported that about half of the families that left welfare after 1996 experienced a drop in income, contributing to overall income declines among the poorest fifth of female family heads with children (Bavier 2001). These results are based on the 1996 Survey of Income and Program Participation and exclude net tax effects and child care expenses. More recent data from the Current Population Survey show that incomes (excluding taxes and child care expenses) of single-mother families in the bottom quintile began improving after 1998 (Bavier 2001). Using cash income as a measure of poverty among female high school dropouts, a third study found that incomes increased as a result of welfare reform, but "only among women in the middle or upper part of the income distribution among less-skilled women" (Schoenie and Blank 2000, 26). In a review of the literature on income change since TANF, Haskins (2001, 3) concludes that while many families are better off, "there is a group of mother-headed families of small to moderate size that are worse off than they were before welfare reform."

How Have Changes in Income Supports Affected Poverty?

The official measure of poverty, which considers only pre-tax cash income, paints an unambiguously positive picture of the changing economic status of families between 1996 and 1998. The fraction of all persons in families with children and in independent single-parent families who are living in poverty declined by 3 and 5 percentage points, respectively, between 1996 and 1998 (table 4-4). The percentage of people living in extreme poverty also declined, by almost 1 percentage point for all families and 2 percentage points for independent single-parent families. However, because the official measure of poverty excludes noncash government supports such as food stamps and expenses such as child care and taxes, it does not accurately capture the changing circumstances of low-income families.

Table 4-4. *Persons in All Families with Children and in Independent Single-Parent Families Living in Poverty and Extreme Poverty, 1996–1998*

	Persons in All Families with Children (Thousands)		Persons in Independent Single-Parent Families (Thousands)	
Degree of Poverty	1996	1998	1996	1998
Extreme poverty (under 50 percent of the federal poverty level)				
Cash income	7,514	6,254*	4,007	3,272*
Disposable income				
Food Stamps	3,194	3,189	1,311	1,578*
Federal taxes	2,727	2,800*	1,139	1,401*
Child care expenses	2,838	2,907*	1,234	1,458*
Rate of extreme poverty, cash income only[a]	**5.0%**	**4.1%***	**19.8%**	**18.0%**
Rate of extreme poverty, disposable income[b]	**1.9%**	**1.9%**	**6.2%**	**8.0%***
Poverty (under 100 percent of the federal poverty level)				
Cash income	23,744	19,935*	9,476	7,604*
Disposable income				
Food Stamps	21,405	17,855*	8,743	6,868*
Federal taxes	18,891	15,344*	7,784	5,668*
Less child care expenses	20,036	16,658*	8,208	6,143*
Rate of poverty, cash income only[a]	**16.3%**	**13.2%***	**46.8%**	**41.8%***
Rate of poverty, disposable income[b]	**13.7%**	**11.0%***	**40.5%**	**33.8%***

Source: The Urban Institute's National Survey of America's Families for 1997 and 1999, representing income years 1996 and 1998, respectively, augmented by the Transfer Income Model, version 3 (TRIM3). TRIM3 corrects for underreporting of government benefits and estimates the value of food stamps and federal taxes (including the EITC).

[a] The Census Bureau's definition of poverty includes cash income from earnings, self-employment, assets, social insurance, and welfare.

[b] This expanded definition of poverty is based on disposable income; it includes income from food stamps and the EITC and subtracts federal taxes paid and out-of-pocket child care expenses. (Housing assistance is excluded because of lack of comparability between the questions in the 1997 and 1999 surveys.)

* Difference between estimated poverty rates in 1996 and 1998 is significant at the 90 percent confidence level or higher. Standard error calculations take into account the NSAF sample design but not error due to microsimulation estimates.

The broader measure of poverty used in this chapter is based on disposable income, and reveals a different situation. According to this broader measure, the percentage of persons in families with children living in poverty declined significantly, but the percentage living in extreme poverty remained flat. This percentage translates into almost 100,000 more people living in extreme poverty in 1998.

Similarly, the broader measure shows a significant drop in the proportion of people in independent single-parent families living in poverty. However, the number living in extreme poverty grew by 1.8 percentage points, or 224,000 people. Food stamps lifted over a million more people in this group out of extreme poverty in 1996 than in 1998, a reflection of the significant decline in the number of even very poor people who receive food stamps. On the other hand, child care expenses reduced disposable income for fewer persons in independent single-parent families in 1998 than in 1996. The lessening burden of these out-of-pocket expenses presumably reflects increased subsidies for child care among very poor families as these parents moved into the labor market.

Poverty declined between 1996 and 1998 in each of the NSAF focal states, but the change in the extreme poverty rate varied. For example, extreme poverty among people in independent single-parent families declined significantly in some states but increased in others. It increased in the four states (California, New Jersey, New York, and Wisconsin) whose cash assistance payments to families on welfare were higher than the extreme poverty income of $526 per month for a family of three in 1996. The average cash benefits in these states were $532 per month, or $726 a month including food stamps. Families may have difficulty maintaining the higher income when they either leave or avoid welfare and rely on earned income, especially if they do not have food stamps and incur higher child care expenses.

In contrast, the two states with the biggest decreases in extreme poverty (Alabama and Texas) provided cash assistance benefits that were below the extreme poverty level. The average maximum monthly benefit for a family of three in these two states was $176 in 1996 (17 percent of the federal poverty level), $476 including food stamps (45 percent of the federal poverty level). Some families in these states moved out of extreme poverty when they left welfare for work. However, the 1998 rates of extreme poverty for independent single-parent families remained higher in Alabama and Texas than in the four states that had more generous benefits.

Food stamps play a key role in these state results. A smaller share of eligible nonelderly families received food stamps in 1996 than in 1998.[14] However, several NSAF focal states saw higher-than-average declines in participation, including Mississippi, New York, and Wisconsin. Had eligible families, especially extremely poor ones, remained in the Food Stamp program, poverty would have been reduced significantly in these states.

Summary and Caveats about Income Change

While family income since passage of the welfare reform bill in 1996 generally improved, outcomes for independent single-parent families are alarming. Welfare reform, the strong economy, and government policies that focused on increasing the take-home pay of low-wage workers have produced many positive results. Disposable incomes have increased, on average, for families with children, and the percent living in poverty has declined. However, a look beneath the averages for all families shows that disposable income for those most at risk for welfare—independent single-parent families in the bottom income quintile—declined by 8 percent between 1996 and 1998. The number of persons in independent single-parent families who lived in extreme poverty increased by 224,000.

The increase in extreme poverty seems to stem from families either leaving or avoiding welfare and food stamps without sufficient earnings or income supports to offset the loss of these benefits. Ironically, this increase is largest in states that provide generous welfare benefits, where movement from welfare to a low-paying job may mean moving into extreme poverty. Chapter 2 describes research showing a subset of former welfare recipients who neither work nor live with another adult who works. Only about half of the extremely poor families that left welfare receive food stamps (Zedlewski 2001). Some families may have left government assistance programs because they were sanctioned (cut off for not cooperating with their state's welfare program), faced temporary benefit time limits, misunderstood how the new welfare system worked, or chose to remain outside of government assistance programs, at least those delivered at a welfare office.

The story about the effects of welfare reform on family incomes is far from complete. Income data for the most recent years are not available, and it is possible that the incomes of independent single mothers improved between 1998 and 2000. Nor are the effects of the economic downturn since 2000 clear. More important, these data cannot tell what will happen when time limits on benefits begin to take effect. Although the federal government allows states to exempt 20 percent of their caseloads from time limits, and a few states guarantee assistance to all families that play by the rules but are not able to move off welfare, in the long run it will be difficult for states to cover benefits for all families that need assistance for more than five years.

Policy Implications

Welfare reform has intensified interest in government policies that support low-income working families. The strong focus on work as the primary means of support for all but the most severely disabled has wide acceptance and fits with mainstream thinking. However, there is also a growing recognition that some families need assistance beyond their earnings to support their families. Child support provides some of this additional assistance to single-parent families, but many noncustodial parents of low-income children do not have the means to pay support (see chapter 3, and Sorensen and Zibman 2001).

GOVERNMENT COULD STREAMLINE THE PATCHWORK OF INCOME SUPPORT PROGRAMS TO ENSURE THAT MORE FAMILIES NEEDING ASSISTANCE GET IT. The federal government and state governments offer significant support to low-income working families in the form of food stamps, the EITC, Medicaid and SCHIP, and child care, but these programs operate independently of each other, and government does little to help low-income families make their way through the resulting maze of work supports. Consequently, these benefits do not reach all low-income families. Some of the programs require applications in a welfare office, with benefits contingent upon detailed and frequently reviewed reports of earnings, assets, and household expenses. Benefits delivered through the tax system require a family first to know they are available and then to either slog through pages of complex instructions, pay an independent tax preparer, or seek free tax help from a community service agency. Recent analysis reveals that Hispanics benefit from the EITC less than other groups (Ross Phillips 2001).

Families need help in making sense of the safety net and obtaining access to the supports designed to fulfill their needs. Simple, straightforward information about available income supports should be widely available. Federal regulations that overemphasize payment accuracy and underemphasize access to supports need to be reassessed. Recent changes in the Food Stamp program moved in this direction, reducing state penalties when errors are made in benefits paid to working families and encouraging states to lighten reporting burdens on recipients. Experiments that have mandated work and supplemented family incomes have improved outcomes for families and children, but supplements were delivered to families through a coordinated, guaranteed package (see Berlin 2000).

STATES AND THE FEDERAL GOVERNMENT NEED TO ASK WHETHER THEY ARE DOING EVERYTHING POSSIBLE TO PREVENT SOME FAMILIES FROM LEAVING THE INCOME SUPPORT SYSTEM BEFORE THEY ARE READY. As noted in chapter 1, some states are beginning to recognize that the work-first approach to finding a job is not suitable for all welfare recipients. The most severe problems seem to occur among the most vulnerable families—those headed by single parents with limited education, relatively few hours of work, and very low earnings. These families require interventions to bring them back into a more structured system of supports. Some need intensive education and training. Some may require basic cash assistance until they can work more hours or earn a higher wage. More generous child care assistance, especially for single parents living independently, would help some families avoid extreme poverty. Many of those unable to work require assistance with disabilities, job skills, and other barriers to employment, as well as food and health care assistance.

Federal policy could lift limitations on states' ability to use federal TANF dollars for education and training. More states could expand welfare recipients' earned-income deductions and benefits to allow more of them to keep some cash assistance (and the coordinated set of supports that go with it) while they begin to earn income. Of course, this policy will only be effective if welfare recipients who work a substantial number of hours and receive reduced welfare benefits have their federal benefit time-limit clock stopped while they are working.

POLICYMAKERS NEED TO TAKE A CRITICAL LOOK AT THE SYSTEM OF SUPPORTS FOR THE DISABLED. The SSI program covers only people who are unable to engage in any work. It excludes the partially disabled who can do some work but not enough to support their families. A few states guarantee cash assistance to such families indefinitely, but most do not. It is not equitable that the most vulnerable families with children face disparate safety nets across the 50 states, nor is it equitable that the states bear so large a share of supporting the partially disabled with children. The SSI definition of disability could be revised to include adults who are capable of some work, with a careful eye toward providing incentives that encourage work over indefinite assistance.

OTHER POLICIES SHOULD FOCUS ON THE ADEQUACY OF SAFETY NET BENEFITS. Many families with children have very low incomes, even when earnings and government benefits are taken into account. The EITC provides significant help to working families, but increased tax liabilities and child care expenses eat away at this benefit. Child care expenses are particularly high relative to the income of single parents with no other adults to help. Two policies could increase disposable incomes for working families with children:

- Ten states now provide a refundable EITC, and two use TANF dollars to pay for the refundable portion. More states could consider this course.
- Out-of-pocket child care expenses could be reduced by making free and subsidized child care more readily accessible to working poor families. Families need to understand what is available, and states need to streamline access to benefits. Sufficient federal and state dollars should be available to provide free care for all very low income working families.

In short, Congress will need to take a critical look at family income during TANF reauthorization discussions and in future welfare policy debates. Legislators must look beneath the generally bright picture of the average family with children to discover the increased economic hardship among single parents struggling to work and raise children on their own. Families leaving welfare need solutions that not only replace the income they lose as they move to work but that also increase their disposable income. Legislators also need to seek solutions for partially disabled parents who cannot work enough to support their families. Some of these families need long-term income support, not the temporary assistance that TANF provides.

NOTES

The author thanks Linda Giannarelli, Joyce Morton, and Laura Wheaton for their untiring efforts in adapting the NSAF for use in the TRIM3 model, and Desiree Principe for her excellent research assistance.

1. The food stamp benefit cuts for immigrant children, the elderly, and disabled persons living in the United States when PRWORA was passed were rescinded by the federal government in 1998. During 1997, 11 states, including most of those with large populations of immigrants (California, Colorado, Florida, Maryland, Massachusetts, Minnesota, Nebraska, New Jersey, New York, Rhode Island, and Washington), paid for food stamps for these groups and sometimes for a broader group of legal immigrants, such as all who were eligible for TANF. The immigrant provisions in PRWORA accounted for about half of the predicted 1.2 million-person increase in the number of children living in poverty (Zedlewski et al. 1996, 14). Thus, new state coverage and federal rescisions substantially mitigated this effect of the welfare law.

2. The studies that estimated the effects of the pending legislation followed the current Congressional Budget Office assumptions showing that states would have about $5 billion less to spend on TANF than was projected under then-current AFDC law. However, the final legislation included a block grant formula more generous to states by allowing them to base their block grant on the highest level of spending since 1994.

3. Some states adopted time limits on benefits that are shorter than the federal limit; these were not anticipated in the original projections of the effects of welfare reform. However, in most states, these time limits have been softened considerably by exemptions and extensions. It is unlikely that federal time limits will mimic this experience, at least in the long run, because federal dollars will not be available to fund benefits beyond five years except for 20 percent of each state's caseload.

4. The Urban Institute's Transfer Income Model, version 3 (TRIM3), is used to simulate eligibility for and receipt of SSI, TANF, and food stamps, and to calculate federal income and payroll taxes. The simulations correct for the underreporting of welfare benefits that plagues all surveys (see Wheaton and Giannarelli 2000) by using individual state rules to simulate eligibility, and adjusting the number receiving benefits to match control totals developed using state and federal administrative data. Taxes are calculated using detailed rules of federal programs. Respondents report out-of-pocket child care expenses for the month of the survey. The ratio of child care expenses to parents' earnings in the month of the survey is applied to the last year's earnings to estimate child care expenses in the prior year. These results exclude state income taxes, which can have significant effects on low-income family incomes (Maag and Rogers 2000), and they exclude housing assistance (the questions about this source of income were faulty on the first round of the NSAF). The exclusion of housing assistance should not have a significant effect, because the level and receipt of housing assistance did not change appreciably between 1996 and 1998 (U.S. Department of Housing and Urban Development 2001).

5. The National Academy of Sciences (see Citro and Michael 1995) recommends a measure of family economic resources and poverty that includes the value of noncash government supports and deducts out-of-pocket spending for work expenses and health. Estimates of transportation expenses and health care are not included in the definition of

income used here. In addition, as noted earlier, housing assistance is not included in these estimates.

6. The 2001 tax law increases the child tax credit to $600 in 2001, $700 in 2005, $800 in 2009, and $1,000 in 2010. In addition, new rules allow families to receive a refundable credit of 10 percent of the amount by which their earnings exceed $10,000, beginning in 2001 and indexed to inflation after 2002. The tax law also reduced the marriage penalty in the EITC by increasing the amount of income above which the credit begins to phase out for married couples.

7. This list excludes social insurance programs that assist families that have earned "insurance" by meeting requirements for minimum work histories and that provide benefits without regard to income (such as Social Security Disability and Survivor's Insurance and Unemployment Insurance). It also excludes General Assistance, a program offered in 35 states that primarily serves destitute individuals without children who cannot work and often are awaiting eligibility for SSI (Gallagher et al. 1999).

8. See Burt, Pindus, and Capizzano (2000) for a description of how the system worked in 1997.

9. Families were sorted into five approximately equal groups based on their disposable incomes. For example, 20 percent of families with the lowest incomes fell into the bottom income quintile. Quintiles were defined separately for families with children and single parents living alone and for each year.

10. For simplicity I refer to demographic status in 1996 and 1998, the years for which the NSAF measured income, even though demographic status is measured at the time of the survey (sometime in 1997 and 1999, respectively).

It is possible that the composition of independent single parents in 1998 differed from 1996 in such a way that it would affect their income status. For example, more higher-earning single parents may have lived with partners in 1998 than in 1996. Tabulations of the characteristics of independent single-parent families in both years did not show significant differences in their family size, age, or health status. However, a significantly larger share of single parents living independently in 1998 had some education beyond high school, compared with the 1996 cohort (21 percent in 1998 versus 14 percent in 1996). This difference would lead us to expect that the 1998 cohort had somewhat more earning capacity than the 1996 cohort.

11. Garrett and Holahan (2000) and Zedlewski (2001) discuss the connection between leaving welfare and leaving the Medicaid and Food Stamp programs, respectively. As families lose the connection to a welfare caseworker, many do not understand that they may still be eligible for health and food stamp benefits.

12. All income values were converted to real 1999 dollars using the increase in the Consumer Price Index for Urban Families since 1996.

13. The decline in social insurance may simply mean that independent single-parent families with income from social insurance were more likely to fall into the second income quintile in 1998 than in 1996, on average; indeed, results for the second income quintile do show an increase in this source of income.

14. The TRIM/NSAF model does not include the changes in immigrant eligibility provisions outlined in note 1. It simulates pre-PRWORA immigrant eligibility law and therefore overestimates program eligibility in 1998. While program targets are based on federal administrative data (and exclude state-only recipients), the model retains benefits

for all persons who report benefits as long as they pass the model's eligibility test. Thus, participating immigrants will *not* be excluded here as long as they reported benefits. Therefore, the omission of the immigrant rules is unlikely to have had a large effect on state-specific results.

REFERENCES

Acs, Gregory, Norma Coe, Keith Watson, and Robert I. Lerman. 1998. *Does Work Pay? An Analysis of the Work Incentives under TANF.* Washington, D.C.: The Urban Institute. *Assessing the New Federalism* Occasional Paper No. 9.

Acs, Gregory, and Sandi Nelson. 2001. " 'Honey, I'm Home': Changes in Living Arrangements in the Late 1990s." Washington, D.C.: The Urban Institute. *Assessing the New Federalism* Policy Brief B-38.

Bavier, Richard. 2001. "Welfare Reform Data from the Survey of Income and Program Participation." *Monthly Labor Review* 124 (7): 13–23.

Berlin, Gordon. 2000. *Encouraging Work, Reducing Poverty: The Impact of Work Incentive Programs.* New York: Manpower Development Research Corporation.

Burt, Martha, Nancy Pindus, and Jeffrey Capizzano. 2000. *The Social Safety Net at the Beginning of Federal Welfare Reform.* Washington, D.C.: Urban Institute. *Assessing the New Federalism* Occasional Paper 34.

Citro, Constance F., and Robert T. Michael, editors. 1995. *Measuring Poverty: A New Approach.* Washington, D.C.: National Academy Press.

Economic Report of the President. Transmitted to the Congress in February 1999. Washington, D.C.: U.S. Government Printing Office.

Gallagher, Jerome L., Cori E. Uccello, Alicia B. Pierce, and Erin B. Reidy. 1999. *State General Assistance Programs, 1998.* Washington, D.C.: Urban Institute. *Assessing the New Federalism* Discussion Paper 99-01.

Garrett, Bowen, and John Holahan. 2000. "Welfare Leavers, Medicaid Coverage, and Private Health Insurance." Washington, D.C.: The Urban Institute. *Assessing the New Federalism* Policy Brief B-13.

Haskins, Ron. 2001. "Effects of Welfare Reform on Family Income and Poverty." In *The New World of Welfare,* edited by Rebecca M. Blank and Ron Haskins (103–36). Washington, D.C.: Brookings Institution Press.

Maag, Elaine, and Diane Lim Rogers. 2000. *The New Federalism and State Tax Policies toward the Working Poor.* Washington, D.C.: The Urban Institute. *Assessing the New Federalism* Occasional Paper No. 38.

Primus, Wendell, Lynette Rawlings, Kathy Larin, and Kathryn Porter. 1999. *The Initial Impacts of Welfare Reform on the Incomes of Single-Mother Families.* Washington, D.C.: Center on Budget and Policy Priorities.

Ross, Donna, and Laura Cox. 2000. *Making It Simple: Medicaid for Children and CHIP Income Eligibility Guidelines and Enrollment Procedures.* Washington, D.C.: Center on Budget and Policy Priorities.

Ross Phillips, Katherin. 2001. "Who Knows about the Earned Income Tax Credit?" Washington, D.C.: The Urban Institute. *Assessing the New Federalism* Policy Brief B-27.

Schoenie, Robert, and Rebecca Blank. 2000. "What Has Welfare Reform Accomplished? Impacts on Welfare Participation, Employment, Income, Poverty, and Family Structure." Ann Arbor, Mich.: University of Michigan, Ford School of Public Policy. Working Paper 00-016.

Sorensen, Elaine, and Chava Zibman. 2001. "Poor Dads Who Don't Pay Child Support: Deadbeats or Disadvantaged?" Washington, D.C.: The Urban Institute. *Assessing the New Federalism* Policy Brief B-30.

U.S. Department of Health and Human Services. 1996. "The Effects of Congressional Actions to Reform Welfare on Family Incomes and Poverty." Washington, D.C.: U.S. Department of Health and Human Services.

U.S. Department of Housing and Urban Development. 2001. "A Picture of Subsidized Households: U.S. Summaries." Data accessed from http://www.huduser.org/data/picture.html.

Wheaton, Laura, and Linda Giannarelli. 2000. "Underreporting of Means-Tested Transfer Programs in the March CPS." In *Proceedings of the Sections on Government Statistics and Social Statistics* (236–41). Alexandria, Va.: American Statistical Association.

Zedlewski, Sheila, Sandra Clark, Eric Meier, and Keith Watson. 1996. "Potential Effects of Congressional Welfare Reform Legislation on Family Incomes." Washington, D.C.: The Urban Institute.

Zedlewski, Sheila. 2001. "Former Welfare Families and the Food Stamp Program: The Exodus Continues." Washington, D.C.: The Urban Institute. *Assessing the New Federalism* Policy Brief B-33.

5

How Are Children Faring under Welfare Reform?

Martha Zaslow, Kristin Anderson Moore, Kathryn Tout,
Juliet P. Scarpa, and Sharon Vandivere

Concern for the well-being of children has been, and remains, an important component of welfare policy in the United States. Yet it is only in the past decade that research has focused on the effects of welfare reform on children. The earliest predictions by researchers anticipated a range of possible outcomes, from positive to negative, for children, depending on family characteristics and the degree to which families successfully made (or did not make) the transition to work; increased (or decreased) their economic resources; and decreased (or increased) parental stress (Zaslow et al. 1998). Recent studies on welfare reform's effects on children are enabling researchers to begin to gauge the effects of welfare reform and to fine-tune predictions of future effects. Information from this research is useful to policymakers at all levels as they discuss TANF reauthorization and the future of welfare policy.

To present a more complete picture of how children are faring under welfare reform, this chapter draws on a composite of experimental and nonexperimental approaches to research. Each approach addresses distinct types of research questions, and each has particular strengths and limitations (for a detailed discussion, see National Research Council 2001). The chapter first describes the impact various welfare-to-work programs have on children, drawing on data from experimental evaluations. It then examines national trends in the home environments of children overall and also in low-income families, drawn from (nonexperimental) survey and administrative data. Key findings from these two types of research provide the context for the third section: new analyses of NSAF data that portray children from current and former welfare families in the early years of welfare reform. Finally, the chapter discusses the implications of these findings for welfare policy.

Research Strategies

Experimental evaluations of welfare-to-work programs have the advantage of attributing outcomes to specific causes. A well-designed experimental evaluation can point to a particular welfare program as the source of differences in outcomes between children in the program and children in control groups. Further, because experimental evaluations cover a range of welfare-to-work programs, it is possible to discern how different programs affect children. Yet the impacts documented in these studies pertain to selected programs, in selected places, carried out in particular time periods. They do not reflect the full range of welfare programs in existence, programs implemented very recently, or the well-being of children nationally.[1] It is not appropriate to use experimental data to reach general statements about whether welfare reform has benefited or harmed children; rather, these data should be used to discuss the benefits or harms of the particular programs studied.

Nationally representative survey and administrative data, in contrast, have the advantage of yielding descriptive information on an entire population—for example, on all children from families receiving welfare or that recently left welfare. When collected at intervals, these national data can reveal changes in child well-being over time.[2] Yet such data cannot be used to attribute levels of child well-being or changes in well-being to specific welfare programs or policies: The differences reflect numerous other influences on low-income families, such as the strength of the economy, changes in the welfare caseload, and the Earned Income Tax Credit. Moreover, national surveys and particularly administrative data typically do not provide in-depth information, limiting their questions to a single respondent and including brief markers of child well-being or risk.

In seeking to provide a composite picture of child well-being, this chapter uses findings from experimental studies to ask what impacts different programs have on children. Findings from national survey and administrative data are used to ask how children in general, and particularly children in families receiving and leaving welfare, have fared in the years following welfare reform.

Effects of Welfare-to-Work Programs on Children

A recent review of evidence from seven experimental studies examining a range of welfare-to-work programs concludes that these differing programs have not had widespread effects on children (Zaslow, Brooks, et al. 2001; Zaslow et al. forthcoming).[3] This is perhaps not surprising, given that welfare-to-work programs generally do not include services targeted directly at children, such as early childhood intervention or developmental screening.

Nevertheless, the programs did have some significant effects, both positive and negative, particularly on children's cognitive and behavioral development. These effects were similar in size to those of some programs that target children directly, but not to those of high-intensity early childhood intervention programs. Furthermore, the effects on children tended to differ by type of program and by the impact of the program on adult employment, earnings, income, and sometimes educational attainment. Finally, the effects of these welfare-to-work programs tended to vary with both family and child characteristics. A key challenge for policymakers, practitioners, and researchers, then, is to identify the factors that tip the balance of impacts in a favorable rather than an unfavorable direction.

Effects on Young Children

Favorable cognitive and behavioral impacts tended to occur among preschool or school-age children whose mothers enrolled in programs that not only increased employment but also improved the family's overall economic well-being (increasing family income, diminishing the proportion of families in the program in poverty, or both). Programs that had strong financial work incentives often—though not always—improved economic outcomes for families as well as cognitive and behavioral outcomes for young children. Programs that resulted in increased maternal education were also sometimes associated with favorable impacts on young children's cognitive development.

Unfavorable impacts on young children were associated with programs in which mothers did not make progress in any of the key economic outcomes (employment, earnings, and overall income or family poverty level) or experienced setbacks on one or more of them. This suggests that young children may be adversely affected when their mothers fail to make expected or required progress in terms of employment and economic resources.

Effects on Adolescents

Two unexpected findings emerged from the review of experimental studies. First, adolescent children of adult recipients tend to be unfavorably affected by welfare-to-work programs, according to the three programs that have reported data on adolescents. Each of these programs has implemented very different policies, and two of them (both involving strong financial work incentives) have had favorable impacts on young children. Several hypotheses for the unfavorable effects on adolescents appear plausible (Brooks, Hair, and Zaslow 2001). The welfare-to-work programs may have altered the quality of parent-child relations, by increasing harshness in interactions, for example. Parental monitoring and supervision may have diminished (a factor that is important to adolescent development in general and that may be especially important in high-risk neighborhoods). And adolescents may be taking on substantial adult responsibilities within the family (e.g., providing regular care for younger children, having major responsibilities for cooking and cleaning, or even contributing economically) before they are ready for them. Distinguishing among these possibilities will be critical to putting in place appropriate policy and program responses. For example, after-school mentoring and activity programs will not help adolescents who cannot participate because they are urgently needed at home.

Effects in Light of Risk of Long-Term Dependency

A second unexpected finding concerns families' risk of long-term welfare dependency (defined on the basis of previous work history, educational attainment, length of previous welfare receipt, and other such factors). Specifically, children from families at lower risk of long-term dependency were more likely to be unfavorably affected by this set of welfare-to-work programs than children from higher-risk families, even though children from higher-risk families tended to show less positive overall developmental status. This finding raises the possibility that the concept of risk as it applies to welfare recipients needs to be re-evaluated. Families labeled "lower risk" may indeed be less disadvantaged in terms of parents' educational attainment or previous work experience, but they may face other, more recent stressors such as job loss, domestic violence, or divorce or separation. The addition of a work requirement may result in unfavorable impacts upon the children in these families. While a great deal of attention is being paid to the important question of how best to help parents with multiple enduring barriers to employment make the transition from welfare to work, these unexpected findings suggest that other families may be facing different stressors (perhaps acute as opposed to more chronic) and need different supports.

Changes in Family Context

National trends in employment, poverty, welfare receipt, and family structure show clearly that the family context of children has changed substantially in the period surrounding welfare reform. However, careful examination of these trends indicates that the changes may not have affected the family factors that experimental studies suggest may be of greatest importance in bringing about changes in child well-being, or may not have been of sufficient magnitude, to date, to alter the well-being of children.

Trends in Employment

The trend toward increased labor force participation and preparation (i.e., full-time schooling) among single mothers has resulted in "enormous changes within a relatively short period of time" (Blank 2000, 5). While employment and preparation for work among married women with children under age 6 increased steadily from 1979 to the mid-1990s, the rate of increase slowed from the mid- to late 1990s. In contrast, between 1989 and 1999, a decade that includes the period surrounding welfare reform, the rate of labor force participation and preparation rose by 34 percent for never-married women with young children and by 20 percent for widowed, divorced, or separated women with young children. These changes reflect the confluence of several possible factors, including the influence of welfare reform (beginning with the waivers that preceded congressional action), a strong economy, and the EITC.

Employment specifically among welfare recipients increased after welfare reform, from 22 percent in 1997 to 32 percent in 1999 (Zedlewski and Alderson 2001). Among former recipients, employment increased from 61 percent to 64 percent in those years (Loprest 2001).[4]

These trends can be viewed from the perspective of the experimental studies summarized above. These studies suggest that although the transition to employment is important in understanding welfare reform's effects on children, employment should be considered in terms of the changes it brings about in a family's overall economic status. In general, welfare-to-work programs that increased employment without improving overall economic well-being had few or no effects on preschool and school-age children. In these studies, increased employment per se appeared to have few harmful (or beneficial) effects on young children. Rather, unfavorable impacts on children tended to occur in families where parents did not or could not respond to program requirements for increased employment and where overall economic well-being did not improve, or even deteriorated. Favorable impacts on children, when they did occur, tended to be concentrated in families where increased employment was accompanied by improvements in overall family income, a decrease in the proportion of families in poverty, or both.

Trends in Income and Poverty

Findings from the experimental studies highlight the importance of looking not only at changes in labor force participation, but also at indicators of overall income and poverty. National data on family income and poverty are somewhat mixed. Using both the official definition of poverty and a broader one that incorporates food stamps, the EITC, and other government benefits, Haskins and Primus (2001) have found that the proportion of children living in poverty fell during a period of economic expansion in the mid-1980s, rose to about 20 percent in the late 1980s and early 1990s, and has declined steadily since 1993, when states began to experiment with welfare reform by obtaining waivers. By 1999, child poverty was the lowest it had been since 1979. Poverty among minority children has also fallen, to 1979 rates for Hispanic children and to the lowest rates since data were first collected, in 1961, for black children.

While overall child poverty has declined substantially, some low-income families have not kept pace (see chapter 4). Although annual earnings increased by an average of about $2,300 among the poorest 40 percent of single-mother families between 1993 and 1999, their disposable income rose by only $292 (Haskins and Primus 2001). The "increased earnings are not translating into greater disposable income, because these families are losing most of their cash welfare income and much of their food stamp income as well" (ibid., 6).

Poverty declined among families that left welfare, from 48 percent in 1997 to 41 percent in 1999 (Loprest 2001). However, much of this decline is attributable to small increases in income that pushed families from just below the poverty line to just above it. Loprest notes that the changes were not accompanied by increases in median monthly earnings or by increases in median monthly income, which includes earnings plus child support receipts, Supplemental Security Income, Social Security, and pension and investment income. In addition, more former welfare recipients reported worrying about food or having difficulty paying mortgage, rent, or utility bills in 1999 than in 1997 (ibid.). Other studies have also found that while economic circumstances for some families have improved since welfare reform, they have worsened for others (Blank 2000). Porter and Primus (1999) note that the decline in child poverty rates has been slower than the decline in welfare caseloads.

The increase in disposable income among low-income, single-parent families since welfare reform may be generally too small to improve the overall economic picture of many of these families, and is therefore unlikely to lead to substantial improvements in child well-being—even though the proportion of children living in poverty has fallen (see discussion in Haskins and Primus 2001). Continued monitoring of the trends in child poverty and in disposable income is important: A further decline in child poverty accompanied by more substantial improvements in disposable income may provide a basis for improvements in child well-being, while economic deterioration may have opposite implications.

Trends in Welfare Receipt

The number of people on welfare declined substantially in the early years after reform, leading many observers to expect that those remaining on the rolls faced more barriers to employment than earlier recipients. Contrary to expectations, however, the proportion of welfare recipients with barriers to employment has not increased (Zedlewski and Alderson 2001). If the characteristics of the caseload have not changed substantially, there is little reason to expect that the risk status of children on welfare has increased in recent years.

Trends in Family Structure

Numerous studies over the years have established that, on average, children benefit from living in stable families with both biological parents in a low-conflict marriage (Amato 2000; Seltzer 2000). Moreover, research consistently finds that children in step-families fare about the same in terms of developmental outcomes as children in single-parent families and that both groups have somewhat less positive outcomes than children raised by two biological parents (Coleman, Ganong, and Fine 2000; Nelson, Clark, and Acs 2001). Living with a mother and the mother's boyfriend in a cohabiting relationship has also been found to be associated with poorer outcomes among teens, compared with teens living with both biological parents, with a single parent, or in a blended family (Nelson et al. 2001). An exception may be black adolescents who live with married step-parents: These young people fare better on some outcomes than their counterparts who live with a single mother or with a mother and her boyfriend in a cohabiting relationship (ibid.). Although studies have not identified changes in family structure as likely mediators of welfare reform's impacts on child well-being, reductions in childbearing outside of marriage and increases in family formation, particularly marriage of a child's biological parents, could be expected to enhance children's development.

Two promising trends in family structure, fertility, marriage, and living arrangements during the 1990s deserve mention here (see also chapters 3 and 11). One is the decline in teen childbearing since 1991. The other is an overall decline in black women's childbearing outside of marriage across the 1990s. Birth rates outside of marriage increased slightly among white women in their twenties and among Hispanic women in the late 1990s (Martin, Hamilton, and Ventura 2001). Though promising, it is too early to tell whether or how these changes will translate into improved well-being of children as they get older. Since the timing of these declines does not track with welfare reform, though, there is little indication that welfare reform has contributed to either of these declines. Furthermore, while welfare reform policies are associated with declines in the percentage of children living with a single mother, some of the declines may result from increases in cohabitation and step-parenting, rather than marriage of biological parents.

Trends in Child Abuse

Welfare receipt and child poverty are both strongly related to child maltreatment (Geen et al. 2001). Many people concerned with child welfare anticipated that child maltreatment would increase under welfare reform because the new requirements would increase stress on parents and poverty among children. Child poverty in fact decreased in the 1990s, as noted above, and a recent study has found no evidence of increased referrals to child welfare agencies (ibid.). Nationwide, reported cases of child abuse have declined (U.S. Department of Health and Human Services 2001).

The Well-Being of Children in Current and Former Welfare Families

The research findings described above provide a context for new analyses of NSAF data involving a nationally representative sample of children grouped by family income and welfare status. These new analyses are designed to answer questions regarding children's risk of poor developmental outcomes, how that risk might differ by family income, whether or how risk differs for children in families that have left welfare versus those in families still receiving welfare, and whether the degree of risk for children in current and former welfare families has changed from 1997 to 1999.

Measures of Developmental Risk

To assess developmental status of children, the survey asked the adult respondent most knowledgeable about the children in the household a series of questions about specific children's behavioral and emotional adjustment, engagement in school and extracurricular activities, and health. This chapter reports on eight measures of developmental risk derived from their answers. In the area of behavioral and emotional adjustment, two measures are covered: high levels of behavioral and emotional problems, calculated separately for children age 6 to 11 and 12 to 17. (Separate scores for these two age groups were calculated, because the NSAF asked age-appropriate questions for each group.) Four measures are included to assess adjustment to school and participation in extracurricular activities. The first measure indicates the proportion of children age 6 to 17 not participating in any extracurricular activities. The second indicates the proportion of children age 6 to 17 exhibiting low engagement with school. The third and fourth identify the proportion of children age 12 to 17 who had skipped school two or more times and the proportion who had been suspended or expelled in the past year.[5] In the area of health, two measures are used, both for children under age 17. The first identifies whether the child has a physical, mental, or health condition that limits his or her activity. The second identifies children who the respondents characterized as being in fair or poor health.

This chapter presents findings in terms of the percentage of children who display risk on each measure. This strategy makes it possible to determine whether risk of poor developmental outcomes differs for children in families currently receiving welfare and those in families who have left welfare, to ask whether risk levels in these two groups differ from that in other poor and higher income families, and to examine whether risk for these two groups has changed over time.

Family Groups

Children are divided into five mutually exclusive family groups, depending on welfare status and income.

- Current recipients—families that have received welfare continuously for the past two years or longer, new recipients, and families that left welfare and returned one or more times and were receiving welfare at the time of the survey.
- Former recipients—families that have left welfare within the past two years.
- Other poor families—those with incomes below the federal poverty level but with no history of welfare receipt within the past two years.
- Near-poor families—those with incomes between 100 percent and 199 percent of the federal poverty level, including only those who have never received welfare or who had not received it in the two years prior to or at the time of the survey.
- Higher-income families—those with incomes at or above 200 percent of the federal poverty level, including only those who have never received welfare or who had not received it in the two years prior to or at the time of the survey.

Risk Status of Children in 1999

Table 5-1 shows the percentage of children in each family group who were at risk of poor developmental outcomes in 1999, as determined by the eight measures of well-being. Table 5-2 provides an overview of sta-

(*text continues on page 92*)

Table 5-1. *Percentage of Children under Age 18 at Risk of Poor Developmental Outcomes, by Family's Welfare Receipt Status and Income, 1999 (weighted estimates)*

Measure of Risk	Current Recipients	Former Recipients	Other Poor Families	Near-Poor Families	Higher-Income Families	All Family Categories
High level of behavioral and emotional problems						
Age 6 to 11	23	14	8	6	4	6
Age 12 to 17	20	21	9	8	6	7
Participation in no extracurricular activities (age 6 to 17)	41	31	35	25	10	18
Low school engagement (age 6 to 17)	29	30	24	22	16	19
Suspended or expelled in last year (age 12 to 17)	27	43	21	20	9	14
Skipped school two or more times in last year (age 12 to 17)	18	22	14	12	7	9
Health condition that limits activity (age 0 to 17)	21	14	12	10	7	9
Current health is fair or poor (age 0 to 17)	11	8	9	6	2	5

Source: Child Trends calculations from the 1999 National Survey of America's Families.

(continued)

Table 5-2. *Differences in the Risk of Poor Developmental Outcomes for Children under 18, by Family's Welfare Receipt Status and Income, 1999 (Continued)*

Measure of Risk	Do Current and Former Recipients Differ?	Do Current and Former Recipients Differ from Other Poor Families?		Do Current and Former Recipients Differ from Near-Poor and Higher-Income Families?			
				Current Recipients		Former Recipients	
		Current Recipients	Former Recipients	Near-Poor	Higher-Income	Near-Poor	Higher-Income
High level of behavioral and emotional problems (age 6 to 11)	No	Yes	(Yes)	Yes	Yes	Yes	Yes
High level of behavioral and emotional problems (age 12 to 17)	No	(Yes)	Yes	Yes	Yes	Yes	Yes
Participation in no extracurricular activities (age 6 to 17)	No	No	No	Yes	Yes	No	Yes
Low school engagement (age 6 to 17)	No	No	No	No	Yes	Yes	Yes

Suspended or expelled in last year (age 12 to 17)	Yes	No	Yes	No	Yes	Yes	Yes
Skipped school two or more times in last year (age 12 to 17)	No	No	No	No	Yes	(Yes)	Yes
Health condition that limits activity (age 0 to 17)	(Yes)	Yes	(Yes)	Yes	Yes	Yes	Yes
Current health is fair or poor (age 0 to 17)	No	No	No	Yes	Yes	No	Yes

Source: Child Trends calculations from the 1999 National Survey of America's Families.

Note: Differences were statistically significant at $p < .05$. Differences in parentheses were statistically significant at $p < .10$.

tistically significant differences across groups of families on the eight measures.

Children in families currently receiving welfare and children in families that had left welfare within the past two years were at consistently greater risk than children in higher-income families. The magnitude of the differences is considerable: For example, while 23 percent of children age 6 to 11 in families currently receiving welfare and 14 percent of children in families that had left welfare showed high levels of behavioral and emotional problems, only 4 percent of children in higher-income families did. As can be seen in table 5-1, this pattern held across all eight measures.

In general, children in families that had left welfare did not appear to have fared better than children in families currently receiving welfare. In fact, children in these groups differed significantly on only two of the eight measures of developmental risk. First, adolescents in families that had left welfare were more likely than those in current welfare families to have been suspended or expelled in the past year. This difference is of interest given the unfavorable effects seen in adolescents whose parents participate in welfare-to-work programs. Second, children of current recipients were more likely than children of former recipients to have a health condition that limits their activities. A child's poor health may be a barrier to the parent's obtaining and keeping employment. It is important to recall that the leaver group studied here had left welfare within two years prior to the survey. One study raises the possibility that outcomes for children of former recipients may improve in time (Hofferth, Smith, and McLoyd 2000).

Some differences emerged between children in current and former recipient families and children in other poor families. Children of current and former recipients were more likely than children in other poor families to have a health condition that limited their activity. In addition, the proportion of children showing high levels of behavioral problems was larger in both current and former recipient families than it was in other poor families, regardless of age group. Adolescents in former recipient families—though not in current recipient families—were more than twice as likely to have been suspended or expelled as children in other poor families (which, again, aligns with the finding that mothers' participation in welfare-to-work programs tends to have negative effects on adolescents).

Most of these differences between current or former recipients' children and those in other poor families occur in the behavioral realm. Hair and colleagues (forthcoming) hypothesize that measures of child behavior tend to reflect changes in family circumstances more quickly than cognitive or health measures, which tend to reflect cumulative influences over time. Children in families currently or recently receiving welfare may have experienced greater family change and instability in recent years than children in other poor families, putting them at greater risk of behavioral problems. Yet it is important to note that, on a majority of measures, comparable proportions of children in current and former recipient families and in poor families are at risk. Thus, as previous research indicates, poverty seems to be an important risk factor for poor developmental outcomes (Brooks-Gunn and Duncan 1997; Moore et al. 1995; McGroder et al. 2000), and this appears to be the case regardless of a family's welfare status.

Finally, children in current and former recipient families were more likely to be at risk than children in near-poor families. Differences were statistically significant on five measures for children in current recipient versus near-poor families and on six measures for children in former recipient versus near-poor families. Children in families of current and former welfare recipients did not fare better than children in near-poor families on any measure.

Changes in Children's Risk Status between 1997 and 1999

Table 5-3 shows changes in the risk status of children from current and former welfare families between 1997 and 1999. Examination of these changes helps answer two important questions. First, has risk among children in current recipient families worsened over time, given the possibility that families on welfare in 1999 may be families that are more disadvantaged than those who were on welfare in 1997, given declining caseloads? Second, have children in former welfare families fared progressively better on measures of developmental risk as supports for working as well as requirements have strengthened?

The NSAF analyses do not support either possibility. There are no statistically significant changes in children's risk between 1997 and 1999, regardless of whether they are in current or former welfare families (table 5-3). These findings are in accord with other results from the 1997 and 1999 NSAF rounds, particularly those suggesting that barriers to employment and disadvantage have not intensified over time in the caseload of current recipients, or have done so only in subtle ways. The findings also agree with data indicating that very serious risk, as mani-

Table 5-3. *Change from 1997 to 1999 in Percentage of Children under age 18 at Risk of Poor Developmental Outcomes, by Family's Welfare Receipt Status (weighted estimates)*

Measure of Risk	Current Recipients			Former Recipients		
	1997	1999	Statistically Significant Difference?	1997	1999	Statistically Significant Difference?
High level of behavioral and emotional problems						
Age 6 to 11	16	23	No	13	14	No
Age 12 to 17	23	20	No	25	21	No
Participation in no extracurricular activities (age 6 to 17)	33	41	No	34	31	No
Low school engagement (age 6 to 17)	33	29	No	32	30	No
Suspended or expelled in last year (age 12 to 17)	39	27	No	39	43	No
Skipped school two or more times in last year (age 12 to 17)	23	18	No	28	22	No
Health condition that limits activity (age 0 to 17)	15	21	No	14	14	No
Current health is fair or poor (age 0 to 17)	9	11	No	8	8	No

Source: Child Trends calculations from the 1997 and 1999 National Survey of America's Families.
Note: Differences were statistically significant at $p < .10$.

fested by child abuse, has not increased during the years of welfare reform. At the same time, the findings are in accord with Loprest's (2001) results indicating that median monthly earnings and income have not increased from 1997 to 1999, despite a decline in poverty among former recipient families.

The findings do leave open the important possibility that subgroups of families are beginning to diverge. Looking at average risk only within family groups, such as those used here, could mask such differences. For instance, the finding that a greater proportion of former welfare families experienced material hardship in 1999 than in 1997, while a smaller proportion reported being in poverty in 1999, points to the presence of diverging subgroups. Research is underway examining this possibility (Chase-Lansdale et al. 2001). In addition, following data through 2001 might reveal that early trends in family structure, child poverty, or both (particularly if accompanied by increased income) do contribute to child well-being over a longer period.

Policy Implications

The persistently high risk of poor developmental outcomes among children of current and former welfare recipients raises a fundamental policy issue: How and to what extent will welfare policies seek to support the well-being and development of children in families receiving and moving off of welfare? From the perspective of children, it may be important to consider several approaches.

CONSIDER PROVIDING ECONOMIC SUPPORTS IN CONNECTION WITH EMPLOYMENT SO THAT OVERALL FAMILY INCOME INCREASES WHEN PARENTS MAKE THE TRANSITION FROM WELFARE TO WORK. In several programs that had strong financial work incentives (within or outside of the welfare system), young children showed improvements in their behavior and academic performance. These programs include the Minnesota Family Investment Program (Gennetian and Miller 2000), the Canadian Self-Sufficiency Program (Morris and Michalopoulos 2000), and New Hope (Bos et al. 1999; Huston et al. 2001). The term "strong" must be qualified, in that the improvement in overall income is not enormous—about $110 a month on average in the Minnesota program—but it is enough to make a difference in children's developmental outcomes (Moorehouse 2001).

RECONSIDER APPROACHES DESIGNED TO ENHANCE WELFARE RECIPIENTS' EDUCATIONAL ATTAINMENT. Welfare reform initially focused on moving recipients rapidly into employment rather than preparing them for employment through education and training. The findings from experimental studies suggest that young children may benefit, especially in terms of their cognitive development, when parents increase their educational attainment as part of a welfare-to-work program. Some programs for hard-to-employ welfare recipients are now considering education and training; such approaches may be particularly beneficial for children whose parents have few basic skills (Magnuson and McGroder 2001).

TAKE INTO ACCOUNT THE NEEDS OF ADOLESCENTS AND INFANTS AS WELL AS YOUNG CHILDREN IN FAMILIES MOVING FROM WELFARE TO WORK. Successive waves of welfare reform have required mothers of younger and younger children to meet work requirements. Therefore concern, and indeed research, has tended to focus on the impacts of welfare-to-work programs on preschool and school-age children. Research reveals that these programs tend to have favorable effects on young children but, unexpectedly, unfavorable effects on adolescents. The reasons for the negative effects on adolescents are not yet clear. Several explanations seem plausible, including increased friction in parent-child relations, decreased parental supervision, and adolescents' assumption of substantial responsibilities in the household (Brooks et al. 2001). For some young people, after-school programs may represent a solution, while for others, participation may not be possible, because of their other roles and responsibilities. More research is needed to shape policies and programs that will benefit adolescents.

The recent extension of work requirements to mothers of infants has not been carefully studied from the perspective of its impacts on child development. This is a serious gap in knowledge. The National Academy of Sciences' Committee on Integrating the Science of Early Development (Shonkoff and Phillips 2000) has called for careful review of this policy. Implementation and systematic evaluation of differing approaches, such as varying the timing and extent of the work requirement in the first year of life, could be quite important.

PROVIDE SUPPORTS NOT ONLY FOR FAMILIES FACING MULTIPLE, PERSISTENT BARRIERS TO EMPLOYMENT, BUT ALSO TO FAMILIES FACING RECENT, HIGHLY STRESSFUL SITUATIONS. Increasing numbers of welfare programs are considering what kind of assistance will be needed for each member of a family in order to make the transition to work succeed (Corbett 2001). These family support approaches should focus both on families facing multiple and often enduring barriers to employment (such as low educational attainment and literacy, mental health problems, and substance abuse) and families facing acutely stressful situations (such as job loss or a recent separation or divorce).

Efforts to support the hard-to-employ have taken on increasing importance as work requirements are applied with greater vigor and time limits begin to run out. Children can benefit from programs that address parental barriers to employment, such as low maternal literacy or depressive symptoms (Hair et al. forthcoming; Zaslow, Hair, et al. 2001), but programs that also address children's developmental needs directly (through high-quality early childhood care and education, for example) are particularly promising (Smith 1995). Research on such two-generation programs cautions that both the adult and the child components need to be of sufficiently high quality and duration to affect both generations positively (St. Pierre, Layzer, and Barnes 1995).

Child abuse is more likely among poor families and families receiving welfare (Geen et al. 2001). Therefore, caseworkers and others working with welfare families, especially with hard-to-employ families, should be alert to the possibility of "dual-system clients" (Ehrle et al. 2001)—that is, families involved with both welfare and child welfare agencies. Communication among such agencies has improved in recent years (ibid.), but family support programs should give further consideration to planning and developing joint programs and services.

Several welfare-to-work programs have had unexpected negative impacts on children in families traditionally considered at low risk of long-term welfare dependency. These families may be experiencing risks or stressors different from those currently used to measure risk, but little is known at this point about the nature of the stressors. Determining the needs of children and adults in such families and evaluating means of addressing those needs are essential steps to developing effective programs and policies.

Clearly, recent research on the well-being of children affected by welfare reform has much to contribute to the debates surrounding TANF reauthorization. Future research can be made even more informative by focusing on such issues as the effects of programs on infants and adolescents, and by providing more fine-grained measures of children's development. Surveys to date show that children in families receiving and leaving welfare in recent years face significant developmental risk. Other studies reveal the positive and negative effects of particular welfare-to-work programs. Armed with this knowledge, policymakers can use the opportunity provided by TANF reauthorization to support the healthy development of children while continuing to pursue economic self-sufficiency for their parents.

NOTES

The authors would like to thank Alan Weil, Kenneth Finegold, and Jennifer Brooks for their thoughtful comments. We appreciate the Clark and Packard Foundations' support of our synthesis work, and would like to acknowledge the evaluation studies completed by the Manpower Demonstration Research Corporation, Abt Associates, and Mathematica Policy Research, which we have drawn upon.

1. See discussion of this issue in Morris and colleagues (2001), and Finegold and Scheuren (2001).

2. The National Survey of America's Families uses repeated cross-sectional portrayals rather than longitudinal analyses.

3. See also Morris and colleagues (2001); Duncan and Chase-Lansdale (2001); and Sherman (2001).

4. The increase for former welfare recipients during this period was not significant, whereas the increase for recipients was.

5. Previous work with these measures has indicated good psychometric characteristics (see Ehrle and Moore 1999). This earlier work guided the choice of cut points to distinguish between scores considered to indicate risk of poor developmental outcomes and those not indicating such risk. The measures of behavioral and emotional problems for 6- to 11-year-olds and 12- to 17-year-olds, as well as the measures of school engagement and participation in extracurricular activity for 6- to 17-year olds, are scales based on multiple interview items.

REFERENCES

Amato, Paul R. 2000. "The Consequences of Divorce for Adults and Children." *Journal of Marriage and the Family* 62 (4): 1269–87.

Blank, Rebecca M. 2000. "Fighting Poverty: Lessons from Recent U.S. History." *Journal of Economic Perspectives* 14 (2): 3–19.

Bos, Hans, Aletha C. Huston, Robert Granger, Greg Duncan, Tom Brock, and Vonnie McLoyd. 1999. "New Hope for People with Low Incomes: Two-Year Results of a Program to Reduce Poverty and Reform Welfare." New York: Manpower Demonstration Research Corporation.

Brooks, Jennifer, Elizabeth Hair, and Martha Zaslow. 2001. "Welfare Reform's Impact on Adolescents: Early Warning Signs." Washington, D.C.: Child Trends.

Brooks-Gunn, Jeanne, and Greg J. Duncan, 1997. "The Effects of Poverty on Children." *Future of Children* 7 (2): 55–71.

Chase-Lansdale, P. Lindsay, Rebekah Levine Coley, Brenda J. Lohman, and Laura D. Pittman. 2001. "Welfare Reform: What About the Children?" Paper presented at the Association for Public Policy Analysis and Management meeting, November 2001, Washington, D.C.

Coleman, Marilyn, Lawrence Ganong, and Mark Fine. 2000. "Reinvestigating Remarriage: Another Decade of Progress." *Journal of Marriage and the Family* 62 (4): 1288–1307.

Corbett, Thomas. 2001. "Evaluating Welfare Reform in an Era of Transition: Are We Looking in the Wrong Direction?" *Focus* 21 (3): 1–5.

Duncan, Greg J., and P. Lindsay Chase-Lansdale. 2001. "Welfare Reform and Child Well-Being." In *The New World of Welfare,* edited by Rebecca M. Blank and Ron Haskins (391–417). Washington, D.C.: Brookings Institution Press.

Ehrle, Jennifer, and Kristin Anderson Moore. 1999. *Benchmarking Child and Family Well-Being Measures in the National Survey of America's Families.* Washington, D.C.: The Urban Institute. NSAF Methodology Report No. 6.

Ehrle, Jennifer, Karin Malm, Lynne Fender and Roseana Bess. 2001. *Welfare Reform and Opportunities for Collaboration between Welfare and Child Welfare Agencies.* Washington, D.C.: The Urban Institute. *Assessing the New Federalism* Occasional Paper No. 53.

Finegold, Kenneth, and Fritz Scheuren. 2001. "Three Ways to Research PRWORA: A Response to Peter H. Rossi." In *Four Evaluations of Welfare Reform: What Will Be Learned,* edited by Douglas J. Besharov and Peter Germanis (75–86). College Park, Md.: University of Maryland School of Public Affairs.

Geen, Rob, Lynne Fender, Jacob Leos-Urbel, and Teresa Markowitz. 2001. *Welfare Reform's Effect on Child Welfare Caseloads.* Washington, D.C.: The Urban Institute. *Assessing the New Federalism* Discussion Paper 01-04.

Gennetian, Lisa A., and Cynthia Miller. 2000. *Reforming Welfare and Rewarding Work: Final Report of the Minnesota Family Investment Program: Volume 2. Effects on Children.* New York: Manpower Demonstration Research Corporation.

Hair, Elizabeth C., Sharon M. McGroder, Martha J. Zaslow, Surjeet K. Ahluwalia, and Kristin Anderson Moore. Forthcoming. "How Do Maternal Risk Factors Affect Children in Low-Income Families? Further Evidence of Two-Generational Implications." *Journal of Prevention and Intervention in the Community.*

Haskins, Ron, and Wendell Primus. 2001. "Welfare Reform and Poverty." Washington, D.C.: Brookings Institution. *Welfare Reform and Beyond* Policy Brief No. 4.

Hofferth, Sandra L., Julia Smith, Vonnie C. McLoyd. 2000. "Achievement and Behavior among Children of Welfare Recipients, Welfare Leavers, and Low-Income Single Mothers." *Journal of Social Issues* 56 (4): 747–74.

Huston, Aletha C., Greg J. Duncan, Robert Granger, Johannes Bos, Vonnie McLoyd, Rashmita Mistry, Danielle Crosby, Christina Gibson, Katherine Magnuson, Jennifer Romich, and Ana Ventura. 2001. "Work-Based Antipoverty Programs for Parents Can Enhance the School Performance and Social Behavior of Children." *Child Development* 72 (1): 318–36.

Loprest, Pamela. 2001. "How Are Families That Left Welfare Doing? A Comparison of Early and Recent Welfare Leavers." Washington, D.C.: The Urban Institute. *Assessing the New Federalism* Policy Brief B-36.

Magnuson, Katherine A., and Sharon M. McGroder. 2001. "Intergenerational Benefits: The Effect of Maternal Education on Children's School Readiness." Paper presented at the Population Association of America annual meeting, March 2001.

Martin, Joyce A., Brady E. Hamilton, and Stephanie J. Ventura. 2001. "Births: Preliminary Data for 2000." *National Vital Statistics Report* 49 (5). http://www.cdc.gov/nchs/data/nvsr/nvsr49/nvsr49_05.pdf.

McGroder, Sharon M., Martha J. Zaslow, Kristin Anderson Moore, and Suzanne Le Menestrel. 2000. *National Evaluation of Welfare-to-Work Strategies: Impacts on Young Children and Their Families Two Years after Enrollment: Findings from the Child Outcomes Study.* Washington, D.C.: U.S. Department of Health and Human Services, Administration for Children and Families and Office of the Assistant Secretary for Planning and Evaluation; and U.S. Department of Education, Office of the Under Secretary and Office of Vocational and Adult Education.

Moore, Kristin Anderson, Martha J. Zaslow, Mary Jo Coiro, S. Miller, and E. Magenheim. 1995. *How Well Are They Faring? AFDC Families with Preschool-Aged Children in Atlanta at the Outset of the JOBS Evaluation.* Washington, D.C.: U.S. Department of Health and Human Services and U.S. Department of Education.

Moorehouse, Martha. 2001. Discussant comments made during the "Effects on Children of Differing Welfare and Employment Policies Symposium" (V. Knox, chair). Biennial Meeting of the Society for Research on Child Development, Minneapolis, Minn. (April).

Morris, Pamela A., and C. Michalopoulos. 2000. *The Self-Sufficiency Project at 36 Months: Effects on Children of a Program That Increased Parental Employment and Income.* Ottawa, Canada: Social Research and Demonstration Corporation.

Morris, Pamela A., Aletha C. Huston, Greg J. Duncan, Danielle A. Crosby, and Johannes M. Bos. 2001. *How Welfare and Work Policies Affect Children: A Synthesis of Research.* New York: Manpower Demonstration Research Corporation.

National Research Council. 2001. *Evaluating Welfare Reform in an Era of Transition: A Report of the National Research Council.* Washington, D.C.: National Academy Press.

Nelson, Sandi, Rebecca L. Clark, and Gregory Acs. 2001. "Beyond the Two-Parent Family: How Teenagers Fare in Cohabiting Couple and Blended Families." Washington, D.C.: The Urban Institute. *Assessing the New Federalism* Policy Brief B-31.

Porter, Kathy, and Wendell Primus. 1999. *Changes since 1995 in the Safety Net's Impact on Child Poverty.* Washington, D.C.: Center on Budget and Policy Priorities.

Seltzer, Judith A. 2000. "Families Formed Outside of Marriage." *Journal of Marriage and the Family* 62 (4): 1247–68.

Sherman, Arloc. 2001. *How Children Fare in Welfare Experiments Appears to Hinge on Income.* Washington, D.C.: Children's Defense Fund.

Shonkoff, Jack P., and Deborah A. Phillips. 2000. *From Neurons to Neighborhoods: The Science of Early Childhood Development.* Washington, D.C.: National Academy Press.

Smith, Sheila. 1995. *Two Generation Programs for Families in Poverty.* Norwood, N.J.: Ablex.

St. Pierre, Robert G., Jean I. Layzer, and Helen V. Barnes. 1995. "Two-Generation Programs: Design, Cost, and Short-Term Effectiveness." *The Future of Children: Long-Term Outcomes of Early Childhood Programs* 5 (3): 76–93.

U.S. Department of Health and Human Services, Administration on Children, Youth and Families. 2001. *Child Maltreatment 1999: Reports from the States to the National Child Abuse and Neglect Data System.* Washington, D.C.: U.S. Government Printing Office.

Zaslow, Martha J., Jennifer L. Brooks, Kristin Anderson Moore, Pamela Morris, Kathryn Tout, and Zakia Redd. 2001. *Impacts on Children in Experimental Studies of Welfare-to-Work Programs.* Report to the Edna McConnell Clark and David and Lucille Packard Foundations.

Zaslow, Martha J., Elizabeth C. Hair, M. Robin Dion, Surjeet K. Ahluwalia, and Jennifer Sargent. 2001. "Maternal Depressive Symptoms and Low Literacy as Potential Barriers to Employment in a Sample of Families Receiving Welfare: Are There Two-Generational Implications?" *Women and Health* 32: 211–51.

Zaslow, Martha J., Kristin Anderson Moore, Jennifer L. Brooks, Pamela Morris, Kathryn Tout, Zakia Redd, and Carol Emig. Forthcoming. "Experimental Studies of Welfare Reform and Children." *Future of Children.*

Zaslow, Martha J., Kathryn Tout, Christopher Botsko, and Kristin Anderson Moore. 1998. "Welfare Reform and Children: Potential Implications." Washington, D.C.: The Urban Institute. *Assessing the New Federalism* Policy Brief A-23.

Zedlewski, Sheila R., and Donald W. Alderson. 2001. "Before and After Reform: How Have Families on Welfare Changed?" Washington, D.C.: The Urban Institute. *Assessing the New Federalism* Policy Brief B-32.

6

Work Opportunities for People Leaving Welfare

Demetra Smith Nightingale

One defining characteristic of the new welfare system is its emphasis on work as the route off welfare and out of poverty. Many observers who opposed PRWORA were concerned that jobs would not be available for large numbers of welfare recipients. Thus far, those fears have not been borne out. Similarly, there were concerns that families would reach the welfare time limit and still not be employed. As the first families reach their five-year lifetime limits, it will soon become clearer whether those concerns were valid.

What is evident is that welfare caseloads nationwide have declined by over 50 percent since 1996 (see the introduction to this book), and that most adults who have left the rolls are attached to the labor market (see chapter 2). However, there are a number of important short- and long-term questions beyond whether welfare recipients are getting jobs. What kinds of jobs are these individuals getting? Are there opportunities for them to move up in the job market? What strategies help people get jobs, keep jobs, and get good jobs? What are state and local programs doing to help TANF recipients make the transition to work, succeed in the workplace, and become economically self-sufficient? What happens when the economy slows down? This chapter looks beyond the drop in caseloads by examining what kinds of jobs low-income workers can expect to obtain, what programs are doing to help welfare recipients find employment, and what other strategies government can use to help low-income families achieve financial stability.

Are Welfare Recipients Getting Jobs?

Most observers agree that the reduction in welfare caseloads during the 1990s reflected both the strong economy and welfare reform's focus on employment, work requirements, and time limits. Although analysis of the causes of the caseload decline will undoubtedly continue, it is clear that many of those individuals who left the rolls after 1996 have entered the job market. According to an analysis of NSAF data, more than 60 percent of those who left welfare in 1997 and 1999 were employed (Loprest 2001). This finding corroborates the results of most state studies that track welfare recipients who leave the rolls (Loprest 1999).

In fact, since the early 1990s, employment has increased for all single mothers, not just for those leaving welfare. This increase reflects the continuing strong economy, low unemployment rate, and high demand for workers. As shown in figure 6-1, the percentage of single mothers who were employed increased from about 59 percent to 73 percent between 1993 and 1998 (Lerman 2001).

Analysts generally agree that sufficient numbers of jobs are available nationwide to absorb welfare recipients entering the labor market (Burtless 2000; McMurrer, Sawhill, and Lerman 1997). A study of 20 large metropolitan areas found that most could incorporate the increase in employment by welfare recipients and other low-income mothers without eroding the job market for other low-skilled workers (Lerman and Ratcliffe 2000). Of course, the results vary across cities, depending on the size of the labor market, the area's industrial and occupational makeup, and the characteristics of the local workforce. A large influx of welfare recipients into the job market could cause an increase in the overall unemployment rate in some metropolitan areas, including Baltimore, New York City, St. Louis, and Washington (Lerman, Loprest, and Ratcliffe 1999).

Surveys of employers provide further evidence that the labor market should be able to accommodate most welfare recipients. Initial concerns about employers' reluctance to hire welfare mothers now appear unfounded. Between 30 and 40 percent of all employers surveyed in four large metropolitan areas report having hired welfare recipients in the past two years (Holzer and Stoll 2001). More than 80 percent of employers

Figure 6-1. *Employment/Population Ratio and Unemployment Rate, Ages 19–64, 1993–2001*

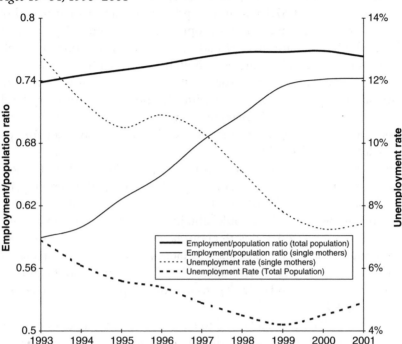

Source: Lerman 2001.

with high proportions of entry-level jobs nationwide report recently hiring welfare recipients, and virtually all these employers indicate that they would be willing to hire welfare recipients (Regenstein, Meyer, and Hicks 1998). The labor market's ability so far to absorb welfare recipients, and the willingness of employers to hire such individuals, suggests that demand for such workers is strong. But what kinds of jobs can these workers expect to obtain?

What Kinds of Jobs Do Welfare Recipients Get?

Although welfare recipients are leaving public assistance and going to work, the types of jobs they are entering generally offer limited growth opportunities. In most cases, welfare recipients enter the secondary labor market, where wages, benefits, and job security are relatively low. Among workers who recently left welfare, the median wage in 1999 was between $7.00 and $7.15 an hour, and the pre-tax median monthly income was a little over $1,100 (Loprest 2001). About 52 percent of those who left welfare in 1999 had incomes below the poverty level. Many of these individuals are poor, both because their hourly wages are low and because they are not working full-time and year-round. A 1997 national survey of 500 employers with high proportions of entry-level jobs found that nearly half their entry-level positions were filled by part-time workers, and that most entry level workers earned $6.00 an hour or less (Regenstein et al. 1998).

Low-wage workers are also less likely than other workers to have access to health insurance and other benefits through their employers. The Families and Work Institute, for instance, found that about 60 percent of low-wage workers could obtain job-related health insurance for their family, compared with about 88 percent of all other workers (Kaye and Nightingale 2000, appendix table 4.6). A survey of entry-level employers found that only half offered health insurance, about half provided paid vacation, and only 17 percent provided paid sick leave (Regenstein et al. 1998).

Because welfare recipients tend to have less education and fewer skills than workers in general, they are likely to move into jobs that require limited skill. They tend to work in business services, personal services (including health), wholesale/retail trade (including stores and eating establishments), and manufacturing. Very few former welfare recipients work in jobs in the construction, communication, transportation, or government sectors. In terms of occupations, former welfare recipients are concentrated in clerical/administrative and services jobs, as shown in figure 6-2 (Loprest 1999).

Many of these low-skill occupations offer low wages. The median weekly earnings for all full-time workers was $494 in 1996, about 200 percent of the official federal poverty level for a family of three, but the median weekly earnings for full-time jobs held by workers with limited education or skills was $308, just barely over the poverty level for a family of three (Nightingale 2001).

Former welfare recipients have additional difficulties once they start a job. The four-city survey of employers cited earlier found that between one-quarter and one-third of employers reported that job performance was a problem among former welfare recipients (Holzer and Stoll 2001).

Figure 6-2. *Types of Jobs Obtained by Former TANF Recipients, 1995–1997*

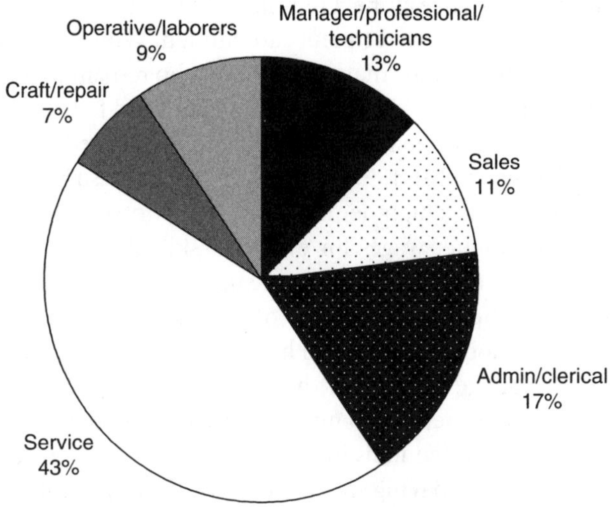

Source: Loprest 1999.

In particular, absenteeism, which is often linked to child care and transportation issues, was a concern.

Do Low-Skilled Workers Move Up in the Job Market?

One premise of current federal welfare policy is that working, even in entry-level jobs, creates opportunities to move up the job ladder. Many workers, especially younger individuals, do acquire experience and move to better jobs. However, workers with less education have limited upward job mobility. Moreover, many jobs in today's technology- and services-driven economy require higher-skilled workers than in the manufacturing-centered economy of the past.

Of course, many low-wage workers do move up the job ladder, but education, rather than experience, is increasingly the most important determinant of wage increases. Since the late 1970s, workers without a college degree have had fewer opportunities for wage increases than those with a degree (Blank 1995; McMurrer et al. 1997).

Few studies specifically address whether welfare recipients with low skills and limited education have difficulty advancing in the job market based on work experience alone. Preliminary evidence suggests, however, that the options for welfare recipients are limited. While many low-wage workers advance in the labor market, the ones who remain in jobs with little or no wage increases for long periods of time tend to be less educated and disproportionately female, features shared by the welfare population as a whole (McMurrer et al. 1997). In the late 1990s, the sustained strength of the economy and the high demand for labor contributed to increased employment and higher wages for even low-skilled workers. This prosperity, however, did not necessarily create upward occupational mobility.

The limited occupational mobility of low-skilled women may partly reflect the types of jobs these women hold. Occupations offering workers without some college education the greatest wage potential, such as machinist, equipment repairer, and truck driver, tend to be held by men (Nightingale 1999). Individuals in sales and administrative clerical positions can obtain better-paying supervisory positions through work experience. But only a small portion of sales and administrative jobs are supervisory, so few non-supervisory workers can expect to move up to such positions. In general, unless low-educated females work in nontraditional jobs or pursue higher education, their upward mobility is limited.

What Policies and Strategies Are States Using to Promote Work and Upward Mobility?

PRWORA gave states increased flexibility to design their own welfare programs, including the freedom to develop specific work requirements, work incentives, work services, and support systems. Thus far, state programs have primarily emphasized moving recipients into jobs as quickly as possible (see chapter 1), although many states are beginning to move beyond the rapid-employment strategy. Once large numbers of former recipients entered the workforce, program administrators and staff became more aware of the need to help new workers keep their jobs. As more families reach their lifetime limit on welfare, one of the highest priorities is to develop strategies that will help welfare leavers and other low-income parents increase their incomes. States are exploring several ways of achieving this goal, including helping workers remain in the labor market, helping workers with jobs advance in the labor market, and, in some places, supplementing wages with other income transfers and supports. Federal policy increasingly supports such efforts, in part by providing special grants to states, local programs, and agencies focusing on post-employment retention and advancement strategies.

Many programs are also beginning to provide ongoing support to ease the transition to work, especially to individuals with serious difficulties, and to improve clients' work skills. A number of states, such as Wisconsin and Massachusetts, are using welfare reform as an opportunity to redefine their family support policies by expanding programs to encompass more poor families with children, particularly working families, and to emphasize services and activities aside from cash benefits.

Expanded Role of Work in Welfare

Historically, welfare recipients have combined work and public assistance in various ways. Since the 1970s, federal and state welfare policies have increasingly emphasized work and, to varying degrees, education and job training. PRWORA expanded the emphasis on work, primarily by stressing the importance of moving recipients as quickly as possible into jobs in the regular labor market. By the late 1990s, some states had begun to broaden their focus on work by providing post-employment services to improve job retention and by incorporating strategies to improve individuals' skills and earning potential.

Even before PRWORA, most welfare recipients had some labor force activity. An analysis of mothers who had received welfare in the late 1980s found that about 70 percent had worked at some point in the previous 24 months (Spalter-Roth et al. 1995). In addition, throughout the 1980s about 15 percent of recipients participated in a work-welfare program (Nightingale 1997). But few welfare recipients before welfare reform worked and received cash welfare at the same time. For example, from 1983 to 1993 only about 5 to 7 percent of welfare adults each year also had earnings from employment (U.S. Congress 1994).

To reinforce the importance of work, PRWORA established state performance standards in the form of work participation rates. By 1999, 35 percent of all TANF families and 90 percent of two-parent cases in each state were expected to be employed in regular jobs or involved in work-related activities. The target rate rises to 50 percent of all families in 2002 (the rate for two-parent cases stays at 90 percent). States that do not reach these rates risk losing part of their TANF grant.

One development since the enactment of federal welfare reform is that a higher proportion of public-assistance recipients than in the past are involved in work and work-related activities. More families are combining work and welfare; by 1999, more than 30 percent of welfare recipients also had earnings from employment (U.S. Department of Health and Human Services [DHHS] 2000b). While some of this increase in the number of working recipients likely reflects the strong economy and other policies, such as the expanded earned income tax credit, welfare reform's emphasis on work undoubtedly played a role.

The emphasis on work and the TANF work participation rates have also contributed to the increased number of welfare recipients participating in activities intended to help them become employed. States have wide discretion in deciding how to meet their TANF work participation rates, including strategies to encourage or require work. To count toward a state's federally specified participation rate, a person must participate at least 20 hours a week in one or more of the following activities: regular work, job-search assistance, a community service job, school (for teenage parents), or employment-related education or training. No more than 30 percent of the persons counted towards a state's participation rate can be active only in education or training.

State TANF agencies, however, decide what is required of individual welfare applicants and recipients. States can implement work requirement policies and work programs that allow a broader range of training and education activities than what federal policies will "count" for state participation rates. States also have the flexibility to broadly define work activities to include education and training to help clients obtain and retain jobs, as long as the state meets its federal participation rate. States also have the discretion to exempt individuals from work requirements, and some, such as Massachusetts, exempt large numbers of cases from work activity requirements, though these recipients are usually still subject to the time limit.

Reports on TANF block grant spending and on the numbers of welfare recipients in various activities reflect the emphasis on work. In fiscal year 1999, $1.8 billion (or 8 percent) of the $23 billion in TANF block grant and state maintenance of effort spending was spent on work activities (DHHS 2000a). That is about half a billion dollars more than the average annual federal and state spending in the 1980s for the Job Opportunities and Basic Skills (JOBS) Training Program under AFDC (Nightingale 1997). In fiscal year 1999, an average of about 885,000 persons each month (42 percent of TANF adults nationwide) were in a federally countable work activity, including 28 percent of TANF adults who were working in regular jobs and 16 percent who were in job search and other work activities (DHHS 2000b).[1] This is 20 percent more work activity participants than were in JOBS in 1994 (Nightingale 1997)—even though the total welfare caseload in 1999 was about 50 percent lower than in 1994.

An analysis of NSAF data confirms that most welfare recipients are involved in work-related activities: In 1997, 21 percent of adults receiving TANF benefits reported that they were working, 25 percent said they were looking for work, and about 10 percent reported being in school or training (Zedlewski 1999). About 28 percent of welfare recipients reported that they had participated in some skill-building activity in 1996. Two-thirds of these respondents were active in vocational training, college courses, or high school/GED classes (Bell 2000).

Although most former welfare recipients work, the employment situation varies by state. Leaving welfare for work is easier in some states than in others, just as working one's way out of poverty is easier in certain states. As discussed in chapter 4, some states have set TANF earned income disregard levels high, meaning a certain amount of earnings are ignored when officials are considering whether a family's income is low enough to qualify for welfare. A high disregard policy allows families to extend the income range within which they can work and still receive some cash welfare. In several states, other policies to support working families, such as state earned income tax credits and minimum wage and living wage provisions, complement TANF policies.

Expanded Population: Beyond Cash Assistance

Welfare reform's target population has gradually expanded beyond families receiving a welfare check to include former welfare recipients, noncustodial parents of TANF recipients and other poor children, families at risk of going on welfare, and working poor families. Some of this shift has resulted from federal policies. For example, a number of federal initiatives provide special grants to fund program development for employment retention and advancement, services to noncustodial parents, and rural service delivery.

The Department of Labor administers the Welfare-to-Work (WtW) Grants program, which has provided $3 billion in funding to states and to hundreds of local programs. The WtW initiative complements TANF efforts by funding services to improve the long-term employability of welfare recipients and other low-income parents who have particularly serious labor market problems. The availability of WtW grants, retention and advancement grants, and grants for serving noncustodial parents has provided impetus to develop new strategies for the TANF population and for non-welfare poor parents as well (Nightingale 2001).

In some states, the target population has expanded as TANF caseloads have shrunk. With less of the total block grant funds paying for cash grants to families on welfare, several states have begun using TANF funds to provide longer-term support services, crisis intervention, and case management to former recipients, noncustodial fathers who also have employment barriers, other non-welfare families who might be at risk of needing welfare, and working poor families in general. These efforts are still being developed, and there is little information yet on the scale of the programs or the results.

Expanded Scope of Work Programs: Beyond "Work First"

The most dramatic declines in TANF caseloads occurred before 1998. Caseload levels stabilized after that year, and as the first families began to reach state-imposed time limits, many—but not all—states modified their initial TANF work-first focus to consider broader human capital development and worker support strategies. One concern behind these modifications is that individuals remaining on welfare may have relatively more serious barriers to employment than do those already working. Research is somewhat mixed on this point, with some evidence suggesting that on most measurable factors today's welfare recipients are similar to those of the 1990s. At the state and local levels, however, where programs are charged with requiring more clients to work and providing more individuals with employment services, there is a strong sense that work-requirement caseloads are harder to employ than in the past. Many states are trying to identify and address those with special needs (see chapter 9). Welfare administrators also increasingly recognize that if work is to be the primary route to economic self-sufficiency, then work advancement must also be part of welfare-to-work strategies. Parents must move beyond entry-level, low-wage jobs in order to achieve long-term financial stability.

Even before PRWORA, national policy and many state programs had adopted what has been referred to as work-first approaches. Such approaches are premised on promoting work as an immediate goal, arguing that "any job is a good job" and that "the best way to succeed in the labor market is to join it . . . as quickly as possible" (Holcomb et al. 1998).

The focus on immediate job entry was the dominant program approach in the first few years of TANF. While various types of work-first models emerged, the most common ones involved mandatory work requirements, with states typically requiring an individual to begin working (a regular job or unpaid work experience assignments) or participating in other work-related activities (job search, education, or training) soon after he or she applied for welfare. Some analysts have concluded that the work-focused welfare policies, along with the strong job market during the economic boom of the 1990s, contributed to the large decline in caseloads (Wallace and Blank 1999).

Given the drop in the number of welfare cases, many state and local programs are now implementing more service-focused programs or are developing new strategies that are designed to address serious employment and family problems, incorporate skills development into employment, and provide longer-term follow-up and case management to improve job retention. New programs are being developed within the TANF agencies, other public agencies, and nonprofit organizations, particularly among agencies that receive federal program grant funds, such as WtW grants, or that participate in special demonstrations, such as training for young fathers or post-employment services.

One promising strategy is to incorporate work-based skills development into employment preparation programs. In Boston, the WtW grant has been used to develop nearly two dozen employer partnerships involving firms in financial services, retail trade, hospitality, health services, and other sectors. The firms collaborate with the workforce investment agency to design a pre-employment, occupation-specific curriculum, which is then followed by a workplace-based internship. Participating employers commit to hire all participants who complete the program (Nightingale 2001).

Another promising strategy is to operate paid supportive employment programs. Philadelphia's Transitional Work Corporation has developed a comprehensive program that provides pre-employment services, paid work experience assignments with close supervision, and ongoing counseling and support to hundreds of TANF recipients who have not been able to successfully move into the labor market through other programs. The program is supported with funds from TANF, WtW, and private foundations. In the state of Washington, WtW and TANF funds are being used to fund paid community-service jobs, which are administered by nonprofit community organizations and designed to improve work skills (Martinson and Holcomb forthcoming).

Not all TANF agencies have adopted broad or comprehensive perspectives. Some have made only minor adjustments to what existed under AFDC to bring programs into compliance with PRWORA. Observers and experts continue to debate whether strategies that are aimed at improving skills or upward mobility are increasing employment, income, or family well-being. Research and evaluations now under way should provide insight into these issues in the future.

What Happens When the Economy Slows Down?

Since PRWORA was passed, employment and wage trends for welfare recipients and other low-income mothers have been impressive. The recent economic slowdown, however, has raised concerns about the strength of the job market for low-wage workers. In general, less-educated workers have substantially higher unemployment rates than other workers. For example, between 1981 and 1995, the unemployment rates of workers without a high school diploma were about twice those of workers with a college degree (Smith and Woodbury 2000). Moreover, unemployment rates for former welfare recipients and for low-income parents are generally about twice the national unemployment rate (Holzer 2000; Vroman 1998; Kaye 1997). The full effect of an economic downturn on welfare will depend on how severe the contraction is and how long it lasts. Two likely effects, however, are a rise in welfare caseloads and, as time limits begin to take effect more fully, an increase in the number of poor families who do not qualify for TANF.

Just as the strong economy over the past several years contributed to the decline in welfare caseloads, a downturn in the economy will have some reverse effect, increasing caseloads. Wallace and Blank (1999) suggest that a 1 percentage point increase in the national unemployment rate is likely to result in a 6 to 7 percent increase in the welfare caseload in the subsequent two years. A higher increase in unemployment would have a greater effect on caseloads.

In theory, unemployment insurance is the first line of support for workers who lose their jobs. In reality, however, many unemployed people, especially low-wage workers, do not qualify for benefits. Only about 30 to 40 percent of all unemployed workers qualify for unemployment insurance, and that rate is even lower for low-wage workers, such as former welfare recipients or low-skilled noncustodial parents of welfare children

(Vroman 1998; Kaye 1997). Low-wage workers do not qualify for unemployment insurance for different reasons: Some do not have enough quarters of work to qualify, while some have left their jobs under conditions that disqualify them for benefits. As more former welfare recipients gain experience and remain in the workforce, a greater number should qualify for unemployment insurance. In the near term, many former welfare recipients who have entered the workforce will not qualify for unemployment insurance if they lose their jobs.

Before the 1996 reforms, most former welfare recipients who lost their jobs could return to public assistance. The TANF time limits make returning more difficult. Since late 2001, families have been reaching the five-year federal time limit, and some families have already reached shorter time limits imposed by certain states. Because many families go on and off welfare, and in and out of jobs, not everyone on welfare will reach the time limit at once. Thus, the full impact of the federal time limits will not emerge for several years.

Many states have policies in place to temper the effects of the federal time limit. For example, by using state rather than federal funds to pay for some welfare cash grants, states may continue to provide families with welfare eligibility and cash assistance without imposing a time limit, as long as federal funds are used to pay for a family's benefit for no more than five years. In addition, the federal clock stops when an individual earns enough from a job to leave welfare completely, as many have done. The federal clock keeps running, though, for those who combine work and some welfare receipt. A few states, such as Illinois, have chosen to use state funds to pay for benefits to working welfare recipients, meaning their federal clock stops. Still, some recent estimates suggest that a 1 point increase in unemployment might result in a 20 to 25 percent increase in the number of poor unemployed parents who are ineligible for either TANF or unemployment insurance (Nightingale et al. 2001). The obvious implication is that the income safety net may be inadequate during a severe economic downturn, since many unemployed low-income parents would not qualify for either TANF or unemployment insurance.

Policy Implications

Welfare reform has gradually broadened beyond the cash assistance system. Many TANF work programs and policies now provide services to more individuals than just those receiving a welfare check. In many states, for example, TANF funds are used to provide employment, job retention, and supportive services to former recipients as well as current recipients. Several state TANF work programs also serve, or collaborate with other programs that serve, noncustodial fathers.

In addition, programs providing employment services to welfare recipients are not all operated by TANF agencies; and many do not use TANF funds alone. In many places, funds from TANF, WtW grants, workforce investment programs, and fatherhood programs are combined to provide services to low-income parents with employment needs, regardless of their formal welfare status. In particular, the federal WtW grants program is funded separately and operates independently from TANF, but is considered a partner in welfare reform. Workforce investment boards, community or faith-based organizations, and educational institutions operate many WtW-funded programs.

The broadening of publicly supported programs to help low-income families in general is not entirely new. Employment and training programs have historically served welfare recipients along with other low-income persons. What is new is that since 1996 there has been considerable funding—especially from TANF block grants and from WtW grants—to operate work-related programs for welfare recipients and other low-income parents. In the narrowest sense, welfare refers to the actual cases receiving cash grants through TANF welfare agencies. In a broader sense, however, welfare in the post-PRWORA era encompasses financial assistance as well as a range of work-related services provided in partnership with federal, state, and private agencies to a wide group of low-income families.

Welfare has also become broader in another sense: The types of services and activities offered through TANF's work programs and other programs serving welfare recipients involve more than simply requiring individuals to go to work. Increasingly, programs offer a range of employment-related services—including pre-employment preparation, post-employment services, job retention services, and employment services to low-skilled noncustodial fathers. Such activities are more complex, and typically more costly, than approaches that primarily require clients to conduct job searches.

In many states and communities, some of the more promising employment-related programs for welfare families are just beginning to mature. In the upcoming reauthorization process and in future welfare policy debates, it will be important to avoid making policy changes that might disrupt or stifle innovative programming, and to encourage more innovation where it is still needed. For example, TANF regulations that require more detailed reports to track individual clients might divert resources away from program operations. Similarly, if federal TANF funding to states is reduced, or if allowable expenditures are more narrowly defined, states might be forced to halt promising programs for working poor non-welfare families. By contrast, more program innovation might be encouraged if Workforce Investment Act funds could be more easily combined with TANF funds at the local level to provide more comprehensive and seamless employment, training, and supportive services.

Although caseloads have declined considerably since the enactment of welfare reform in 1996, recent economic weakness and the changing nature of welfare provide some justification for maintaining federal TANF funding at the current level. Welfare programming at the state and local levels has expanded to include many noncash assistance services. Fewer families may be receiving cash assistance, but more parents are receiving employment assistance and support services. In addition, fewer dollars are being spent on cash assistance benefits, and more are being spent on employment-related activities. This shift in funding suggests that while welfare caseloads have declined, many families still need assistance.

Using federal welfare funds for employment-related services in addition to cash assistance for the most needy may mean that the costs per person are higher than in the past. Average monthly welfare benefits in fiscal year 2001 were $357. The average monthly cost of TANF work activities was about $500, divided almost evenly between costs of work-related services and costs of child care (DHHS 2000b).[2] In the long run, the investment is expected to pay off by increasing employment and ultimately reducing welfare costs. But in the short run, the costs per case will continue to be higher than the costs of simply providing a welfare check.

Because employment-related assistance has become such an important part of welfare reform, it would be shortsighted to scale back federal resources. Welfare and work activities cost more than welfare alone. States already have ample discretion to use TANF resources to fund employment, education, and skills training. To date, however, most states have focused on employment, and have devoted few resources to skills development. Some are beginning to consider more intensive approaches to address barriers to employment and improve skills.

In addition to maintaining the level of resources devoted to individuals on welfare, a simple change to the welfare law could encourage further investment in employability development. By broadening the definition of work activities that are allowable under the TANF work participation provisions, the federal government would encourage states to develop innovative skills development activities. Without stronger work skills or higher education, most people who leave welfare for work will remain in the low-wage labor market. By encouraging working parents to enroll in programs that will increase their skills and earning potential, public policy can more directly help low-income working parents establish long-term economic self-sufficiency.

NOTES

1. Percentages do not add to 100 because some individuals participate in more than one component category.
2. Calculations are based on fiscal and program activity data reported by DHHS in the 2000 Report to Congress (DHHS 2000b).

REFERENCES

Bell, Stephen H. 2000. "The Prevalence of Education and Training Activities among Welfare and Food Stamp Recipients." Washington, D.C.: The Urban Institute. *Assessing the New Federalism* Policy Brief B-24.
Blank, Rebecca M. 1995. "Outlook for the U.S. Labor Market and Prospects for Low-Wage Entry Jobs." In *The Work Alternative: Welfare Reform and the Realities of the Job Market*, edited by Demetra Smith Nightingale and Robert H. Haveman (33–71). Washington, D.C.: Urban Institute Press.
Burtless, Gary. 2000. "Can the Labor Market Absorb Three Million Welfare Recipients?" In *The Low-Wage Labor Market: Challenges and Opportunities for Economic Self-Sufficiency*, edited by Kelleen Kaye and Demetra Smith Nightingale (65–83). Washington, D.C.: Urban Institute Press.
DHHS. See U.S. Department of Health and Human Services.
Holcomb, Pamela A., LaDonna Pavetti, Caroline Ratcliffe, and Susan Riedinger. 1998. *Building an Employment-Focused Welfare System: Work First and Other Work-Oriented Strategies in Five States*. Washington, D.C.: U.S. Department of Health and Human Services.
Holzer, Harry J. 2000. "Unemployment Insurance and Welfare Recipients: What Happens When the Recession Comes?" Washington, D.C.: The Urban Institute. *Assessing the New Federalism* Policy Brief A-46.

Holzer, Harry J., and Michael A. Stoll. 2001. *Employers and Welfare Recipients: The Effects of Welfare Reform in the Workplace.* San Francisco: Public Policy Institute of California.

Kaye, Kelleen. 1997. "Unemployment Insurance as a Potential Safety Net for Former Welfare Recipients." Conference of U.S. Department of Health and Human Services.

Kaye, Kelleen, and Demetra Smith Nightingale, eds. 2000. *The Low-Wage Labor Market: Challenges and Opportunities for Economic Self-Sufficiency.* Washington, D.C.: Urban Institute Press.

Lerman, Robert I. 2001. *Jobs and Wages Up Sharply for Single Moms, Gains Especially High After Welfare Reform.* Washington, D.C.: The Urban Institute. *Single Parents' Earnings Monitor,* July 25.

Lerman, Robert I., and Caroline Ratcliffe. 2000. "Did Metropolitan Areas Absorb Welfare Recipients without Displacing Other Workers?" Washington, D.C.: The Urban Institute. *Assessing the New Federalism* Policy Brief A-45.

Lerman, Robert I., Pamela Loprest, and Caroline Ratcliffe. 1999. "How Well Can Urban Labor Markets Absorb Welfare Recipients?" Washington, D.C.: The Urban Institute. *Assessing the New Federalism* Policy Brief A-33.

Loprest, Pamela. 1999. *Families Who Left Welfare: Who Are They and How Are They Doing?* Washington, D.C.: The Urban Institute. *Assessing the New Federalism* Discussion Paper 99-02.

———. 2001. "How Are Families That Left Welfare Doing? A Comparison of Early and Recent Welfare Leavers." Washington, D.C.: The Urban Institute. *Assessing the New Federalism* Policy Brief B-36.

Martinson, Karin, and Pamela Holcomb. Forthcoming. "Strategies for Moving Welfare Recipients to Work in the TANF Program." Washington, D.C.: The Urban Institute.

McMurrer, Daniel P., Isabel V. Sawhill, and Robert I. Lerman. 1997. *Welfare Reform and Opportunity in the Low-Wage Labor Market.* Washington, D.C.: The Urban Institute. *Opportunity in America* Brief 5.

Nightingale, Demetra Smith. 1997. "Work-Related Resources and Services: Implications for TANF." Washington, D.C.: The Urban Institute. *Assessing the New Federalism* Policy Brief A-7.

———. 1999. "Low-Wage and Low-Skill Occupations: Identifying the Best Options for Welfare Recipients." Washington, D.C.: The Urban Institute. Unpublished discussion paper, November.

———. 2001. "Program Structure and Service Delivery in Eleven Welfare-to-Work Grant Programs." Washington, D.C.: The Urban Institute. Photocopy.

Nightingale, Demetra Smith, Wayne Vroman, Kelly S. Mikelson, Burt S. Barnow, and Shayne Spaulding. 2001. "The Employment Safety Net for Families in a Declining Economy: Policy Issues and Options." Washington, D.C.: The Urban Institute. Photocopy.

Regenstein, Marsha, Jack A. Meyer, and Jennifer Dickemper Hicks. 1998. *Job Prospects for Welfare Recipients: Employers Speak Out.* Washington, D.C.: The Urban Institute. *Assessing the New Federalism* Occasional Paper 10.

Smith, David M., and Stephen A. Woodbury. 2000. "Low-Wage Labor Markets: Changes over the Business Cycle and Differences across Region and Location." In *The Low-Wage Labor Market: Challenges and Opportunities for Economic Self-Sufficiency,* edited by Kelleen Kaye and Demetra Smith Nightingale (41–61). Washington, D.C.: Urban Institute Press.

Spalter-Roth, Roberta, Beverly Burr, Heidi Hartmann, and Lois Shaw, with Jill Braunstein and Robin Dennis. 1995. *Welfare that Works: The Working Lives of AFDC Recipients*. Washington, D.C.: Institute for Women's Policy Research.

U.S. Congress. 1994. House Committee on Ways and Means. *1994 Green Book: Background Material and Data on Programs Within the Jurisdiction of the Committee on Ways and Means*. 103rd cong., 2d sess., July 15. Table 10.29.

U.S. Department of Health and Human Services. 2000a. *Accountability Report: Fiscal Year 1999*. Washington, D.C.: U.S. Government Printing Office. February.

————. 2000b. *Temporary Assistance for Needy Families (TANF) Program*. Washington, D.C.: U.S. Government Printing Office. August.

Vroman, Wayne. 1998. "Effects of Welfare Reform on Unemployment Insurance." Washington, D.C.: The Urban Institute. *Assessing the New Federalism* Policy Brief A-22.

Wallace, Geoffrey, and Rebecca M. Blank. 1999. "What Goes Up Must Come Down? Explaining Recent Changes in Public Assistance Caseloads." In *Economic Conditions and Welfare Reform*, edited by Sheldon H. Danziger (49–89). Kalamazoo, Mich.: W.E. Upjohn Institute for Employment Research.

Zedlewski, Sheila R. 1999. *Work-Related Activities and Limitations of Current Welfare Recipients*. Washington, D.C.: The Urban Institute. *Assessing the New Federalism* Discussion Paper 99-06.

7

Child Care and Welfare Reform

Gina Adams and Monica Rohacek

C hild care is an essential support for many parents who need help caring for their children while they work. Consequently, policy-makers have increasingly invested in child care subsidies for low-income families, usually in the form of vouchers that help parents purchase care from a broad range of child care options. Though these subsidies are not usually limited to families on welfare, they play a key role in welfare reform efforts because they can support work among families trying to leave welfare and can prevent welfare receipt for low-income working families at risk of receiving welfare. In addition, the child care that families use with these subsidies affects their children's development. Therefore, subsidy policies and funding levels have implications for the development and safety of millions of low-income children and youth.

Child care funding and policies are an integral part of the national debate on TANF reauthorization. State child care subsidy programs that support low-income families are funded by the federal Child Care and Development Fund (the CCDF)—which is also scheduled for reauthorization in 2002—as well as by the TANF block grant. (The CCDF is also known as the Child Care and Development Block Grant.) States are increasingly using TANF funds for child care, either by spending them directly out of TANF or by transferring them to the CCDF. Consequently, funding and policy decisions about TANF have direct implications for the success of child care policy strategies, and funding and policy decisions for the CCDF have implications for the success of efforts to reform welfare.

This chapter describes the major child care issues that face policy-makers as they debate the reauthorization of TANF and the CCDF. It provides background on the larger child care context, as well as on recent developments in federal and state policy and funding. It then describes some of the challenges that remain and some of the key issues to be addressed in the reauthorization debate.

Child Care in Context

Child care subsidy policies operate within the context of the larger child care market, which provides a framework for understanding the current policy debate. One of the main forces driving the use of child care in the United States has been the increase in employment of parents, especially mothers, in the last few decades. Between 1992 and 2000, for example, the proportion of single women with children under age 6 who were employed rose from 46 percent to 69 percent (figure 7-1) (U.S. Bureau of Labor Statistics [BLS] 1997; BLS 2001). In addition, many parents who do not work outside the home use child care to provide an educational and social environment for their children (Tout et al. 2001).

Data from the 1999 NSAF show that over 20 million children under age 13 whose mothers are employed receive some form of child care, whether in a child care center, in the home of an unrelated adult (known as a family child care home), in their own home by a nanny or babysitter, or by a relative in their own or the relative's home (figure 7-2). Child care arrangements vary widely, depending on the age of child, family income, parental work schedules, availability of another parent or relative, cultural beliefs, local child care markets, access to financial assistance (or free care), and policies such as licensing and subsidies. These factors interact in complex ways to affect the preferences, options, and constraints that parents face. They also shape the quality of care, which affects the safety, development, and well-being of children.

For many families, cost is an important factor in their choice of child care arrangements. NSAF data show that, in 1997, about half of all working parents with children under age 13 paid for child care, and that families paying for care spent an average of 9 percent of their earnings. Poor families that paid for care spent an even larger portion—23 percent—

Figure 7-1. *Maternal Employment, 1992–2000*

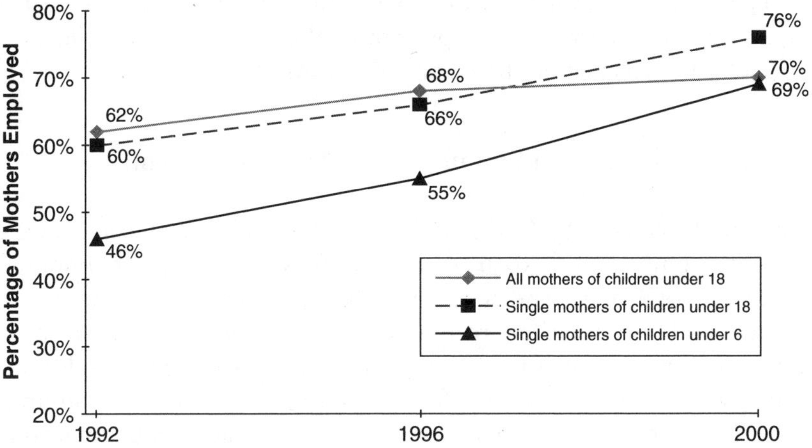

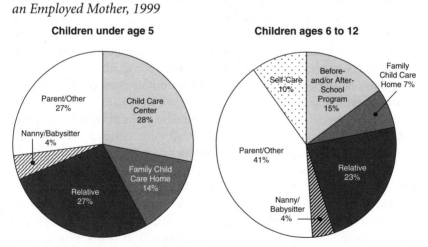

Percentage of Mothers Employed

- ◆ All mothers of children under 18
- ■ Single mothers of children under 18
- ▲ Single mothers of children under 6

Source: BLS (1994; 1997; 2001).

Figure 7-2. *Child Care Arrangements for Children under Age 13, with an Employed Mother, 1999*

Children under age 5

- Parent/Other 27%
- Child Care Center 28%
- Nanny/Babysitter 4%
- Family Child Care Home 14%
- Relative 27%

Children ages 6 to 12

- Self-Care 10%
- Before- and/or After-School Program 15%
- Family Child Care Home 7%
- Parent/Other 41%
- Relative 23%
- Nanny/Babysitter 4%

Source: Sonenstein et al. (forthcoming).

Notes: Figures report the percentage of children with each type of arrangement as their primary child care arrangement. The arrangements of 5-year-olds are not included because this age group is transitioning between the preschool and school-age populations.

of their earnings (Giannarelli and Barsimantov 2000). Even poor families that got help paying for care from other sources (such as relatives or subsidies) spent an average of 21 percent of their earnings for child care (unpublished calculations based on 1997 NSAF).

Child Care Policy and Funding under Welfare Reform

The Family Support Act (FSA) of 1988 initiated a new era of federal interest and investment in child care subsidies, after several decades of minimal federal involvement. The act created two child care entitlements for current and former welfare recipients, both of which relied upon combined federal and state funds. Congress passed two additional child care initiatives in 1990. These four federal programs were overlaid upon a remarkably uneven and diverse landscape of state child care funding, policies, and programs. Prior to 1988, some states had a long history of investing significant state and optional federal funds in child care. Other states had virtually no child care subsidy program for low-income working families. For instance, as FSA was being implemented, funding of child care subsidies ranged from 24 cents per child in Idaho to $152 per child in Massachusetts (Adams and Sandfort 1992).

The situation changed again in 1996 with the passage of welfare reform. First, the four existing federal programs were combined into the CCDF, giving states even greater flexibility in setting up and administering their programs. Second, the federally mandated entitlements to child care for current and former welfare recipients were eliminated, thus increasing states' discretion in determining who would be given priority in receiving subsidies. Simultaneously, parents on TANF were required to meet work participation requirements, even if they had very young children.

Third, funding for child care increased in two ways. Appropriations for the CCDF exceeded the combined total of the previous four federal programs, and states were allowed to use TANF money for child care, either directly or by transferring up to 30 percent of their TANF block grant to the CCDF. These changes, combined with subsequent increases, resulted in a significant rise in total funding for child care. In fiscal year 2000, for example, a total of $7.4 billion in federal child care funding was allocated to states (including the District of Columbia) through the CCDF, and by states through TANF[1]—in contrast to $2.1 billion in fiscal year 1997 (based on Schumacher, Greenberg, and Duffy 2001; U.S. Department of Health and Human Services [HHS] 1997a; HHS 2000).[2]

Examining CCDF and TANF funding patterns separately provides further insight into state and federal commitments. Specifically, direct federal support for child care via CCDF allocations to states rose from $1.9 billion in FY 1997 to $3.5 billion in FY 2000 (HHS 1997a; HHS 2000). In addition, almost every state has consistently met or exceeded the requirements that allow them to draw down all of the federal CCDF funds for which they are eligible (HHS 2001c).[3]

Almost all states spend at least some TANF funds for child care; in FY 2000, 44 states transferred a total of $2.4 billion from TANF to the CCDF, and 35 states spent $1.5 billion in federal TANF dollars directly on child care (Schumacher et al. 2001).[4] Only two states spent no TANF funds on child care in that year. TANF has become the largest source of increases in federal child care funding, and child care has accounted for the "single biggest redirection" of TANF funds (ibid.). In fact, TANF now rivals the CCDF as the primary federal funding source for child care; in FY 2000, total TANF funds allocated by states for child care exceeded the total federal CCDF funding (figure 7-3) (ibid.).

States also use their own funds to subsidize child care. State spending in response to federal CCDF matching and maintenance-of-effort requirements totaled $1.8 billion in FY 2000 (HHS 2000). While a number of states have continued to spend more of their own money than required,[5]

Figure 7-3. *Federal TANF and CCDF Funds Allocated for Child Care*

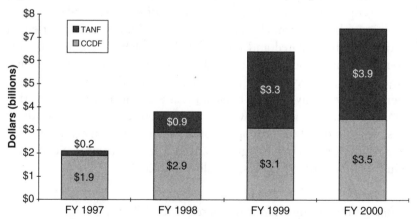

Notes: Based on figure in Schumacher et al. (2001). Estimates verified with HHS (1997a; 1997b; 1998; 2001b). TANF allocations include funds transferred to the CCDF, as well as TANF funds spent directly on child care in each year.

and while research suggests that some states have allocated additional funds since 1996 (Collins et al. 2000), data limitations make it difficult to determine how common these increases are. Nor is it possible to estimate the total amount that states are spending on child care. There are indications that the slowdown in the economy is causing some states to cut back on their investments in child care, and administrators and others are worried about states' ability to sustain the growth in funding.

Who Is Receiving What Kind of Care?

Not surprisingly, the growth in funding for child care has been accompanied by significant growth in the number of children receiving child care subsidies. In FY 2000, states provided subsidies to an estimated average of 1.9 million low-income children per month through the CCDF alone (HHS 2001b)—an increase of 90 percent over the estimated 1 million served each month in 1996 (Schumacher et al. 2001). These children ranged in age from birth to 13 years. In FY 1999, 28 percent of the children in subsidized child care each month were under age 3, 37 percent were age 3 to 5, and 35 percent were age 6 to 13 (school age) (HHS 2001a). Recent research suggests that subsidies generally appear to be going to families with the lowest incomes; in some states, the median income of recipients is one-third that of the eligibility cutoff for child care subsidies (Layzer 2001).

Subsidies are generally provided through vouchers[6] that help parents obtain care from legal providers in their communities. Parents usually make a copayment that is determined by a sliding-fee schedule. Children receiving subsidies through the CCDF are cared for in a wide variety of settings, both regulated and unregulated. In 1999, 71 percent of children receiving subsidies were in child care centers or licensed family child care homes; 29 percent were in legally unregulated child care arrangements, fairly evenly divided between relatives and nonrelatives (HHS 2001a). These patterns vary widely by state. For example, one study of 16 states found that the proportion of subsidized children being cared for by a relative or in-home caregiver[7] ranged from 4 percent in North Carolina to 64 percent in Michigan (Collins et al. 2000).

What Other Changes Have Occurred since 1996?

All states have responded to the increased funds in recent years by serving additional children. However, change has not been so clear or consistent in other policy areas. For example, while a number of states have reduced parent copayments, raised income eligibility limits, raised reimbursement rates, funded major quality enhancement initiatives, or initiated some combination of these actions, others have moved in the opposite direction (Schulman, Blank, and Ewen 2001).

Despite the elimination of the child care entitlements, most states continue to give higher priority to current and former welfare recipients. However, a few—including Illinois, Rhode Island, Vermont, and Wisconsin—have moved toward a system that gives all low-income families equal priority. They have done this in two ways: by determining eligibility solely on the basis of income and work status (thus breaking the historical link between child care eligibility and welfare), and by investing sufficient funds to make this promise a reality. However, there are indications that some of these states may have difficulty continuing to meet their commitments.

Finally, while most states set child care policies at the state level, Texas and Colorado have recently joined New York in devolving more decision-making to the local level. Texas, for example, lets local administrative units set eligibility levels within a range set by the state.

Consistent Themes

Despite all of these developments and changes over the last decade, federal and state support for child care has been consistently characterized by several important themes:

- *Supporting "parent choice."* Since 1988, the child care subsidy system has been predicated on allowing parents to choose any legal provider that would accept the subsidy, whether licensed or not, and ranging from relatives to child care centers.
- *Supporting parents' ability to work.* The child care subsidy system focuses primarily on enabling low-income parents to work and far less on ensuring that parents have access to care that supports their children's development.
- *Giving highest priority to families leaving welfare for work.* Before 1996, states were required to give child care subsidies to current and former welfare recipients, while low-income working families that had *not* received welfare were given such support at the state's discretion. Although the entitlement was eliminated in 1996, most states continue to give highest priority to current and former welfare

recipients rather than other low-income working families. This is largely due to federal work participation requirements, which give states incentives to support families subject to these work requirements and time limits.

- *Allowing state diversity and variation.* Because states have always had significant latitude in structuring their child care services, variation is a hallmark of child care policy. Such variation appears in how much money states commit to child care, how they administer and structure their programs, the proportion of eligible families they serve, and such policies as who is eligible for the benefit, how much they have to pay, and the amount of the state's subsidy.

Ongoing Challenges and Issues

Despite the growth in funding for child care, a number of issues remain. Three of them—all related to the adequacy of the current system for meeting the needs of low-income working families—are discussed below.

Are Low-Income Families That Need Child Care Assistance Getting Help?

One of the first steps necessary to assess the adequacy of current funding is to establish which families "need" assistance. In this process, it is important to recognize that child care assistance is broadly designed to serve low-income working parents, not just current or former welfare recipients. Under federal law, for example, states can serve families up to 85 percent of the state median income (SMI). This allows subsidies to support families moving from welfare to work, as well as to prevent welfare receipt among low-income working families that need help staying in the labor force.

Despite increases in funding and services, research suggests that large proportions of eligible low-income families are still not getting help. The National Study of Child Care for Low-Income Families (NSCCLIF) found, for example, that none of the 16 states studied in 1999 served more than 25 percent of the families eligible under *federal* guidelines, and some states served fewer than 10 percent of those eligible. Even when the proportion of children served who were eligible under *state* eligibility requirements—which are usually lower than the federal limit—is examined, 13 of the 16 states were serving 30 percent or less of the eligible children (Collins et al. 2000).

While some eligible families may not want or need subsidies, two multistate studies—the ANF child care case studies and the NSCCLIF—suggest that there are a number of ways in which the current system limits access for those eligible families that do want help. Largely as a consequence of insufficient funding, states have devised a variety of formal and informal ways to ration child care subsidies.

One approach states use to ration services is to restrict the number of people who are eligible for subsidies. In March 2000, 47 states (including the District of Columbia) had income eligibility limits below the federal limit. In 22 states, a family of three earning $25,000 did not qualify for assistance (Schulman et al. 2001). States also restrict eligibility in other ways. For example, a low-income parent who was not receiving welfare and who wanted child care assistance in order to find a job was not eligible in 35 states, and 18 states required low-income parents who were employed to be working a minimum number of hours to be eligible (ibid.).

States also ration services indirectly by limiting outreach efforts; thus, some eligible families do not receive child care assistance because they do not know that subsidies are available. Respondents in most states studied by ANF and NSCCLIF reported limited outreach or public education about the availability of subsidies, particularly for low-income working families that had not received welfare. Former and current welfare recipients were more likely to have heard about child care assistance because they had come into contact with state agencies, which have an incentive to tell them about subsidies. Agency staff responding to the ANF study attributed the limited outreach to inadequate funding for child care, and suggested it was unethical to create demand for a service they were unable to provide.

Finally, states may use other rationing tools, such as creating waiting lists, setting priorities for categories of applicants, or freezing intake for the program. Seventeen states had waiting lists or had frozen intake as of March 2000 because they had insufficient funds to serve everyone who had applied (Schulman et al. 2001). In these cases, current and former welfare recipients are typically assigned higher priority and receive assistance, whereas other low-income families are put on waiting lists or denied service.

How Well Is the Child Care Subsidy System Working?

Some eligible families that try to apply for child care subsidies may not actually receive assistance because they are unable to complete the initial application process or because meeting all of the requirements to keep subsidies proves too challenging, the ANF case studies found (Adams, Snyder, and Sandfort 2002). These findings may explain other research showing that many families receive subsidies for relatively short periods (an average of three to seven months, in one study [Meyers et al. 2001]) and that usage may be low even among families ranked high-priority for service (Schumacher and Greenberg 1999).

State and local policies and practices can make it quite difficult for families to get and keep child care subsidies. First, parents must take a number of steps, including those below:

- *Application.* The application process includes applying for child care, finding a provider, and getting the provider approved. While this process is relatively straightforward in some places, it is much more difficult in others, involving multiple office visits and extensive paperwork.
- *Periodic recertification.* Subsidies are given for a limited period, and parents must regularly demonstrate eligibility in order to renew them. While policies may require parents to recertify every 3 to 12 months, caseworkers may require parents to recertify more frequently.
- *Reporting of any change in circumstances.* Parents are generally required to report any change that would affect the amount of, or their eligibility for, a subsidy, including all changes in income, work schedules, employment, child care providers, and welfare status, though locales vary in how strictly they enforce these requirements. Such changes can occur very often in the lives of low-income parents, requiring them to be in frequent contact with the state in order to remain in compliance.
- *Meeting additional TANF requirements.* Families on welfare can face an additional layer of requirements because their eligibility for child care subsidies depends upon their eligibility for TANF. If the TANF and child care agencies are not coordinated, parents may have to navigate both systems in the process of getting and keeping a subsidy.

Second, depending on the site, each of these steps may require that parents take time off work or comply with other burdensome requirements, such as in-person visits or extensive paperwork. These requirements stem from various sources, including policy requirements, agency resources, and/or local agency implementation and leadership. For example, in addition to varying policy requirements and resources, local agencies vary widely in the extent to which they focus on service and efficiency, thereby contributing to or lessening the burden on parents. Parents who consistently encounter disrespectful, inefficient, or poorly trained caseworkers, lost paperwork, long waits in the office, complex administrative systems, or other such problems can find it challenging to stay in the program. Such problems can deter families from applying in the first place, and—to the extent that they require families to choose between taking time off work and retaining their subsidies—directly contradict the larger goals of the subsidy program.

Third, while these problems are likely to challenge all families, they seem particularly likely to affect certain parents who have the greatest need for support and who are of particular concern to policymakers. Among these are parents who change employment or family situations frequently; who face transportation, language, or other barriers to work; who are TANF recipients and have to navigate two systems; or who have entry-level jobs and are trying to become securely established in the workforce.

Overall, these findings suggest that if subsidies are to succeed in helping low-income parents work—and in meeting the welfare reform goal of helping recipients move into work—they will need to be focused more on access to and retention of assistance. However, improving access and retention without increasing funds for subsidies is likely to increase the number of eligible parents who end up on waiting lists or not being served.

Does the Current System Help Families Get Good Quality Child Care?

Despite the major role that child care subsidies play in affecting the development of almost 2 million low-income children, child care subsidy policies place a higher priority on supporting work than on supporting access to good quality child care. This is troublesome because evidence strongly suggests that, in addition to being shaped by their home environment, children's short- and long-term development is related to the quality of their nonparental care. There is also evidence that low-income children in particular reap developmental benefits from participating in high-quality child care programs (Vandell and Wolfe 2000; Phillips and Adams 2001).

Despite its importance, studies have found that many programs, across a range of settings, do not adequately support children's development

(Vandell and Wolfe 2000) and that turnover among child care staff is generally high (Whitebook et al. 2001) because of low wages and benefits. This situation presents a serious problem for children's development, given the importance of good quality care and of developing nurturing relationships with stable caregivers.

While not designed to ensure quality care, state licensing laws provide an important base in that they protect children from harm. However, these laws have gaps. Some states exempt smaller family child care homes from any regulation or oversight; many states have relatively low standards (31 do not require staff in child care centers to have training prior to starting employment [Center for Career Development in Early Child Care and Education at Wheelock College 1999]); and enforcement can be minimal.

While good quality care may be difficult for any family to find, it can be particularly hard for low-income families, families living in rural areas, families with infants and toddlers, and families that need child care during nontraditional work hours (Clark and Long 1995; U.S. General Accounting Office [GAO] 1995; GAO 1997). Low-income families are more likely to be constrained by the cost of care, inadequate child care options in their communities, and such barriers as nontraditional or irregular work hours, limited English skills, and lack of public transportation (Fuller et al. 1997; GAO 1995; GAO 1997).

It is not surprising, therefore, to find that low-income parents are more likely to rely upon low-cost or free options, such as relatives. The 1999 NSAF finds that only 16 percent of children under age 5 in low-income families with working parents are in center-based care, in contrast to 29 percent of children in higher-income families (Sonenstein et al. forthcoming). The survey does not provide information on the quality of these settings, nor is it possible to determine the extent to which these child care patterns reflect the preferences of low-income families. However, it is likely that the constraints of cost and supply play an important role in these patterns.

The quality of child care was a major topic in the policy debate surrounding welfare reform. As a result, states are required to spend at least 4 percent of their CCDF funding to improve the quality and supply of care. Yet 4 percent is a small fraction of CCDF funds, and it seems even smaller in the context of total spending in the child care market.

Most of the remaining 96 percent of CCDF funding helps low-income families pay for child care. Although the goal of these funds is to help give low-income families "equal access" to the kinds of child care choices a wealthier family would have, the way the CCDF is set up and administered makes it hard to realize this goal. First, the vast majority of child care funds are spent through vouchers that give parents access to the child care choices in their communities. However, low-income communities tend to offer fewer choices, particularly in regard to licensed facilities (Fuller and Strath 2001; Queralt and Witte 1998); there is also evidence that children from low-income families who are not in center-based care are more likely to be in lower-quality arrangements than children from higher-income families in such settings (National Institute of Child Health and Development Early Childhood Research Network 1997; Galinsky et al. 1994). The problem of limited choices is even more severe for low-income parents who work odd hours or who have very young children or children with special needs.

Second, families receiving child care subsidies are unlikely to have access to the full range of providers in their communities. The CCDF encourages states to set their maximum reimbursement rates for child care providers at or above the 75th percentile of current fees charged in the market. This should ensure that parents have access to all providers except those whose fees fall in the top 25 percent of local market rates. However, nearly half of all states have set their reimbursement caps below that (Schulman et al. 2001), so subsidized families have access to an even smaller proportion of providers than recommended by the CCDF. Because higher-quality care is generally more expensive, these policies are likely to limit the quality of care available to parents receiving subsidies unless those parents can afford a higher copayment to cover the additional charges.[8] (High-quality care is generally more expensive because facilities are better and employees are better compensated and have more experience, training, and materials.)

Finally, choice may be limited even further by the way in which subsidy payments are implemented (Adams, Snyder, and Tout forthcoming). As long as they fall below the caps described above, child care providers are supposed to be reimbursed the full amount they charge parents who do not receive subsidies. In practice, however, providers may get less. Respondents in the 1999 ANF case studies in several states described frequent miscommunication about when families' subsidies are to begin or end, resulting in providers not getting paid for the full period of service. Some localities do not pay for days when children are absent, or pay only partial subsidies. These and similar problems, plus the paperwork required for payment, appear to make some providers unwilling to serve children receiving child care subsidies, and could affect providers' ability to provide good quality care.

In addition to the issues related to the "equal-access" goal, there are two other issues with the quality of care funded by the CCDF. First, many families receive child care subsidies only for short periods, which may result in their children receiving unstable care. Having a stable relationship with caregivers is important to the healthy development of children. While the precise causes of these short spells are unclear, they are likely to be related to the fact that eligibility is closely tied to income and work status, which change frequently, as well as to the process challenges of retaining subsidies described earlier. Interrupted receipt of subsidies may also hamper efforts to blend funding from the CCDF with Head Start and state prekindergarten funds, a strategy for improving the care received by at least some preschool-age children who receive subsidies.[9]

Second, the 29 percent of subsidized children who are in unregulated settings are of particular concern. While research shows that the quality of unregulated care varies widely (Galinsky et al. 1994), it is hard for states to ensure that children in these settings are protected from harm, much less getting care that enhances their development. The freedom to choose a relative or other unregulated caregiver is particularly important for low-income parents, who are more likely to work hours when other child care options are not available (Acs, Ross Phillips, and McKenzie 2000). Consequently, states must carefully balance parents' need for such care with the need to protect children's well-being.[10]

Addressing any of the problems described in this section requires either increased funding for child care or a reduction in the number of families served. Because funding is inadequate, states have consistently had to choose between improving the quality of care and serving more children.

Policy Implications

Several important issues should be discussed as policymakers debate the reauthorization of the CCDF and TANF. These include the overall level and stability of child care funding, the adequacy and equity of subsidies, and whether greater emphasis should be placed on funding child care that supports children's development. Many of these issues exist because of the ongoing challenges of confronting difficult tradeoffs and resolving fundamental uncertainties about what child care subsidies are designed to accomplish.

The Financial Commitment to Child Care

Three funding issues will need to be part of the debate. The first concerns overall funding. Although federal funds for child care have increased significantly since the passage of welfare reform, they are not sufficient. As a result, significant numbers of eligible families are not receiving child care assistance, and there is reason to be concerned about the quality of care available to low-income children receiving subsidies.

The second issue concerns the trade-off between funding flexibility and stability. Much of the recent expansion in access to child care subsidies came about because states were free to use large amounts of TANF funds for child care. An economic downturn or a reduction in TANF funding could result in substantial amounts of money being diverted away from child care and back into cash assistance. Many child care subsidy administrators face this possibility. In 31 states, TANF accounted for more than one-third of combined federal CCDF and TANF funding for child care; in 15 of those states, TANF accounted for at least half of the combined year 2000 funding (Schumacher et al. 2001). In addition to posing threats to the current system, the unstable nature of child care funding may be preventing some states from further expanding and improving their subsidy systems.

The third issue concerns the trade-off between devolution and equity. State variability and devolution have been key elements of child care policy in recent decades. As a result, states differ significantly in numerous aspects of their child care systems, including eligibility for and amount of subsidies. While it is likely that this approach has allowed a number of states to develop more generous and innovative models than a single national approach would have produced, it has also resulted in a child care situation that is fundamentally inequitable across states.

Who Should Get Help Paying for Child Care?

Although child care assistance is widely agreed to be an important work support for all low-income families, the reality in many states is that parents on welfare are more likely to get assistance than low-income working parents who need assistance to avoid going on welfare. In the 17 states with waiting lists or frozen intake, a low-income working parent who urgently needs child care assistance is most assured of getting it by quitting his or her job and applying for welfare—a perverse incentive that undercuts welfare reform's stated goals.

Several steps are necessary to continue moving toward child care subsidies that effectively support work for all low-income families:

- Providing sufficient funding to ensure that all low-income working parents who want and are eligible for a child care subsidy can receive it, regardless of their welfare status;
- Reducing or eliminating the administrative barriers that prevent low-income families from getting or keeping subsidies; and
- Reaching out to non-welfare families with information about their eligibility for child care subsidies.

Support for Child Development as Well as Parents' Work

In recent years, there has been a remarkable convergence of opinion across parties and disciplines about the importance of the preschool years for learning, literacy, and school readiness, as well as about the importance of after-school time for the development, school achievement, and safety of school-age children. Nonetheless, there continues to be a fundamental disconnect between these concerns and the way funds are being spent to support child care for low-income children. Even though subsidies influence the care of almost 2 million low-income children every month, the quality of that care is not a central focus of child care subsidy policies.

Using the reauthorization process to move toward a child care subsidy system that effectively supports children's development as well as parents' ability to work would require the following:

- Ensuring that funding is adequate to support families' choices of good quality child care, and allocating additional resources to improve the quality of that care;
- Giving states incentives or directives to reimburse all child care providers at full and current market rates, and to pay higher rates for care in short supply (e.g., higher-quality care, care for infants and toddlers, care of children with special needs, care in low-income communities, and care provided during nontraditional work hours);
- Changing policies and practices that do not support access to or use of stable, good quality care (e.g., payment policies or practices that undercut provider reimbursement levels, limit the willingness of providers to participate in the subsidy system, or lead to frequent disruptions in subsidy);

- Facilitating the development and ongoing support of good quality care in low-income communities, thus expanding the options available to families;
- Allocating resources to recruit and retain providers through compensation and education initiatives;
- Investing in strategies to support the quality of child care in unregulated settings; and
- Improving coordination with other entities, such as Head Start, that can provide comprehensive services for children in child care.

NOTES

The authors would like to thank Sarah Adelman for her assistance and support, as well as Helen Blank, Mark Greenberg, Joan Lombardi, Karen Schulman, Rachel Schumacher, Kathleen Snyder, Matthew Stagner, and Karen Tvedt for their thoughtful review and comments.

1. Head Start funds are not included in this analysis because they primarily fund part-day, part-year programs for 3- to 4-year-olds and are not designed to meet the child care needs of working families.

2. Federal funding available for child care in a given fiscal year may be described either in terms of funding *spent* or in terms of funding *allocated*. Because federal rules allow states to obligate and spend CCDF and TANF funding within a specific period of time after the fiscal year in which funds are allocated, the total amount allocated in a particular year will not be equal to the total amount spent in that year. The data presented in this chapter (with the exception of TANF direct child care spending levels) are allocation data and thus may differ from reported spending data. Although spending data more precisely describe how much is actually spent for child care in a specific fiscal year, the difference between spending and allocations in recent years has been relatively small. In addition, because of the rules that allow spending of CCDF allocations in subsequent fiscal years, it is difficult to determine what portion of CCDF funds spent in a specific year were originally TANF funds and what portion were originally CCDF funds.

3. In FY 2000, two states did not accept their full matching allotment, resulting in $10 million being reallocated to other states (HHS 2001c). This reallocated amount represented a small fraction of the $3.5 billion in total CCDF funding allocated to states in FY 2000.

4. These figures from Schumacher et al. are as of September 2001, and differ from the amounts in chapter 12 of this volume, which rely on data reported to the Administration for Children and Families (ACF) by states immediately after the close of FY 2000. The figures in this chapter are based on those initial reports to ACF, as well as on amended reports submitted later. The largest difference may be attributed to California, whose reported transfer from TANF to the CCDF changed from $61 million in the original report to $520 million in the amended report (HHS 2001d, Schumacher et al. 2001).

5. In FY 2000, states counted $1.7 billion in state child care spending toward TANF maintenance-of-effort requirements; some of this spending was also counted toward the

$1.8 billion in state maintenance-of-effort and matching requirements for the CCDF (Schumacher et al. 2001).

6. A few states pay through a contract mechanism, whereby they obligate funds to programs to pay for slots for a certain number of children.

7. As with other forms of care, the extent to which families use in-home child care, whether provided by a relative or an unrelated babysitter, varies widely. The NSCCLIF found that half of the 14 states for which they had data reported more than 5 percent of their subsidy going to in-home caregivers; Illinois and Louisiana were the highest, at 21 and 23 percent (Collins et al. 2000). In-home care can present problems for states because of a federal requirement that they comply with the Fair Labor Standards Act for these caregivers (in addition to other issues noted in the text). It is not clear whether this law is enforced, however, and states vary in how they have responded to it.

8. A number of states are experimenting with paying higher rates to providers who provide higher-quality care—though research has not yet shown whether such policies have an impact (Schulman et al. 2001).

9. Blending subsidy funds with funds from Head Start or state prekindergarten programs is one way to improve the quality of care for some children in the subsidy system: namely, the low-income 3- to 4-year-olds who are eligible for those programs. Yet the possibility that changes in a parent's work status and income could cause a child to lose eligibility for subsidies in the course of the program year is one factor that can make it difficult for programs to blend funds. Some states are experimenting with changing the CCDF requirements for children enrolled in Head Start to facilitate such coordination.

10. While the CCDF does require that states have minimal health and safety protections in place for unregulated caregivers (except for some relatives) who receive subsidies, states vary in how they implement this requirement. It is even more difficult to improve the quality of care above this baseline, as these settings are usually small (making quality improvement efforts costly), and turnover rates can be high.

REFERENCES

Acs, Gregory, Katherin Ross Phillips, and Daniel McKenzie. 2000. "On the Bottom Rung: A Profile of Americans in Low-Income Working Families." Washington, D.C.: The Urban Institute. *Assessing the New Federalism* Policy Brief A-42.

Adams, Gina, and Jodi R. Sandfort. 1992. *State Investments in Child Care and Early Childhood Education.* Washington, D.C.: Children's Defense Fund.

Adams, Gina, Kathleen Snyder, and Jodi Sandfort. 2002. *Getting and Retaining Child Care Assistance: How Policy and Practice Influence Parents' Experiences.* Washington, D.C.: The Urban Institute. *Assessing the New Federalism* Occasional Paper No. 55.

Adams, Gina, Kathleen Snyder, and Kathryn Tout. Forthcoming. *Child Care Providers and the Child Care Subsidy System.* Washington, D.C.: The Urban Institute. *Assessing the New Federalism.*

BLS. See U.S. Bureau of Labor Statistics.

Center for Career Development in Early Child Care and Education at Wheelock College. 1999. *Child Care Licensing: Training Requirements for Roles in Child Care Centers and*

Family Child Care. Boston, Mass.: Center for Career Development in Early Child Care and Education.

Clark, Sandra, and Sharon Long. 1995. *Child Care Prices: A Profile of Six Communities—Final Report.* Washington, D.C.: The Urban Institute.

Collins, Ann, Jean I. Layzer, J. Lee Kreader, Alan Werner, and Fred B. Glantz. 2000. *National Study of Child Care for Low-Income Families: State and Community Substudy Interim Report.* Cambridge, Mass.: Abt Associates.

Fuller, Bruce, and Annelie Strath. 2001. "The Child Care and Preschool Workforce: Demographics, Earnings, and Unequal Distribution." *Educational Evaluation and Policy Analysis* 23 (1): 37–55.

Fuller, Bruce, Casey Coonerty, Fran Kipnis, and Yvonne Choong. 1997. *An Unfair Head Start: California Families Face Gaps in Preschool and Child Care Availability,* 2d ed. Berkeley: PACE Center. *Growing Up in Poverty Project.*

GAO. See U.S. General Accounting Office.

Galinsky, Ellen, Carollee Howes, Susan Kontos, and Marybeth Shinn. 1994. *The Study of Children in Family Child Care and Relative Care: Highlights of Findings.* New York: Families and Work Institute.

Giannarelli, Linda, and James Barsimantov. 2000. *Child Care Expenses of America's Families.* Washington, D.C.: The Urban Institute. *Assessing the New Federalism* Occasional Paper 40.

Layzer, Jean. 2001. *Child Care Funding: How Much Is Needed and Is There Enough?* Washington, D.C.: The Brookings Institution, June 13. Transcript. Moderated by Ron Haskins. http://www.brook.edu/comm/transcripts/20010613.htm. (Accessed August 28, 2001.)

Meyers, Marcia K., Laura Peck, Ann Collins, J. Lee Kreader, Annie Georges, Elizabeth E. Davis, Roberta Weber, Deanna Schexnayder, Daniel Schroeder, and Jerry A. Olson. 2001. *The Dynamics of Child Care Subsidy Use: A Collaborative Study of Five States.* A report prepared for the Child Care Bureau, Administration on Children, Youth and Families, Administration for Children and Families, Department of Health and Human Services. New York: Columbia University, National Center for Children in Poverty.

National Institute of Child Health and Human Development Early Child Care Research Network. 1997. "Poverty and Patterns of Child Care." In *Consequences of Growing Up Poor,* edited by Greg Duncan and Jeanne Brooks-Gunn (100–31). New York: Russell Sage Foundation.

Phillips, Deborah, and Gina Adams. 2001. "Child Care and Our Youngest Children." *The Future of Children* 11 (1): 35–51.

Queralt, Magaly, and Ann Dryden Witte. 1998. "Influences on Neighborhood Supply of Child Care in Massachusetts." *Social Service Review* 72 (1): 17–47.

Schulman, Karen, Helen Blank, and Danielle Ewen. 2001. *A Fragile Foundation: Child Care Assistance Policies.* Washington, D.C.: Children's Defense Fund.

Schumacher, Rachel, and Mark Greenberg. 1999. *Child Care after Leaving Welfare: Early Evidence from State Studies.* Washington, D.C.: Center for Law and Social Policy.

Schumacher, Rachel, Mark Greenberg, and Janellen Duffy. 2001. *The Impact of TANF Funding on State Child Care Subsidy Programs.* Washington, D.C.: Center for Law and Social Policy.

Sonenstein, Freya, Stefanie Schmidt, Natalya Bolshun, and Gary Gates. Forthcoming. "Primary Child Care Arrangements: Findings from the National Survey of America's Families." Washington, D.C.: The Urban Institute. *Assessing the New Federalism.*

Tout, Kathryn, Martha Zaslow, Angela Romano Papillo, and Sharon Vandivere. 2001. *Early Care and Education: Work Support for Families and Developmental Opportunity for Young Children.* Washington, D.C.: The Urban Institute. *Assessing the New Federalism* Occasional Paper No. 51.

U.S. Bureau of Labor Statistics. 1994. *Table 9. Families with Children under 18 Years Old, by the Employment Status of Parent(s) and Type of Family, 1992–1993 Annual Averages.* "Employment and Earnings Characteristics of Families: Fourth Quarter 1993." Feb. 1. ftp://146.142.4.23/pub/news.release/History/famee.020194.news. (Accessed August 31, 2001.)

———. 1997. *Table 4. Families with Own Children: Employment Status of Parents by Age of Youngest Child and Family Type, 1995–1996 Annual Averages.* "Employment Characteristics of Families:1996." June 16. ftp://146.142.4.23/pub/news.release/History/famee.061697.news. (Accessed August 31, 2001.)

———. 2001. *Table 4. Families with Own Children: Employment Status of Parents by Age of Youngest Child and Family Type, 1999–2000 Annual Averages.* "Employment Characteristics of Families in 2000." Apr. 19. http://stats.bls.gov/news.release/famee.nr0.htm. (Accessed August 31, 2001.)

U.S. Department of Health and Human Services, Administration for Children and Families. 1997a. "Final Fiscal Year 1997 State Allocations for the Child Care and Development Fund." Dec. 4. http://www.acf.dhhs.gov/programs/ccb/policy1/archives/salloc97.htm. (Accessed August 28, 2001).

———. 1997b. "Child Care and Development Fund Final FY 1998 State Allocations." Dec. 4. http://www.acf.dhhs.gov/programs/ccb/policy1/archives/salloc98.htm. (Accessed August 28, 2001.)

———. 1998. "FY 1999 Child Care and Development Fund Estimated Allocations." http://www.acf.dhhs.gov/programs/ccb/policy1/archives/pi9804/chart.htm. (Accessed August 28, 2001.)

———. 2000. ACF Information Memorandum # ACYF-IM-CC-00-01. Jan. 11. http://www.acf.dhhs.gov/programs/ccb/policy1/archives/im0001/im0001.pdf. (Accessed August 31, 2001.)

———. 2001a. "Child Care Development Fund (CCDF): FFY 1999 Tables and Charts." Feb. 15. http://www.acf.dhhs.gov/programs/ccb/research/99acf800/cover.htm. (Accessed August 31, 2001.)

———. 2001b. "Final FY 2002 Annual Performance Plan, Revised Final FY 2001 Performance Plan and FY 2000 Annual Performance Report for the Government Performance and Results Act of 1993." Apr. http://www.acf.dhhs.gov/programs/opre/fy2002.htm. (Accessed September 10, 2001.)

———. 2001c. "Fiscal Year 2000 State Spending under the Child Care and Development Fund as of 9/30/00." Aug. 16. http://www.acf.dhhs.gov/programs/ccb/research/00acf696/overview.htm. (Accessed August 27, 2001.)

———. 2001d. *Table A. Combined Federal Funds Spent through the 4th Quarter.* "TANF Program Expenditures in FY 2000 through the 4th Quarter." http://www.acf.dhhs.gov/programs/ofs/data/q400/index.htm. (Accessed September 12, 2001.)

U.S. General Accounting Office. 1995. *Welfare to Work: Child Care Assistance Limited; Welfare Reform May Expand Needs.* GAO/HEHS-95-220. Washington, D.C.: U.S. General Accounting Office.

———. 1997. *Welfare Reform: Implications of Increased Work Participation for Child Care.* GAO/HEHS 97-75. Washington, D.C.: U.S. General Accounting Office.

Vandell, Deborah Lowe, and Barbara Wolfe. 2000. *Child Care Quality: Does It Matter and Does It Need to Be Improved?* Washington, D.C.: Office of the Assistant Secretary for Planning and Evaluation, U.S. Department of Health and Human Services.

Whitebook, Marcy, Laura Sakai, Emily Gerber, and Carollee Howes. 2001. *Highlights: Then and Now: Changes in Child Care Staffing, 1994–2000.* Washington, D.C.: Center for the Child Care Workforce.

8

Health Insurance, Welfare, and Work

Alan Weil and John F. Holahan

The welfare and public health insurance systems have a common pedigree, but policy decisions in the last 15 years have led them to evolve along different paths. Welfare reform redefined and solidified those differences. Despite their differences, the welfare and health care systems must work together if they are to meet the needs of low-income families.

The fundamental question for health policy during an era of welfare reform is how closely eligibility for and administration of the two systems should be connected. Their present close relationship arises from linked eligibility rules and long-standing administrative practices. However, separating the systems, or delinking them, has two advantages. First, the Medicaid program can fulfill its promise of providing health insurance to those who need it only if the program takes a more active approach to outreach than the traditionally passive welfare system. Second, eligibility rules that leave people without health insurance if they find a job and move off welfare create strong disincentives to work. Extending Medicaid eligibility to a broader group than welfare recipients eliminates these disincentives.

This chapter looks at health policy from the perspective of choices made during welfare reform, and examines what needs to be done to make the welfare and health care systems mutually reinforcing. After reviewing the history of Medicaid and welfare eligibility policy, it presents recent data on Medicaid enrollment that suggest problems in the relationship between the two. It then suggests policies designed to improve the role Medicaid plays in supporting the goals of welfare reform.

Medicaid and Welfare Eligibility Policy

For two decades after the enactment of Medicaid in 1965, low-income parents and their children obtained health insurance primarily by means of their eligibility for cash welfare payments, which entitled them to Medicaid coverage.[1] AFDC was available only to families that met the deprivation standard, meaning the death, continued absence, incapacitation, or unemployability of at least one adult in the family. Maximum income standards for eligibility varied across states. On the eve of the 1996 welfare reform law, the median standard for eligibility was an income no greater than 36 percent of the federal poverty level.[2] Thus, Medicaid was originally an ancillary benefit for families that met the very stringent eligibility standards for welfare.

Expanding Medicaid Eligibility prior to Welfare Reform

Two developments in the 1980s led to an expansion of Medicaid eligibility. First, as health care costs continued to rise, health care and health insurance became unaffordable for a much larger segment of the population. Specifically, the lack of health insurance came to be identified with the working poor—those earning too much to be eligible for welfare, but too little to buy coverage on their own when their employers did not provide it. Second, mounting evidence began to indicate that the lack of coverage had negative consequences on health status, access to health services, and children's development.

More than a decade ago, advocates for the poor succeeded in transforming these developments into new policies that set Medicaid and welfare on different paths. Legislation enacted during the late 1980s created two new eligibility categories for Medicaid: children under age 6 and pregnant women with incomes below 133 percent of the federal poverty level (with states having the option of going as high as 185 percent), and children up to age 19, born after September 30, 1983, whose family income was below the poverty level. In addition, a new provision of Medicaid law, Section 1902(r)(2), allowed states to decide what income to disregard when calculating Medicaid eligibility, effectively permitting states to expand eligibility beyond the figures in the federal law.

Three other eligibility policies affected the relationship between Medicaid and welfare. First, the Family Support Act of 1988 created Transitional Medical Assistance, which required states to extend Medicaid coverage for 12 months to families that lost welfare eligibility because of earnings.[3] Second, states could use medically needy programs to cover some people who had incomes above welfare eligibility standards or who had substantial health care costs. Finally, under Section 1115 of the Social Security Act, some states obtained waivers allowing them to expand Medicaid coverage to new populations and to determine eligibility on a different basis from the Medicaid statute.

Protecting Medicaid Eligibility during Welfare Reform

The complex relationship between welfare and health care was highlighted in the final days leading up to enactment of PRWORA. Just two months earlier, both houses of Congress had passed welfare reform bills that converted Medicaid into a block grant. Under such a structure, it would have been entirely up to the states to figure out how to make the two programs work together. But President Clinton threatened to veto any welfare bill that also converted Medicaid into a block grant. Thus, it was only in the late stages of developing the welfare reform law that policymakers turned their attention to the complex challenge of reforming welfare while retaining Medicaid essentially intact.

A number of provisions in the new welfare law affected Medicaid. PRWORA froze state Medicaid eligibility standards as they existed on the date of the law's enactment, although states were permitted to adjust these standards upward with inflation or to lower them to earlier standards. The law allowed states to expand coverage under a new Section 1931. States were given the same flexibility to apply income disregards to family eligibility that they already had for individuals, which gave them the option of covering all members of a family with income that exceeds cash assistance eligibility standards. Federal rules were also changed to make it much easier for states to provide Medicaid eligibility for two-parent families. PRWORA also eliminated Medicaid eligibility for many legal immigrants, and narrowed children's eligibility for SSI, which is accompanied by Medicaid coverage.

One year after the passage of welfare reform, the State Children's Health Insurance Program (SCHIP) was enacted, complicating the relationships among programs even further. Under SCHIP, states were given new federal funds to expand coverage for children, whether by expanding existing state-funded programs or developing new ones, or by extending Medicaid eligibility to more children. With states having spent only one-quarter of available funds three years after SCHIP was enacted (Kenney, Ullman, and Weil 2000), the federal government announced it would consider allowing states to use SCHIP funding to cover some parents as well. As of September 2001, four states had received waivers for this purpose, and another waiver was pending.

An Evolving Relationship

Medicaid began as an adjunct to welfare, but it now covers more people than welfare, and at a greater cost. This evolution has had two effects: Eligibility and enrollment systems have had to adjust to Medicaid's broader role, and the goals of the two programs have diverged.

Aside from making a large number of previously uninsured children eligible for public coverage, Medicaid eligibility expansions in the late 1980s began the delinking of Medicaid eligibility from welfare eligibility. For the first time, a large number of people, primarily children, were eligible for public health insurance coverage even though their families were not receiving cash assistance. Equally important, these eligibility categories were for individuals—some members of the family became eligible for Medicaid while others likely remained uninsured. In Medicaid parlance, these were the noncash, or poverty-related, eligibility groups. In 1996, as welfare reform was being implemented, 53 percent of children and 59 percent of adults enrolled in Medicaid fell into this noncash category.

Welfare and Medicaid also have different objectives now. Cash assistance is explicitly temporary and transitional, and it is targeted to the neediest families with children, a policy shaped by the long-standing tension between providing assistance and preventing long-term dependency on welfare. In contrast, Medicaid benefits are not time-limited. This policy acknowledges that a large share of low-wage jobs do not and never will provide health insurance benefits. Medicaid eligibility is much broader than welfare eligibility, serving many working low-income families.

These differences do not mean that the programs necessarily work at cross-purposes. On the contrary, publicly provided health insurance can support employment, thus furthering a primary goal of welfare policy. Guaranteeing health insurance coverage for families that leave welfare can eliminate one reason some families may prefer to stay on welfare. An analysis of the MinnesotaCare program, which has much broader eligibility than most states' Medicaid programs, concluded that it reduced that state's welfare rolls by just over 5 percent (Minnesota Department of Human Services 1995).

Medicaid Enrollment in the Wake of Welfare Reform

Although families leaving welfare remained eligible for Medicaid, they often lost coverage because they were not aware that their eligibility continued. Moreover, state and county administrative systems did not automatically retain these families on the Medicaid rolls. Why did these systems fail to work together?

Medicaid Enrollment Falls then Rises

National Medicaid caseloads peaked in 1995, after several years of consistent growth. They then fell until 1998, when a slow turnaround began in most states. Enrollment began falling prior to federal welfare reform, presumably through a combination of the strong economy and the state welfare reform efforts that preceded the federal law. Table 8-1 shows that the number of people enrolled in Medicaid at any point in a given year fell from about 42 million in FY 1995 to about 40 million in FY 1998. The number of children and nondisabled adults each fell by about 1 million, with the percentage reduction for adults roughly twice that for children (10 percent versus about 5 percent). The entire decline in Medicaid enrollment is attributable to reductions in the number of cash enrollees—that is, Medicaid enrollees who also receive cash assistance from AFDC or TANF. The number of adult and child cash enrollees fell by about 2 million and 4 million persons, respectively, between 1995 and 1998.[4]

While the number of cash enrollees fell, the number of noncash enrollees increased significantly. Adult noncash enrollees increased by 1 million, while child noncash enrollees increased by almost 3 million (table 8-1). Whether these are the same people who lost welfare benefits is difficult to determine.

Virtually all states experienced reductions in cash enrollees, from 91 percent in Utah to 14 percent in Hawaii,[5] and all states saw increases in noncash enrollment. The net effect was a drop in Medicaid enrollment among children and nondisabled adults in 38 states. The few states with large increases in enrollment were primarily those, such as Oregon,

Table 8-1. *National Medicaid Enrollment, 1995 to 1998*

Enrollee Group	Enrollment (Thousands of People)				Overall Change (%)
	1995	1996	1997	1998	
All Enrollees	**41,677**	**41,295**	**40,591**	**40,381**	**−3.1**
Cash	23,507	22,515	20,157	18,323	−22.1
Noncash	18,170	18,779	20,434	22,057	21.4
Adults	**9,600**	**9,255**	**8,583**	**8,643**	**−10.0**
Cash	5,399	4,934	4,082	3,452	−36.0
Noncash	4,202	4,321	4,501	5,190	23.5
Children	**21,630**	**21,259**	**21,058**	**20,665**	**−4.5**
Cash	11,236	10,474	8,931	7,640	−32.0
Noncash	10,393	10,785	12,127	13,025	25.3
Aged	**4,115**	**4,117**	**4,114**	**4,090**	**−0.6**
Cash	1,847	1,840	1,813	1,783	−3.5
Noncash	2,268	2,278	2,301	2,306	1.7
Disabled Adults and Children	**6,333**	**6,664**	**6,836**	**6,984**	**10.3**
Cash	5,025	5,268	5,331	5,448	8.4
Noncash	1,308	1,396	1,505	1,536	17.4

Source: HCFA Form 2082 data, as edited by the Urban Institute.

Note: Enrollment is defined as the unduplicated number of people signed up for Medicaid at any time in the federal fiscal year.

Massachusetts, Delaware, and Vermont, that had implemented expansions using Section 1115 waivers.

Declines in Medicaid enrollment began to turn around late in 1998. A study of state enrollment data showed that average monthly enrollment increased by 200,000 people from June 1998 to December 1998 (Ellis, Smith, and Rousseau 2000). A year later, Medicaid enrollment had risen by over a million people, to a total of 32 million.

Why Did Medicaid Enrollment Fall?

Four factors played a role in the enrollment trends described above. First, the strong economy was increasing earnings, making fewer people eligible for Medicaid. In addition, the prevalence of employer-sponsored health insurance among low-wage workers, while still low, had risen in recent years (Zuckerman et al. 2001). Even if these families (or at least their children) are eligible for Medicaid on the basis of income, they may choose not to participate if they can obtain affordable coverage through their workplace.

Second, many people were leaving welfare and losing Medicaid coverage as well. Data from the 1997 NSAF show that median family earnings among those who had left welfare were $1,149 per month, or just above the poverty level for a family of three if the workers in the family were employed for an entire year (Loprest 1999). These earnings are low enough to make almost all of the children in these families eligible for Medicaid. In addition, the entire family is eligible for Transitional Medical Assistance for up to a year. Nevertheless, these families may not have known they remained eligible for Medicaid, or they may have faced administrative or other barriers to enrolling in Medicaid as they left welfare.

Third, welfare caseloads were falling in part because families, discouraged by mounting obstacles to obtaining benefits, did not even apply for assistance. Most states either adopted formal diversion programs or added steps—such as a job search or an orientation meeting—that had to be completed before a cash assistance application would be accepted, much less processed. These new steps, with their focus on work and avoiding public assistance, did not always include informing applicants of their likely eligibility for Medicaid.

Finally, Medicaid enrollment of immigrants also fell. PRWORA generally barred legal immigrants who entered the United States after August 22, 1996, from Medicaid. Many immigrants already in the country, who retained eligibility, appear to have dropped Medicaid coverage due to fears their immigration status would be affected because they would be classified as "public charges" (Holahan, Ku, and Pohl 2001).

Two recent studies have attempted to sort out the effects of welfare reform and the economy on declining Medicaid enrollment. These studies, like earlier ones that tried to disentangle the effects of state welfare reform policies and economic growth on declining welfare caseloads, generally found that both factors were responsible (Blank 2000; Council of Economic Advisors 1999; Martini and Wiseman 1997).

The first new study (Davidoff, Garrett, and Yemane 2001) used National Health Interview Survey (NHIS) data from 1994 through 1997 to distinguish the effects on Medicaid enrollment of new eligibility rules, economic expansion, and the changing likelihood of take-up (enrollment by those who are eligible). The authors began by simulating the impact of changes in Medicaid eligibility rules and in the economy. They found that if eligibility rules had not changed, 20.5 million children would have been eligible for Medicaid in 1997, down from 23 million children in 1994, because of rising incomes in the strong economy. In actuality, because of broader eligibility rules, such as expanded income disregards, expansions to older children, and expansions through Section 1115 waivers, 24 million children were eligible. Similarly, the improved economy would have reduced adult eligibility from 7 million to 6 million, whereas expanded eligibility rules made 6.5 million eligible.[6]

The authors then analyzed the effect of changes in administrative practices, diversion efforts, and other welfare reforms on parents' take-up decisions. Using data from 1994 and 1997, they simulated the percentage of eligible children who would have been enrolled, and found that the number would have dropped from 53 percent to 52 percent if take-up behavior had not changed. In reality, take-up rates fell to about 45 percent, a drop the researchers attribute to changes in parents' take-up behavior and state administrative practices. For adults, take-up would have increased from about 56 percent to almost 66 percent if behavior had not changed.[7] Actual take-up was just over 51 percent; thus, changes in behavior resulted in an estimated drop of 14 percentage points in the adult take-up rate (Davidoff et al. 2001).

The second new study used an econometric model to explain the impacts of welfare reform (including measures of whether the state had implemented income disregards, family caps, and job sanctions) and economic variables (such as the unemployment rate and the poverty rate) on declines in Medicaid caseloads (Garrett and Yemane 2001). Using data from 1991 to 1998, the authors conclude that both welfare reform and the economy contributed to the decline in Medicaid enrollees receiving cash assistance, though welfare policies played a larger role. This finding is consistent with the findings of Ku and Garrett (2000), who used data through 1996. One aspect of welfare reform—more generous income disregards—actually increased Medicaid enrollment (Garrett and Yemane 2001).

Taken together, these two studies show that welfare reform led to a decline in Medicaid enrollment. Although the eligibility changes brought about by reform should have increased Medicaid enrollment, they were more than offset by lower take-up, presumably in response to more restrictive administrative practices. Strong economic growth also contributed to the decline in Medicaid enrollment, but it was not as important a factor as welfare reform.

Did Those Leaving Welfare Become Uninsured?

People who left welfare could have kept their Medicaid coverage, obtained private insurance, or become uninsured. According to NSAF data, 22 percent of the women and 47 percent of the children who left welfare retained Medicaid coverage a year later, while 49 percent and 29 percent, respectively, became uninsured.[8] Those who left welfare for work were more likely to have obtained private coverage and less likely to have become uninsured, yet even among this group 34 percent of adults and 24 percent of children were uninsured after a year (Garrett and Holahan 2000).

Another study of changes in insurance coverage found that Medicaid coverage of the nonelderly population declined from 10 percent in 1994 to somewhat over 8 percent in 1998, a drop of about 3 million people (Holahan and Kim 2000) (table 8-2). Among low-income people (those with incomes below 200 percent of the federal poverty level), coverage dropped from almost 25 percent in 1994 to about 23 percent in 1998, a decline of over 3 million people. (Medicaid enrollment among people with incomes above 200 percent of the poverty level actually increased by 200,000.) Employer-sponsored coverage of low-income people increased from about 32 percent to just over 33 percent. The net increase in the number of uninsured low-income people was 800,000—a figure that would have been much larger if the expanding economy had not shifted so many people into higher income groups.

The dynamics of insurance coverage were similar for children and for adults (table 8-2). In low-income families, the proportion of children covered by Medicaid fell from about 37 percent in 1994 to 33 percent in 1998, while adults fell from 17 percent to about 16 percent. The number of children on Medicaid fell by 2 million and the number of adults by just over 1 million. However, the number of uninsured low-income children increased by only 600,000 and the number of adults by 200,000. These figures, together with the data on changes in incomes in table 8-2, suggest that many low-income families leaving Medicaid moved into higher-paying jobs. Thus, although the decline in Medicaid enrollment led to an increase in the number of uninsured children and adults, that increase would have been much greater had it not been for a strong economy.

This picture began to change in late 1998. Although employer-sponsored coverage continued to increase in 1999, from roughly 33 percent of low-income families to 34 percent (Holahan 2001), and private, nongroup coverage also rose, the percentage of people on Medicaid remained relatively constant. Because Medicaid enrollment stabilized,

Table 8-2. Health Insurance Coverage of All Nonelderly Persons, Children, and Adults, by Income, 1994 to 1998

Income group	All nonelderly Persons			Children			Adults		
	Coverage Distribution Within Income Category		Change (Millions of People)	Coverage Distribution Within Income Category		Change (Millions of People)	Coverage Distribution Within Income Category		Change (Millions of People)
	1994	1998	1994–98	1994	1998	1994–98	1994	1998	1994–98
All incomes (millions of people)	**229.7**	**238.6**	**8.9**	**73.9**	**76.0**	**2.1**	**155.8**	**162.6**	**6.8**
Employer	64.3%	65.8%	9.4*	60.5%	63.2%	3.3*	66.0%	67.0%	6.1*
Medicaid	10.0%	8.4%	−3.1*	18.1%	15.2%	−1.9*	6.2%	5.2%	−1.2*
Other public	2.7%	2.4%	−0.5*	2.4%	2.0%	−0.2*	2.9%	2.6%	−0.3*
Private nongroup	5.7%	5.0%	−1.2*	4.5%	4.0%	−0.3*	6.3%	5.5%	−0.8*
Uninsured	17.3%	18.4%	4.2*	14.5%	15.6%	1.2*	18.6%	19.7%	3.0*
Less than 200 percent of FPL[a] (millions of people)	**87.6**	**82.5**	**−5.1**	**34.6**	**33.0**	**−1.7**	**53.0**	**49.5**	**−3.5**
Employer	32.4%	33.1%	−1.1*	32.4%	34.6%	0.2	32.4%	32.1%	−1.3*
Medicaid	24.9%	22.5%	−3.3*	37.1%	33.0%	−2.0*	17.0%	15.5%	−1.3*
Other public	4.1%	3.8%	−0.4*	2.7%	2.3%	−0.2*	5.0%	4.9%	−0.2
Private nongroup	6.8%	5.9%	−1.1*	4.3%	3.6%	−0.3*	8.5%	7.5%	−0.8*
Uninsured	31.7%	34.7%	0.8*	23.4%	26.5%	0.6*	37.2%	40.1%	0.2

	71.5	72.2	0.7	22.9	23.2	0.2	48.6	49.1	0.5
200 to 399 percent of FPL (millions of people)									
Employer	78.4%	76.9%	−0.6	81.8%	81.2%	0.0	76.8%	74.8%	−0.6
Medicaid	1.3%	1.6%	0.2*	1.9%	2.4%	0.1	1.1%	1.3%	0.1
Other public	2.5%	2.1%	−0.2*	2.7%	2.3%	−0.1	2.4%	2.1%	−0.1
Private nongroup	5.6%	5.2%	−0.2	4.9%	4.6%	−0.1	6.0%	5.6%	−0.2
Uninsured	12.1%	14.1%	1.5*	8.6%	9.7%	0.3*	13.8%	16.2%	1.3*
More than 400 percent of FPL	**70.6**	**83.9**	**13.3**	**16.4**	**19.9**	**3.5**	**54.2**	**64.0**	**9.8**
(millions of people)									
Employer	89.4%	88.5%	11.2*	90.3%	89.9%	3.1*	89.1%	88.1%	8.1*
Medicaid	0.3%	0.3%	0.0	0.6%	0.6%	0.0	0.3%	0.2%	0.0
Other public	1.2%	1.1%	0.1	1.0%	1.2%	0.1	1.3%	1.1%	0.0
Private nongroup	4.4%	4.0%	0.2	4.4%	3.9%	0.1	4.4%	4.0%	0.1
Uninsured	4.6%	6.1%	1.8*	3.7%	4.5%	0.3*	4.9%	6.6%	1.5*

Source: Holahan and Kim 2000. Based on data from March Current Population Surveys, 1995–1999.

Note: Excludes persons age 65 and older and those in the Armed Forces.

FPL = federal poverty level.

*Indicates change in percentage is statistically significant between 1994 and 1998 (at p < .10).

[a]The federal poverty level in 2001 was $14,650 for a family of three.

the increase in employer and individual coverage after 1998 translated into an overall reduction of about 1 million in the number of uninsured low-income people.

State and Federal Responses to Falling Enrollment

The political response to falling Medicaid enrollment unfolded quickly and was based upon the limited data available at the time. In the past, a decreasing Medicaid caseload might have received little notice or even have been interpreted as a success, based on the assumption that fewer people needed publicly provided insurance. But this time around, the declines were widely interpreted as a sign of failure. Despite explicit provisions in the welfare reform law designed to protect Medicaid from possible deleterious effects of welfare reform, the policy was not having the intended effect. When Medicaid was viewed as an adjunct to welfare, families' failure to obtain coverage would have been viewed solely as a health care problem. In the context of a work-oriented welfare policy, this failure meant Medicaid was not fulfilling its role as a work support.

The decline in Medicaid coverage prompted a flurry of activity. Some states, realizing families were losing a benefit that was necessary to support them in the move from welfare to work, responded on their own. The federal government stepped into the fray with a Health Care Financing Administration[9] letter instructing states to make sure that enrollees' Medicaid eligibility was redetermined when they stopped receiving cash assistance. Some studies noted that states had made limited use of a $500 million allocation in the welfare reform law designed specifically to effect the delinking of Medicaid and welfare (Ross and Guyer 1999).

The fact that Medicaid enrollment increased throughout 1999 while the economy continued to expand—which should have reduced enrollment— indicates that states were beginning to ensure that more people leaving welfare continued their Medicaid coverage.

Taking Delinking Seriously

The drop-off in Medicaid coverage in the wake of welfare reform demonstrated that delinking had occurred more on paper than in fact (Ellwood 1999). Formally, delinking began in 1987, when eligibility for Medicaid was extended beyond the welfare population. As a practical matter, however, most states simply added new eligibility categories to the Medicaid program while continuing to administer it in the same way they always had. That is, eligibility continued to be determined by traditional welfare agencies using rule-based systems administered by eligibility technicians. Even with the advent of presumptive eligibility, which permitted some hospitals and clinics to confer provisional eligibility when a person came in needing services, paperwork had to be transferred to the county for a final determination.

Bureaucratic inertia is not the only reason delinking did not lead to major new investments in eligibility systems. With Medicaid costs growing faster than state revenues through much of the 1990s, most states were not eager to encourage enrollment. Consistent with the welfare model, Medicaid has historically operated on the premise that those in great enough need will make their way to the social services office or a health care provider to request assistance, while those who do not can be ignored.

For many years, advocates of the poor have expressed concern that states do not actively seek to enroll those who are eligible for Medicaid. Since Medicaid enrollment is automatic for welfare recipients, this concern is focused on people who are not eligible for welfare and those who have left welfare. People who are not eligible for welfare have much lower rates of participation in Medicaid than those who are also eligible for welfare. People who are not eligible for welfare are less likely to be aware that they are eligible for Medicaid, and are harder to find than people who have a regular relationship with a welfare agency. There is another reason for lower Medicaid enrollment among those who have left welfare: Families that make their way off welfare are often happy to be finished with the welfare bureaucracy. Establishing eligibility for Transitional Medical Assistance or poverty-related coverage would require them to continue the unpleasant and time-consuming tasks of reporting and documenting work status and earnings.

Welfare reform added to the complexity. As Matt Salo of the National Governors' Association said, "It was difficult for caseworkers to reconcile two contradictory messages implicit in the 1996 law: 'Medicaid is good, everyone should stay on Medicaid. But welfare is bad, everyone should stay off welfare' " (Pear 1999).

Recent policy changes have given states two new opportunities to fundamentally alter the relationship between Medicaid and welfare and to help those who leave welfare retain their Medicaid coverage. These opportunities came in the form of the SCHIP program and Section 1931.

SCHIP offered states the opportunity to design an entirely new eligibility and enrollment system for children's health insurance that operates separately from the old welfare system, with its emphasis on fraud avoidance and error reduction. Under SCHIP, states may greatly simplify eligibility categories, measures of income, and the documentation required to prove eligibility. They may develop new eligibility systems, separate from welfare agencies and offices; accept electronic, telephone, or mail-in applications; and rely upon private vendors or contractors to conduct enrollment functions. In addition, states have great flexibility in defining the benefits provided under SCHIP, the cost-sharing provisions, and the networks of providers they will use. In some states, lessons learned from SCHIP have been applied to the Medicaid program.[10]

Section 1931 offered a different opportunity: to address the family fragmentation that existed in earlier Medicaid policy. The practical effect of delinking Medicaid eligibility from welfare was to make a large number of children eligible for Medicaid coverage even though their parents were ineligible. Prior to welfare reform, in most states different children in the same family were likely to have had different insurance status, with Medicaid eligibility based upon the child's age as well as the family's income. Section 1931 gave states the option of covering all members of a family using a single Medicaid eligibility standard. That provision, together with new flexibility in measuring income, allowed states to expand their provision of Medicaid coverage to families of almost any income.

It is too soon to know whether simplified eligibility and family coverage will attract significant numbers of uninsured people. Early data are encouraging (Dubay and Kenney 2001; Lambrew 2001; Ku and Broaddus 2000), but there is much more to learn. Setting aside the specific effects of particular policies, these changes demonstrate the potential of delinking—that is, of developing a Medicaid program that encourages enrollment, while welfare is redefined as temporary assistance.

Policy Implications

The Medicaid-related provisions in the welfare law can be characterized as either a failure or a success, depending upon one's perspective. They were a failure in that the stated goals of the legislation—to preserve Medicaid enrollment for eligible people even as welfare was reformed—were not met. The consequences for individuals were in many instances significant, and may never be fully known. Yet the provisions were a success in that states and the federal government, once aware of this failure, seem to have responded by significantly improving their Medicaid systems.

In fact, the data presented above suggest that the problem of declining Medicaid caseloads has been at least partially solved. State administrative practices appear to have improved, as has outreach. Reports from states suggest that enrollment in Medicaid has been rising significantly in the past year, probably because of the slowing economy. Whether enrollment will continue to grow in response to the current economic decline is uncertain.

In the context of TANF reauthorization, it may be tempting to focus welfare policy initiatives specifically on ensuring that families retain their Medicaid coverage when they leave welfare. For example, states could be given performance targets to ensure that a high percentage of those who leave welfare have either private or public insurance coverage. While such policies would certainly benefit some people, this approach is too narrow.

Public policy would do better to complete the process of delinking Medicaid and welfare. The goal should be to make both systems work for all of the people they are intended to serve. Publicly provided health insurance should serve the needs of all who are eligible, whether they are currently on welfare, have recently left the rolls, or have never had any interaction with the welfare system. Excessive emphasis solely on people with a historical connection to welfare distracts administrative attention from the overall goal of enrolling everyone who is eligible for and in need of Medicaid.

Three federal policies are needed to achieve this goal:

- **Continue to encourage states to expand coverage.** Aside from the inherent importance of covering needy populations, expansion of health insurance eligibility beyond the welfare population provides a critical mass that justifies investments in administrative and outreach systems separate from the welfare system. SCHIP has increased the average eligibility of older children from a family income of 76 percent of the federal poverty level to 208 percent. Several states, including California, New Jersey, and Connecticut, have expanded coverage significantly under Section 1931. Other states, including Massachusetts, New York, and Rhode Island, have waivers to expand coverage substantially; the expansions in Massachusetts and New York include childless adults. Older children continue to be added to Medicaid under the expansions enacted in the 1980s. Existing federal incentives for these expansions, in the form of matching funds, should remain in place.

- **Continue to simplify eligibility for Medicaid.** Many states have already taken significant steps in this direction, whether through the design of SCHIP programs, Section 1115 waivers, or Section 1931 expansions. At the same time, participation rates need to be increased. Among people not receiving cash assistance, Medicaid enrollment ranges from 50 percent to 60 percent, with considerable variation among states (Dubay and Kenney 2001). Eliminating asset tests, simplifying eligibility categories, reducing documentation requirements, minimizing cost sharing, and adopting longer periods of eligibility can all make Medicaid more supportive of working families. As states gain experience with outreach, initiated primarily through the SCHIP program, they can learn from each other, and should adopt the most effective approaches.
- **Increase funding to extend insurance coverage to new populations.** Among the many ideas being considered, three warrant mention. The FamilyCare proposal before Congress would not increase matching rates for existing Medicaid populations, but it would extend coverage to parents of Medicaid and SCHIP children at the higher SCHIP matching rate. The Bush administration has proposed tax credits for low-income uninsured people (up to $1,000 for singles and $3,000 for families) to allow them to buy private coverage, although these credits are generally far less than the cost of private policies. The National Governors' Association has proposed higher federal matching rates for some Medicaid populations and services. While none of these proposals is directed at families leaving welfare, they could all reduce work disincentives by expanding coverage to include people whose incomes increase because of employment.

When it comes to expanding coverage or changing administrative systems, the federal government can mandate that states act, give them incentives to act, or leave it up to the states to act. In recent years, the federal government has relied primarily upon financial incentives, and this model has led to progress. But the progress has been uneven, with only 15 states extending coverage to parents with incomes above the poverty level, and just 10 covering adults without children. In addition, financial incentives may be insufficient if state fiscal conditions continue to deteriorate, making the state share of program costs harder to obtain. Still, the federal government should continue providing financial incentives for states to act, although it must recognize that considerable interstate variations in coverage will remain.

The best way to make Medicaid and SCHIP operate as effective work supports for families leaving welfare is to make sure that all families eligible for these programs actually receive benefits. Despite bumps along the road, the nation has made good progress in delinking these programs from welfare and in recognizing that public health insurance meets needs well beyond those of the welfare population. Health policy can best support the goals of welfare reform by continuing to emphasize outreach, coverage, and access to services that support all low-income families that do not have coverage through work and that cannot afford health insurance on their own.

NOTES

The authors thank Mary Pohl for her research assistance and Ron Haskins and Matt Stagner for comments on an earlier draft.

1. Medicaid eligibility is actually far more complex. In fact, most spending is associated with services for older people and people with disabilities—eligibility categories that are not discussed in this chapter.

2. The federal poverty level in 2001 was $14,650 for a family of three.

3. During the second six months of coverage, states may impose a premium or limit the benefit package for families with incomes above the federal poverty level.

4. Enrollment of aged Medicaid beneficiaries was stable. There was a small reduction of 3.5 percent in aged cash enrollees, reflecting longer-term trends in SSI enrollment, but noncash enrollees increased by almost the same amount (1.7 percent). The number of disabled persons continued to rise, by 10.3 percent, with cash and noncash enrollees both increasing during the period.

5. Nebraska is the only state that reported an increase in cash enrollment. This is most likely an error; it is not consistent with data reported on drops in AFDC and TANF recipients.

6. The authors were not able to simulate eligibility for pregnant women or Transitional Medical Assistance, making these estimates somewhat lower than the actual figures.

7. The higher rate for adults is based on historical data showing that eligible adults are more likely to enroll.

8. Children have many more ways to stay on Medicaid than adults do. While eligibility among adults not receiving welfare is limited to Transitional Medical Assistance,

medically needy programs, pregnancy-related programs, or waiver programs, children remain eligible because they are in low-income families, regardless of family structure or health status.

9. The Health Care Financing Administration is now called the Centers for Medicare and Medicaid Services.

10. Many of the simplifications that states implemented in SCHIP eligibility could have been, but were not, made in Medicaid in the past.

REFERENCES

Blank, Rebecca M. 2000. "Declining Caseloads/Increased Work: What Can We Conclude about the Effects of Welfare Reform." Paper prepared for the conference "Welfare Reform Four Years Later: Progress and Prospects" at the Federal Reserve Bank of New York. October.

Council of Economic Advisors. 1999. "Technical Report: The Effects of Welfare Policy and the Economic Expansion on Welfare Caseloads: An Update." Washington, D.C.: The White House.

Davidoff, Amy, Bowen Garrett, and Alshadye Yemane. 2001. *Medicaid Eligibility, Takeup, Insurance Coverage, and Health Care Access and Use before and after Welfare Reform: National Changes from 1994 to 1997.* A report prepared for Office of Research and Demonstrations, Health Care Financing Administration, U.S. Department of Health and Human Services. Washington, D.C.: The Urban Institute.

Dubay, Lisa, and Genevieve Kenney. 2001. *Covering Parents through Medicaid and SCHIP: Potential Benefits to Low-Income Parents and Children.* Washington, D.C.: Kaiser Commission on Medicaid and the Uninsured.

Ellis, Eileen R., Vernon K. Smith, and David M. Rousseau. 2000. *Medicaid Enrollment in 50 States: June 1997 to December 1999.* Washington, D.C.: Kaiser Commission on Medicaid and the Uninsured.

Ellwood, Marilyn. 1999. *The Medicaid Eligibility Maze: Coverage Expands, but Enrollment Problems Persist.* Washington, D.C.: The Urban Institute. *Assessing the New Federalism* Occasional Paper No. 30.

Garrett, Bowen, and John Holahan. 2000. "Health Insurance After Welfare." *Health Affairs* 19 (1): 175–84.

Garrett, Bowen, and Alshadye Yemane. 2001. "National Trends in Medicaid Enrollment and Expenditures." Washington, D.C.: Urban Institute. Unpublished mimeo.

Holahan, John. 2001. *Why Did the Number of Uninsured Fall in 1999?* Washington, D.C.: Kaiser Commission on Medicaid and the Uninsured.

Holahan, John, and Johnny Kim. 2000. "Why Does the Number of Uninsured Americans Continue to Grow?" *Health Affairs* 19 (4): 188–96.

Holahan, John, Leighton Ku, and Mary Pohl. 2001. *Is Immigration Responsible for the Growth in the Number of Uninsured?* Washington, D.C.: Kaiser Commission on Medicaid and the Uninsured.

Kenney, Genevieve, Frank Ullman and Alan Weil. 2000. "Three Years into SCHIP: What States Are and Are Not Spending." Washington, D.C.: The Urban Institute. *Assessing the New Federalism* Policy Brief A-44.

Ku, Leighton, and Matthew Broaddus. 2000. *The Importance of Family-Based Insurance Expansions: New Research Findings about State Health Reforms.* Washington, D.C.: Center on Budget and Policy Priorities.

Ku, Leighton, and Bowen Garrett. 2000. *How Welfare Reform and Economic Factors Affected Medicaid Participation: 1984–96.* Washington, D.C.: The Urban Institute. *Assessing the New Federalism* Discussion Paper No. 00-01.

Lambrew, Jeanne M. 2001. *Health Insurance: A Family Affair.* New York: The Commonwealth Fund.

Loprest, Pamela. 1999. "How Families That Left Welfare Are Doing: A National Picture." Washington, D.C.: The Urban Institute. *Assessing the New Federalism* Policy Brief B-1.

Martini, Alberto, and Michael Wiseman. 1997. "Explaining the Recent Decline in Welfare Caseloads: Is the Council of Economic Advisors Right?" *Challenge* 40 (6): 6–20.

Minnesota Department of Human Services. 1995. "Updated Estimate of the Impact of MinnesotaCare on AFDC." St. Paul, Minn.: Reports and Forecasts Division.

Pear, Robert. 1999. "Poor Workers Lose Medicaid Coverage Despite Eligibility." *New York Times.* April 12, 1999.

Ross, Donna, and Jocelyn Guyer. 1999. "Congress Lifts the Sunset on the '$500 Million Fund,' Extends Opportunities for States to Ensure Parents and Children Do Not Lose Health Coverage." Washington, D.C.: Center on Budget and Policy Priorities.

Zuckerman, Stephen, Genevieve Kenney, Lisa Dubay, Jennifer Haley, and John Holahan. 2001. "Shifting Health Insurance Coverage, 1997–99." *Health Affairs* 20 (1): 169–77.

9

The "Hard-to-Serve":
Definitions and Implications

Martha R. Burt

The term "hard-to-serve" has been used as a catchall phrase to describe welfare recipients who do not move quickly and easily into a job. However, behind this simple phrase lies a broad range of barriers to work and a highly varied set of state and local policies and practices that may or may not identify and serve welfare recipients with these barriers. Examining these barriers and policies is essential, as policymaker attention has moved from immediate job placement to reaching the hard-to-serve population. To this end, this chapter explores the conditions and circumstances that constitute barriers to work, how these barriers interact with TANF sanction and exemption policies, how welfare agencies identify barriers, and what approaches the agencies take to reducing barriers.[1] Finally, the chapter discusses the implications of "hard-to-serve" issues for TANF reauthorization, state actions, and recipient outcomes and well-being.

Barriers to Work or Service Receipt

Discussions of what makes someone hard to serve typically focus on conditions and circumstances that may pose barriers, first to program participation and ultimately to employment. This chapter, therefore, starts on familiar ground. Seeking an organizing principle, this section divides the

163

many possible barriers into three groups, based largely on the types of interventions that would be needed to reduce or eliminate the barrier. The first group includes barriers that can be overcome relatively quickly with appropriate resources. The second group includes treatable, controllable, or reversible barriers that usually require both more resources and more time than those in the first group. The third group includes permanent conditions that require accommodation, as they cannot be removed.

Barriers That Resources Can Overcome Quickly

TANF agencies and their community partners have had considerable success removing some barriers quickly by providing recipients with resources. Difficulty obtaining child care or finding transportation to and from work are usually barriers of this type, as is lack of job search skills.[2] The relative ease or speed of resolution once resources are given distinguishes barriers in this group from those in the next. Success is most likely when recipients face only one barrier from this group.

Before TANF, lack of child care effectively exempted recipients from work. Some states still grant exemptions or deferrals from work requirements if child care is truly unavailable, as may be the case for people who live in remote areas or work unusual hours. Many states have committed TANF, state, and local resources to ensuring that child care does not present a barrier to work. Some states spend more for child care than for TANF cash assistance, and some are taking steps to increase the supply of child care to meet the needs of families with infants, evening and weekend work shifts, and other special circumstances.

Lack of transportation is a serious problem in rural and many suburban areas. Most states have addressed it in several ways, including increasing the value of a car a family may have and still be eligible for TANF, repairing cars, distributing tokens or vouchers for public transportation, and organizing van pools for recipients.

To address lack of job readiness and job search skills, virtually all TANF programs offer assistance with job search, classes to develop job search and job readiness skills, job clubs to encourage persistence, and similar programs. These have a long history of working for some recipients.

Barriers That Are Treatable, Controllable, or Reversible

Many conditions that pose barriers to work, or even to service receipt, are treatable, controllable, or reversible with adequate and appropriate resources. Such conditions include physical and mental illnesses or disabilities, addictions, illiteracy, lack of basic and work-related skills, inability to speak or understand English, lack of work experience, and recent release from a correctional institution. In addition, situations such as domestic violence, homelessness, or involvement with the child welfare system may need to be resolved before a recipient can realistically be expected to find and hold a job.

The time frame for overcoming barriers in this category and being able to participate in work activities is likely to be three to six months, although it may be longer. Further, TANF agencies have less experience with these interventions, and success is not guaranteed even for experienced programs. Some states treat participation in efforts to relieve the barriers in this second group as the equivalent of activities that are strictly work related. In these states, going to counseling, getting substance abuse treatment, taking steps toward obtaining housing, or resolving domestic violence situations become part of the recipient's case plan. Recipients are treated as in compliance with the work requirement if they fulfill these obligations of their case plan.

Some interventions, such as getting a woman and her children safely out of a violent household, may completely eliminate the barrier to employment. Others, such as arranging treatment for mental illness or substance abuse, may need to be combined with continued support if the recipient is to have a realistic chance of remaining stable and holding a job.

TANF agencies that want to bring welfare recipients with treatable, controllable, or reversible conditions into the workforce and keep them there must arrange and pay for appropriate treatments or other interventions to alleviate the conditions.[3] Moreover, the agencies will need to provide support services for at least several months; since recipients likely will not be working during this time, adherence to treatment regimes will have to be accepted as a work-related activity. TANF agencies that take an approach of "get recipients working and offer post-employment support" may have more clients working relatively quickly, but will still have to provide support services for an extended time.

Permanent Conditions: A Different Type of Barrier

Some physical disabilities, mental illnesses, and learning or developmental disabilities are permanent, and may constitute permanent barriers to employment unless accommodations can be made. Many people on welfare have one or more of these conditions (see chapter 2). Though posing real barriers, these conditions are often not severe enough to qualify welfare recipients for federal programs such as Supplemental Security Income (SSI) or Social Security Disability Insurance (SSDI, or just DI). TANF recipients may never have applied for benefits from these programs because the process is even more daunting than applying for welfare. In addition, permanent conditions of a recipient's child or other family member may constitute a barrier to work and make the recipient hard to serve or employ.

Many permanent conditions are covered by the Americans with Disabilities Act (ADA). The ADA is largely untested in the area of welfare rights, but some disability rights activists are beginning to turn their attention to the situation of TANF recipients with disabilities. As a consequence, TANF agencies that do not develop ways to help disabled recipients comply with work requirements are likely to face discrimination lawsuits if they sanction these recipients for not working.[4] The possibility of legal action is becoming a significant motivator for reexamining policies and support services.

Helping people with permanent conditions engage in work-related activities and eventually join the labor force requires both greater attention to matching recipients with work environments and more sophisticated, ongoing relationships with potential employers to create more workplace accommodations. To this end, TANF agency partnerships with vocational rehabilitation agencies, mental health agencies, Goodwill Industries, and other agencies that specialize in helping people with disabilities move into employment are becoming increasingly important.

Interactions among Barriers

Welfare recipients who face more than one barrier to employment often require several kinds of assistance to help them get ready for work and keep a job once they get it. Providing child care or transportation to a recipient with a substance abuse problem may not help until the larger problem of the substance abuse is addressed. Efforts to help a recipient increase literacy or job-related skills may fail because nothing is being done to address an undiagnosed severe learning disability.

Almost two of every five welfare recipients have at least one barrier to work, and one in five has multiple barriers (U.S. General Accounting Office 2000). Moreover, those with multiple *identifiable* barriers may also have more subtle problems, such as difficulty making plans, organizing daily activities, managing money, or meeting complex timetables. Recipients lacking these skills pose a special challenge to TANF programs.

Particularly intractable problems are very likely to occur together (e.g., mental illness and substance abuse, or substance abuse, domestic violence, and child abuse). In such cases it may be hard to arrange appropriate services. Mental health agencies commonly refuse to treat mentally ill substance abusers, and substance abuse treatment programs often refuse to treat people with major mental illnesses. Some programs require a period of residence, which puts them out of reach for most TANF recipients, who have no one with whom they can leave their children during residential treatment.

TANF Status and Barriers: No Easy Mapping

A basic problem for both analysis and policy pertaining to the hard-to-serve is that recipients with the same barrier(s) are being treated very differently in different states. Even within a single TANF agency, recipients with the same barrier(s) may be in different TANF statuses. For example, a person caring for a disabled parent may be exempt from work requirements in one site, sanctioned for failing to follow program rules in another site, and have left the welfare rolls even though she is not working in yet another site. Knowing that a person has a given barrier does not predict TANF status, nor can this knowledge be used in any one-to-one fashion to assign a person to a TANF status.

The broad concept of "hard-to-serve" covers welfare recipients in at least three TANF statuses: those with exemptions or deferrals, those who have been sanctioned (designated "hard-to-engage"), and those who follow TANF rules but still cannot get or keep a job (the "hard-to-employ").

The Exempt and Deferred

In establishing exemption and deferral criteria,[5] state policymakers specify situations they feel make it inappropriate or impossible to ask a parent to go to work. In one sense, people for whom states grant exemptions from work requirements are not hard to serve at all, because they are not usually being given services designed to prepare them for work. In fact, they may not even be hard to employ, but no one knows for sure because they have not been required to seek work.

States vary greatly in the bases they accept for exemption or deferral, with some states requiring work from recipients with conditions that would result in exemptions in other states. This is why this chapter includes exemption and deferral policies as part of a "hard-to-serve" discussion. For example, caring for an infant age 0 to 3 months is grounds for exemption in all but four states (Rowe 2000, table III.B.1). States vary greatly in how much beyond 3 months they are willing to grant an exemption, however, and most lowered cutoff ages under TANF. In 1996, most states (30) exempted a mother until her youngest child reached 3 years of age, whereas in 1999, most states (27) exempted her only until the youngest child was 12 months old (Rowe and Giannarelli 2001).

Many states exempt recipients from work requirements if they are elderly (30 states), pregnant (23 states), sick or incapacitated (31 states), caring for a sick or incapacitated family member (34 states), or in a domestic violence situation where meeting work requirements would pose a danger to the recipient or her children (Rowe 2000, table III.B.1). In most of these states, TANF rules exempt fewer recipients than was true under AFDC. For example, only 18 states used the same exemptions policies for disabled recipients in 1999 that they used before welfare reform (Thompson et al. 1998); the remainder required some or all recipients with disabilities to engage in work activity. Similarly, in 1999 only 22 states used pre-reform criteria to exempt recipients caring for a disabled family member; the remaining states imposed more stringent criteria. These changes have the clear effect of requiring more people to engage in work-related activities, regardless of the barriers they face.

The "Hard-to-Reach" or "Hard-to-Engage"

Most welfare applicants and recipients are now subject to work requirements. They must meet with caseworkers, go through screening and assessment, meet requirements for job search and other job readiness activities, and seek work. Efforts to engage them in such work-related activities generally succeed. But a significant proportion of recipients, the "hard-to-engage," do not cooperate, and receive sanctions as a result. In states with strongly enforced full-family sanctions,[6] many recipients who fail to meet TANF work requirements eventually find themselves and their families dropped from welfare.

It is not easy to find out whether recipients who resist participation in work-related activities (risking sanctions or reaching time limits) do so because they experience barriers, or what barriers they may face. Although there have been numerous studies of former welfare recipients, only a few have covered the period *before* leaving welfare. Those who were dropped as a result of sanctions or having reached their lifetime limit for benefits tend to be younger (18 to 24), less likely to have a high school diploma or its equivalent, and more likely to report being in poor health than those who left welfare for other reasons (Cherlin et al. 2001). Health problems and difficulties with child care and transportation have been cited as reasons for noncompliance leading to sanctions (U.S. General Accounting Office 2000), and by unemployed former recipients as reasons for not working (Loprest 1999; Richardson et al. 2001).

In states that do not have full-family sanctions or that do not enforce them rigorously, "hard-to-reach" or "hard-to-engage" recipients and their families are still on the rolls. Nationally, about 5 percent of current recipients are in sanctioned status at any given time, a number that reaches 10 to 20 percent in a few states (U.S. General Accounting Office 2000). These sanctioned recipients face many of the same barriers as those who were dropped from welfare: lack of a high school diploma or equivalent, health problems, and child care and transportation difficulties (ibid.). Moreover, sanctioned recipients are more than twice as likely as unsanctioned recipients to face barriers to work: 76 percent of sanctioned recipients have at least one such barrier, and 39 percent have multiple barriers. Several states are trying to contact sanctioned families through outreach efforts to learn why they have not complied with work requirements. Outreach staff in some of these programs can link recipients with support services to reduce barriers and help recipients come back into compliance.

The "Hard-to-Employ"

The hard-to-employ can be divided into two groups: recipients who participated in all required program activities but could not get a job, and recipients who found but did not keep a job. Of those who lost a job, some were still on TANF at the time, while others had left TANF but had to return because of the job loss.

Some states wait until recipients fail to get a job before they begin trying to identify barriers to work and helping to overcome them. Others give caseworkers discretion to offer barrier-reducing services, if needed, before sending recipients out into the job market. In addition, a number of states and localities have expanded post-employment services, some of which address barrier reduction as part of this process of preventing return to TANF.

Each approach has its advantages and disadvantages. Since many welfare recipients with potentially restricting conditions do manage to work (chapter 2 and Loprest 1999), failure in the job market may be the most efficient means to identify those who need help. On the other hand, allowing people to fail before offering help may undermine the self-confidence they need to succeed. It may also lead to periods of hardship for their children. States that encourage or require some work-related activity while ensuring that supports are in place when needed may avoid the negative aspects of failure, as well as those of simply exempting people from work requirements without helping them. But monitoring, reassessing, and assembling necessary support services take a lot of caseworker resources, and also require that supportive services be available quickly when it becomes clear that a recipient needs them to maintain employment. Thus, maintaining support services requires considerable time and attention from the TANF agency, along with flexibility and well-developed resource networks.

Identifying Barriers

Even if TANF agencies want to help recipients address a wide variety of barriers or assure that TANF policy does not inadvertently sanction recipients with unaddressed barriers, the agencies often cannot do so because they cannot tell whether a welfare recipient has one or more barriers. Before applying remedies, TANF agencies must answer difficult questions including how to know a barrier exists, how to know which barrier exists, when to inquire, and who should inquire.

Several strategies are useful for identifying barriers. The simplest is to ask directly, without employing any formal questionnaire or screening instrument. This approach usually works best to identify uncomplicated, nonstigmatizing, barriers to work—for instance, child care or transportation difficulties. The second approach is to *screen,* and the third is to *assess* (Thompson and Mikelson 2001). The fourth approach is to see whether the recipient fails to complete some program milestone, such as coming to job club or getting or keeping a job.

Screening usually involves a short initial interview or questionnaire to get an inkling of any conditions or circumstances that may pose barriers to employment. It usually happens when a person first applies for welfare (or when a long-term recipient first encounters TANF requirements). Many TANF offices have an intake form that contains a few questions intended to identify potential barriers.

Initial screening may fail to identify some important barriers for several reasons. Applicants may not see the relevance of some aspects of their lives to their need for welfare. They may not wish to reveal certain information that they consider stigmatizing, illegal, or private. They may not be aware that some barriers exist (e.g., they may never have been diagnosed as having a learning disability). Or something may not be a barrier initially but become a barrier later.

Assessment usually involves a more intensive information-gathering process, and may include the use of formal tools to identify problems such as substance abuse, mental illness, domestic violence, or learning disabilities. Further, assessment may take place not just initially, but also when a recipient reaches a new plateau or fails to reach agreed-upon goals. Assessment is more likely than screening to be oriented toward identifying talents and assets as well as barriers.

Three issues are important in screening and assessment: who does them, when they are done, and what tools are used. States vary in how they approach all of these issues. Some have one worker determine eligibility, a second worker conduct preliminary screening and make placement decisions, and a third worker pursue more in-depth assessment if initial placement fails. Other states combine screening and eligibility determination, and some conduct in-depth assessments of most recipients soon after intake. Further, some have TANF workers conduct screening, and refer recipients to partner agencies with special expertise for assessments, while others have developed in-house assessment expertise. Formal assessment tools used by various states cover between 8 and 13 conditions or circumstances that may constitute barriers to work, and range in length from 15 to 138 questions (Thompson and Mikelson 2001, appendix A).

A final approach to identifying barriers to employment is to require all new recipients to participate in job search and wait to see who does not get a job in the prescribed time. Only after a recipient has failed does the TANF agency take steps to identify and address barriers. Other milestones used to identify failure include receipt of sanctions by recipients who do not follow program rules, lack of a job when recipients are approaching time limits, loss of a job while still on TANF, and return to TANF after job loss by people who left welfare because they got a job. The wait-for-failure

approach reduces the proportion of recipients who receive specialized services to reduce barriers. However, this advantage is balanced by the likelihood that recipients who fail are those with multiple barriers and the most
tenuous hold on functioning. For them, failure is another blow that
reduces the probability of success in the workplace.

Responses to Identified Barriers

TANF agencies can choose to do little or nothing to address barriers. If
they choose to do something, they need to decide how services will
actually be delivered and when they will be made available. The
approaches they take will have serious implications for agency staffing
and administration.

Three options for dealing with barriers to work do not require significant state resources, but also do nothing to help recipients remove barriers. One is to exempt people with barriers from work requirements. There
is a limit to how far a state can take this policy, given federal work participation requirements that states must achieve. States with relatively high
proportions of exempt or deferred recipients are just beginning to face the
effects of time limits on these households. A second option is to withhold
services, have recipients fail, and have them face sanctions and possibly be
dropped from the rolls. A more supportive option is to help recipients
with serious permanent disabilities obtain more appropriate benefits, such
as SSI or DI. TANF programs may try to do this, but many recipients,
although disabled, will not meet the extremely rigorous eligibility criteria
for these federal programs.

Other responses to identified barriers will entail expenditures of
resources to provide recipients with a wide variety of services. These
resources may come from TANF, Welfare-to-Work, or the Workforce
Investment Act, or from partner agencies such as those providing substance abuse or mental health treatment. When TANF began, relatively
few states had a commitment to use significant levels of TANF resources
to support services that help reduce conditions such as mental health or
substance abuse. As states gain more years of experience with TANF, TANF
programs appear to be moving toward providing a wider range of services
and more in-depth services to address the barriers facing those who
remain. A fairly universal outcome is that TANF agencies are now much
more likely to have both formal and informal relationships with a greater

array of nonprofit and for-profit providers, covering a greater variety of services, than was true before TANF. TANF agencies have shown creativity in developing purchase-of-service arrangements for treatment beds, slots, and times that are quickly available to agencies' recipients when a need is identified.

Many states and counties have delegated responsibilities for child care information and referral, eligibility determination, and provider payments to nonprofit child care management or resource and referral agencies. Connections with community-based providers of employment and training services are the most common approach to delivering these core services. Assistance with screening, assessment, and actual service delivery for barriers related to substance abuse, mental health, and domestic violence are most frequently conducted through consultant or contractual arrangements. TANF agencies may arrange to have expert consultants located in agency offices, contract with service providers that have the necessary expertise for service delivery at the provider's location, or both. It may also be necessary to have connections with organizations representing specific subpopulations, such as a community center serving a particular ethnic population. Providers in many communities have been willing to develop services because they know that TANF will be sending them recipients; these services then become resources for the whole community.

TANF agencies have to make agency-level policy decisions about service sequencing and service integration. The former involves deciding who gets what, when; the latter involves deciding whether a TANF case manager or a service provider will be responsible for overall management of a recipient's case. Many states now offer some recipients assistance to remove barriers, but this assistance usually comes only after a recipient has looked for a job and failed. As of summer 2001, less than one-half of states give caseworkers discretion to assign a recipient to services that may help remove barriers as the *first* thing they do, before recipients are sent to job search (Giannarelli 2001). Rarest of all are TANF programs that seek workplace accommodations for recipients with permanently disabling conditions.

Service coordination is now a requirement of the job for both TANF administrators and caseworkers. Administrators must arrange contracts; determine levels of service they wish to purchase, both in total and as maximums for a single recipient; monitor performance; and maintain good working relationships with contract agencies. As recipients get more services, and either achieve or fail to achieve milestones in their case plans, more assessment, more specialty treatment, and more resources could easily be required. Most caseworkers under TANF are being asked to do more—and more complicated—things than they did under AFDC. Caseworkers have to make the actual referrals from among the providers under contract with their agency, often becoming case managers who orchestrate services for their recipients. All of these changes have implications for staff workloads (e.g., people cannot handle as many complicated cases as simple cases) and for training (e.g., managers and caseworkers need a more complex set of skills) that were irrelevant for many states and localities under AFDC.

Policy Implications

People with one or more barriers to employment have always been part of the welfare caseload, but the lifetime limit on benefits under TANF has created new pressures to get them working. Some states address the barriers facing hard-to-serve welfare recipients explicitly, whereas others do so indirectly and perhaps unintentionally.

A number of state policies can mask the existence of hard-to-serve recipients and the severity of the barriers they face. The combination of low benefits, stringent work requirements, and narrow income disregards, for example, creates a situation in which even minimal ability to work can push recipients' income over the eligibility guidelines, forcing them to leave welfare. The combined effect of these policies is to move families off welfare before any of the barriers they face can be identified or ameliorated. As a result, these states may not recognize the extent of barriers until former recipients fail in the workforce and return to welfare.

Two policies that restrict even the possibility of identifying barriers are strictly enforced full-family sanctions and very short time limits. Recipients in states with these policies may find themselves off the rolls before they receive any assistance in addressing barriers. Short time limits may have the same effect when combined with generous exemption policies. In Massachusetts, some recipients are exempt from work requirements and do not receive any work-related services, but they are still subject to the state's 24-month time limit for obtaining cash benefits.

Other jurisdictions, such as Minnesota and California, use a combination of higher benefits, less stringent sanctions, less rigorous application of sanctions, longer time limits before losing benefits, and more generous income disregards as ways to promote the financial well-being of families before they have to leave TANF. These policies also keep families on the rolls longer, enabling them to get more help when it is warranted. States with policies like these often have other policies that expand the variety of activities in which recipients may engage without sanction, and use their TANF resources to offer programs and services that reduce barriers to work.

Many current welfare recipients and their families, as well as other low-income families who have left TANF, do need help—sometimes a lot of help—to reduce barriers to continuous gainful employment. Improvements in family well-being, as opposed to simple reduction of welfare rolls, may be due at least in part to states' willingness to invest in these families. More and more jurisdictions are exploring a skills-development/barrier-reduction approach to welfare policy. Some states are beginning to extend assistance to low-income families who have left TANF, to reduce the likelihood that they will return.

States cannot pursue efforts to improve family well-being without significant resources. Therefore the following measures are needed:

- Congress should maintain current TANF funding levels. Significant reductions might hamper some states' continuing efforts to help hard-to-serve recipients find jobs, and could prevent other states and localities from initiating such efforts;
- Congress should consider expanding the scope of countable TANF work activities to include barrier-reduction activities that help welfare recipients get and keep jobs;
- Congress should consider extending time limits for recipients (and their families) who face multiple barriers to employment, especially intractable or permanent barriers, and should encourage states to do more for these families than simply exempting them from work requirements; and
- Jurisdictions not already using TANF funds to create supports for hard-to-serve families should begin to do so.

The considerable dearth of knowledge regarding hard-to-serve welfare recipients and their families must be remedied. In particular, answers are needed to the following questions. How do states arrive at decisions regarding whether or how to invest in services to reduce barriers? How do the resulting practices affect the well-being of recipients—and their children—

with barriers to work? What proportion of TANF dollars are states and counties spending on barrier reduction? What types of services do these funds support?

The current situation creates great inequities between similar families living in different states—and often in different jurisdictions within the same state. Some states and localities use many TANF resources, and often large amounts of their own resources as well, to address the needs of hard-to-serve TANF recipients, whereas other states and localities do not. Despite having considerable flexibility in how they use TANF funds, some states do not do all they could to help hard-to-serve recipients and their families.

One critical question remains: What will happen to people who *cannot* work? TANF policy is based largely on the premise that those who are not working *could* work if they would just try. The requirement that recipients work, or prepare for work; most states' commitment to a work-first approach; and sanctions for those who do not participate in work-related activities are all policies aimed at recipients' *motivation* to work. Their *ability* to work is addressed in one way by exemption policies, which remove the requirement to try. But exemptions and deferrals do not offer recipients the supports that might make work possible. Approaches that require recipients with significant barriers to participate in work activities and give them the supports they need to do so maximize the likelihood that these recipients will succeed to the extent possible.

Nevertheless, some recipients will never succeed in becoming self-sufficient. What obligations does the public have to them, and what do these recipients have to do before TANF programs are willing to agree that they cannot support themselves and their families? These questions bring into focus the extent to which large parts of the safety net in the United States rely on work-related supports. If one cannot work, one cannot benefit from the Earned Income Tax Credit, which helps lift many low-income working families above poverty level. Nor can one benefit from all of the new investments in child care, either as direct subsidies or as tax credits. Finally, neither SSI nor most states' TANF benefit levels are sufficient to support these families at anything approaching a livable income.

Some states are developing policies to address these issues. Michigan, for instance, has no official time limit, and is committed to using state funds to support all recipients who "play by the rules" but are still on welfare after five years. California guarantees continuation of the child portion of TANF grants even if the household head loses benefits due to time limits. Illinois and some other states use state funds for programs into which they transfer TANF recipients who appear unlikely to move into the workforce.

Federal policymakers should be looking at these programs and policies, and considering circumstances under which time limits will need to be extended, the rule allowing states to exempt up to 20 percent of their caseload from time limits made more flexible, or an alternative program created to support people who truly cannot support themselves and their families. The concept of partial disability could be applied to some TANF recipients facing barriers to work, as it is to disabled veterans, for example. Perhaps policies based on this concept would enable hard-to-employ recipients to earn some income, yet receive cash assistance to compensate for their inability to work full-time.

NOTES

Pam Holcomb and Terri Thompson's help discussing issues in this chapter and reading early drafts is greatly appreciated.

1. The discussion in this chapter owes much to previous analyses by Holcomb and Thompson (2000), Thompson and Mikelson (2001), and Thompson and colleagues (1998), and to the work of TANF/Employment and Training team members for the 1999–2000 round of ANF case studies in focal states.

2. Even these issues may take some time to resolve for some families. Child care becomes more complex when a family has many children; transportation from or within very remote areas may be difficult to arrange; and some people will need much more than a simple job club to achieve employment.

3. Not all states *do* have keeping recipients in the workforce as a goal, and still fewer hold that the elimination of poverty among TANF and former TANF households is a goal of the state's TANF and related policies. But more states are moving toward addressing issues of job retention and returns to welfare as their caseloads change.

4. The Massachusetts TANF agency has been the subject of a class-action discrimination complaint filed with the Office of Civil Rights (OCR), U.S. Department of Health and Human Services, on behalf of TANF recipients with learning disabilities. OCR has issued a "guidance" for TANF agencies on issues related to recipients with disabilities, and the *Georgetown Journal of Poverty Law and Policy* has published an article (LaCheen 2001) that is being received in the field as a manual for advocates in how to represent their TANF recipients administratively and in court (Office of Civil Rights, U.S. Department of Health and Human Services, Complaint Number 01-98-3055. OCR "letter of findings" addressed to Ms. Claire McIntire, Commissioner, Massachusetts Department of Transitional Assistance, dated, January 19, 2001. OCR Memorandum, dated January 19, 2001, addressed to "Entities Involved in Administration or Operation of TANF Programs, Subject: Policy Guidance—Prohibition Against Discrimination on the Basis of Disability in the Administration of TANF"; see *Boston Globe* 2001).

5. There is no systematic, cross-state difference between an exemption and a deferral.

6. For instance, Florida, Idaho, Iowa, Kansas, Maryland, Michigan, Mississippi, Nebraska, Oklahoma, South Carolina, Tennessee, Virginia, and Wyoming eliminate the entire benefit for an *initial* instance of noncompliance.

REFERENCES

Boston Globe. 2001. "U.S. Faults State, Says It Discriminated against Two." January 23.

Cherlin, Andrew, Linda Burton, Judith Francis, Jane Henrici, Laura Lein, James Quane, and Karen Bogen. 2001. "Sanctions and Case Closings for Noncompliance: Who Is Affected and Why?" Baltimore, Md.: Johns Hopkins University. Welfare, Children, and Families Study, Policy Brief 01-1.

Giannarelli, Linda. 2001. Personal communication. Special run of the Welfare Rules Database August 1.

Holcomb, Pamela, and Terri Thompson. 2000. *State Welfare-to-Work Policies for People with Disabilities: Implementation Challenges and Considerations*. Washington, D.C.: U.S. Department of Health and Human Services, Office of the Assistant Secretary for Planning and Evaluation.

LaCheen, Cary. 2001. "Using Title II of the Americans with Disabilities Act on Behalf of Clients in TANF Programs." *Georgetown Journal of Poverty Law and Policy* 8 (1): 1–213.

Loprest, Pamela. 1999. *Families Who Left Welfare: Who Are They and How Are They Doing?* Washington, D.C.: The Urban Institute. *Assessing the New Federalism* Discussion Paper 99–02.

Richardson, Philip, Gregg Schoenfeld, Susan LaFever, Frances Jackson, and Mark Tecco. 2001. *Welfare Leavers and Diverters Research Study: One-Year Follow-Up of Welfare Leavers, Final Report*. McLean, Va.: MAXIMUS, Inc.

Rowe, Gretchen. 2000. "State TANF Policies as of July 1999." In *Welfare Rules Databook*. Washington D.C.: The Urban Institute. *Assessing the New Federalism*.

Rowe, Gretchen, and Linda Giannarelli. 2001. "Variations in TANF Program Rules across the States." Paper presented at the National Association of Welfare Research and Statistics annual meeting. Washington, D.C., August 2001.

Thompson, Terri, and Kelly Mikelson. 2001. *Screening and Assessment in TANF/Welfare-to-Work: Ten Important Questions TANF Agencies and Their Partners Should Consider*. Washington, D.C.: U.S. Department of Health and Human Services, Office of the Assistant Secretary for Planning and Evaluation.

Thompson, Terri, Pamela Holcomb, Pamela Loprest, and Kathleen Brennan. 1998. *State Welfare-to-Work Policies for People with Disabilities: Changes since Welfare Reform*. Washington, D.C.: U.S. Department of Health and Human Services, Office of the Assistant Secretary for Planning and Evaluation.

U.S. General Accounting Office. 2000. *Welfare Reform: State Sanction Policies and Number of Families Affected*. GAO/HEHS-00-44. Washington, D.C.: U.S. Government Printing Office.

10

Assessing Welfare Reform's Immigrant Provisions

Michael Fix and Jeffrey S. Passel

PRWORA rewrote the complex rules that govern immigrants' access to public benefits. The new rules, which take up a full title (Title IV) of the act, did more than tie cash benefits for immigrants to work. They set out a comprehensive new scheme for determining immigrant eligibility for most of the social benefits provided by federal, state, and local governments. Specifically, the new law tied citizenship more directly to the receipt of benefits, shifted new power to determine immigrant benefit eligibility from the federal government to the states, and drew a sharp distinction between immigrants arriving before and after PRWORA's enactment.

Prior to PRWORA's passage, some researchers had argued that public benefits were increasingly influencing immigrants' migration decisions, and that their availability helped explain a perceived decline in the "quality" of new immigrants (i.e., in their education, incomes, and propensity to use benefits) (Borjas and Hilton 1995). In fact, the power of the so-called "welfare magnet," the decline in immigrant quality, and even disproportionately high benefit use among immigrants were all contested in the literature (Duleep and Regets 1994; Fix and Passel 1994; Van Hook, Glick, and Bean 1999). Nonetheless, the perceived link between welfare and immigration flows drove the bill's immigrant provisions and is reflected in PRWORA's premise that "self-sufficiency has been a basic principle of United States *immigration* policies"[1] (emphasis added).

179

Political interest in restricting immigrants' access to welfare evolved in a bipartisan manner through the mid-1990s. Proposals to limit noncitizens' access to SSI[2] and other benefits originated in the Democrat-controlled House of Representatives during the Clinton administration. In due course, more far-reaching restrictions were written into the "Contract with America" (Gillespie and Schellhas 1994), the policy blueprint for the Republican Congress elected in 1994. The final version of the restrictions was drafted by a Republican Congress, and was signed into law on August 22, 1996, by a somewhat uneasy President Clinton, who, despite his goal of "ending welfare as we know it," expressed reservations about the bill's immigrant restrictions.

The political context within which PRWORA's immigrant restrictions were created should also be noted. The law was enacted during a period of anti-immigrant sentiment (following among other things, the 1993 World Trade Center bombing), one that saw the enactment of the 1996 Antiterrorism and Effective Death Penalty Act and the 1996 Illegal Immigration Reform and Immigrant Responsibility Act. Along with other provisions, these laws limited noncitizens' rights of residence and judicial appeal and the ability of undocumented immigrants to adjust to legal status.

Since 1996, attempts to scale back PRWORA's immigrant restrictions have met with mixed success, and many of the law's most far-reaching provisions remain on the books. The policies have had striking effects on benefits usage. Our analysis shows that immigrants' use of all major public benefit programs declined significantly from 1994 to 1999. These declines did not occur because immigrants had suddenly become affluent. According to our analysis, most declines are not explained by rising incomes (Fix and Passel 2001). Indeed, in 1999, half of all immigrant families were poor; low-income legal immigrants were far more likely to be uninsured than their citizen counterparts; and parents of immigrant children were more likely to be worried about having enough food than were the parents of citizen children (Capps 2001).

This chapter describes PRWORA's changes to immigrants' benefit eligibility, and highlights the changes in usage among different immigrant groups. It also examines changes in usage by program and welfare reform's effect on immigrants' decision to become naturalized citizens. Finally, the chapter reviews the proposed restorations and issues that will likely shape the debate over immigrant policy, including the extent of sponsors' responsibilities, welfare reform's impact on successfully integrating immigrant residents into society, and the states' power to decide immigrant benefits eligibility in an era of global competition.

PRWORA's Immigrant Provisions

PRWORA's immigrant provisions redefined the nation's laws governing the access of legal immigrants, refugees, and illegal immigrants to virtually all federal, state, and local benefits that are not universally available. This comprehensive overhaul departed from the piecemeal, program-by-program approach used in the past to establish immigrant eligibility.

The rationale behind PRWORA's immigrant provisions differed from the law's larger goals of discouraging out-of-wedlock births and encouraging able-bodied adults to work. These objectives had less bearing on low-income immigrants, who are more likely to live in intact families and participate in the labor force, than on native-born citizens.[3]

The immigrant provisions incorporated other goals. First, reformers aimed to discourage immigrants likely to seek public assistance from coming to the United States. Second, they wanted to shift support responsibility from the government onto immigrants' sponsors. Third, by reducing immigrant reliance on government assistance, reformers expected to realize a large new stream of cost savings. The Congressional Budget Office estimated that the immigrant restrictions would generate roughly 40 percent of welfare reform's overall savings of $54 billion—despite the fact that in 1996 immigrants represented only 15 percent of all welfare recipients in the United States.

Three Defining Lines

PRWORA drew three new "bright lines" between groups to determine eligibility. The first line divided "unqualified" and "qualified" immigrants. The unqualified group consists of undocumented immigrants, as well as some lawfully present immigrants. The law barred this group from all but a small set of federal and state benefits, such as emergency Medicaid, immunizations, diagnosis and treatment of communicable diseases, and school lunch and breakfast programs. Legal qualified immigrants were made eligible for a wide range of federal public benefits with restricted eligibility, including Social Security, Pell Grants for higher education, and the Earned Income Tax Credit.[4]

Title IV drew a second bright line between legal qualified immigrants and naturalized citizens. Unlike the more restricted eligibility rules for qualified immigrants, PRWORA allowed naturalized citizens to maintain full access to all noncontributory programs defined as "means-tested federal benefits." These programs include Temporary Assistance for Needy Families, Supplemental Security Income, Food Stamps, Medicaid, and SCHIP.

A third bright line was drawn between legal immigrants entering the United States before PRWORA and those individuals entering after. PRWORA granted states the option of extending TANF, Medicaid, and SCHIP to immigrants who had entered the country before August 22, 1996. Over time, this distinction has resulted in tougher restrictions being imposed on the rapidly growing population of legal post-enactment immigrants. Currently, about 3 million post-PRWORA immigrants are living in the United States, representing roughly one-third of all legal permanent-resident aliens.

PRWORA's new eligibility scheme largely exempted three noncitizen populations from the new restrictions: refugees (for their first five to seven years of residency in the United States), immigrants with 40 quarters of work history,[5] and noncitizens who had served in the U.S. military.

In 1997, Congress restored SSI (and the Medicaid benefits that SSI recipients automatically get) to all elderly and disabled immigrants who had been receiving SSI when PRWORA was enacted, and made all pre-enactment legal immigrants eligible to receive SSI if they became disabled in the future.[6] Later that year, Congress also extended food stamp benefits to legal immigrant children and to elderly and disabled immigrants in the United States at the time of PRWORA's signing.[7] The food stamp restoration, however, left out working-age adults, who represented roughly three-quarters of the 935,000 noncitizens who had lost benefits. Moreover, neither the food stamp nor the SSI restoration bills extended benefits to the rapidly growing population of post-enactment immigrants.

New Sponsorship Requirements

For the first time, PRWORA imposed an income requirement on individuals sponsoring new immigrants. The law now requires that the income of all immigrant sponsors—both legal immigrants and citizens—exceed 125 percent of the federal poverty threshold.[8] In addition, the law requires sponsors to sign an affidavit of support pledging to support the entrant until he or she naturalizes or works 40 quarters. Sponsors remain liable for reimbursing public agencies that provide benefits to the immigrant during this initial period. Although similar support requirements were on the books before PRWORA, they had proved legally unenforceable. The new sponsor-income requirement represents a reform to the nation's immigration policies—one intended to keep out family members of the nation's poorest citizens and legal immigrants.

Shift in Responsibility to the States

Title IV, like PRWORA as a whole, devolved broad new powers to the states. In the area of immigrant eligibility, states were granted the authority to discriminate against legal immigrants in federal and state benefit programs, a power the courts had previously denied to states. At the same time, the law authorized (but did not require) states to offer their own food, cash, and health-related benefit programs as substitutes for lost federal benefits. Finally, PRWORA required that state or local governments opting to provide benefits to undocumented immigrants pass a law establishing those immigrants' eligibility for benefits. This provision has proved to be a powerful tool in limiting undocumented immigrants' access to benefits. The federal government invoked the provision to strike down the state of New York's extension of prenatal care to undocumented mothers, and the Texas state attorney general used it to bar Houston's public hospitals from providing nonemergency services to undocumented immigrants.

To the surprise of many observers, after PRWORA almost all states extended Medicaid, SCHIP, and TANF to pre-enactment immigrants. States have been more reluctant to extend benefits to post-enactment immigrants, although the responses vary widely (Zimmermann and Tumlin 1999). The limits of state generosity are evident when the responses of the seven states with the most immigrants are examined. Together, seven large immigrant-receiving states (California, New York, Texas, Florida, Illinois, New Jersey, and Arizona) account for three-quarters of the nation's foreign-born population. California is alone among the seven in providing substitute benefits to post-enactment immigrants in the areas of health, cash assistance, and nutrition. Of the other six states, three now offer substitute health programs for post-enactment immigrants, but little else. Even the most generous states in the nation, such as Massachusetts, restrict immigrant access to substitute programs, sometimes in ways that would be illegal if applied to citizens.[9]

States' differing treatment of pre- and post-enactment immigrants reflects the fiscal incentives built into PRWORA. Under current law, the federal government agrees to share expenditures on pre-enactment immigrants' use of TANF, Medicaid, and SCHIP. Expenditures on legal, post-enactment immigrants must be fully financed with state tax dollars. The patchwork of state responses to PRWORA that has evolved under this financing scheme has meant that noncitizens face wider variation, state by state, in their access to safety net services than citizens.

Court Challenges

PRWORA's immigrant restrictions have withstood numerous legal challenges in the federal courts, where they have been viewed as coming within Congress's far-reaching plenary powers to set immigration policy. Legal challenges at the state court level have produced more mixed results. A New York court has ruled that PRWORA does not authorize the state to bar post-enactment immigrants from the state-funded Medicaid program. Like their federal counterparts, however, most state courts have generally upheld PRWORA.

Benefit Usage following PRWORA

PRWORA has succeeded in reducing immigrants' overall use of public benefits. Several early studies found that noncitizen use of public benefits declined at a faster rate than citizens'. Zimmermann and Fix (1998) documented differential declines in welfare use for Los Angeles County; Fix and Passel (1999), using aggregate national data from the Current Population Survey (CPS), also detected greater declines for noncitizens in use of welfare and food stamps. Subsequent studies, most notably by the Department of Agriculture, confirmed these results, finding that food stamp use among noncitizens fell 72 percent between 1994 and 1998 (Genser 1998).

Shifts in eligibility cannot account for these declines, because most noncitizens in the studies had arrived before 1996 and had retained their eligibility to participate in the programs in question. Rising incomes also fail to explain the degree of change. We have contended that the greater drops in usage among noncitizens are attributable, in part, to welfare reform discouraging some immigrants from using benefits regardless of eligibility. These "chilling effects" likely reflect confusion among immigrants about who is eligible for benefits and fears about the legal consequences of seeking assistance.[10]

Usage Patterns: Five Years Later

Building on research conducted by the Urban Institute over the past decade, this chapter examines patterns in immigrant benefit usage using the Census Bureau's March CPS Supplements for 1995 through 2000.[11] The broad patterns found in the early studies cited above are still apparent. Among all families with one or more adults who are legal permanent-resident aliens (hereafter referred to simply as legal permanent residents or legal noncitizens), there was a notable decline in usage of TANF, SSI, food stamps, and Medicaid between 1994 and 1999.[12] The sharpest decrease occurred in TANF use, with legal noncitizens' participation rate falling from 4.9 percent in 1994 to 2.0 percent in 1999, or 60 percent.[13] The drop in Medicaid usage was the least dramatic, at 15 percent (figure 10-1). Further, the overall declines in participation rates for legal noncitizen families exceeded the declines experienced by citizen families for TANF, SSI, and food stamps, but not Medicaid.

These overall program participation rates, changes in usage over time, and differences in access patterns across groups reflect a number of factors, including poverty rates, family composition (e.g., presence of children or a single head of household), and geographic distribution. To control for some of these factors, most of these analyses focus on families with children whose incomes are below 200 percent of the federal poverty level, comparing usage patterns of low-income legal noncitizen families with those of low-income citizen families. These families have substantial practical and policy import where welfare policy is concerned, since they are the ones most likely to need and to be eligible for public assistance. To unmask differences in usage within the foreign-born population, program participation among refugees, naturalized citizens, and undocumented immigrants is also examined.[14] For Medicaid, this analysis is expanded to focus on individuals, in addition to families.

Differences in participation declines between low-income immigrant and citizen families with children may be less dramatic now than in the

Figure 10-1. *Participation in Means-Tested Benefit Programs among Legal Permanent-Resident Alien Families, 1994 and 1999*

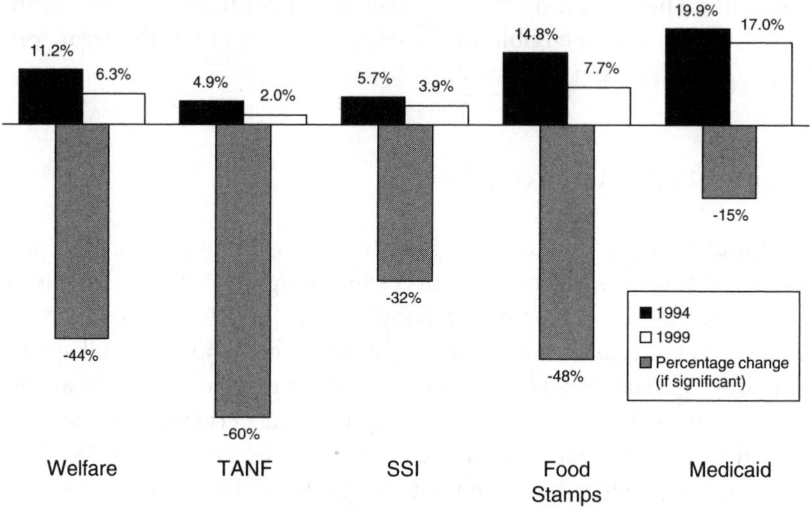

Source: Urban Institute tabulations from March 1995 and 2000 Current Population Surveys, with immigration status imputed with methods based on Passel and Clark (1998).
Note: Welfare encompasses TANF, SSI, and General Assistance.

year immediately following passage of PRWORA. Although this analysis does not provide a definitive reason, actions taken by the federal government in 1999 to lessen the apparent confusion among both providers and beneficiaries may explain the new usage pattern.[15]

At the same time that new federal policies were going into effect, governments at all levels were expanding their outreach under the new SCHIP program to boost enrollment in immigrant and other communities. These two sets of policies may have altered immigrants' trends in benefit use—particularly in the area of health insurance.

Low-Income Families with Children

Families with children with incomes below 200 percent of the federal poverty level experienced large declines in TANF and food stamp use between 1994 and 1999, with legal noncitizen families' use of TANF falling 53 percent, from 18.7 to 8.7 percent, and food stamp usage dropping 38 percent, from 35.1 to 21.9 percent (figure 10-2). Participation in Medicaid—

Figure 10-2. *Participation in Means-Tested Benefit Programs among Low-Income Legal Permanent-Resident Alien Families with Children, 1994 and 1999*

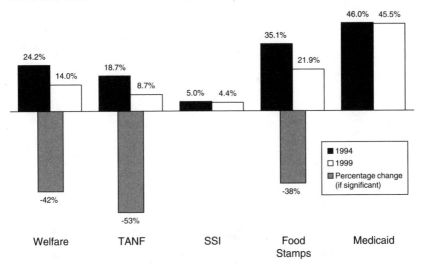

Source: Urban Institute tabulations from March 1995 and 2000 Current Population Surveys, with immigration status imputed with methods based on Passel and Clark (1998).

Note: Welfare encompasses TANF, SSI, and General Assistance. Low-income is defined as family income, excluding welfare income, below 200 percent of federal poverty guidelines.

46.0 percent in 1994 and 45.5 percent in 1999—was statistically unchanged for legal noncitizen families.

Declines for these low-income legal immigrant families with children were not significantly different from those experienced by similarly situated citizen families. Thus, the steep early declines that characterized the immigrant population are now evident for noncitizens and citizens alike (figure 10-3). Although the two groups have now seen comparable drops in usage, program participation rates for low-income legal noncitizen families remain substantially lower than citizens' rates for TANF, SSI, and food stamps; for Medicaid, the two groups do not differ statistically.[16]

Mixed-Status Families

PRWORA not only reduced benefit use among the noncitizens targeted by reform, it also reduced participation among the U.S.-citizen children who live in immigrant families. The U.S.-citizen children of immigrants are a

Figure 10-3. *Participation in Means-Tested Benefit Programs for Low-Income Legal Permanent-Resident Alien and Citizen Families with Children, 1994 and 1999*

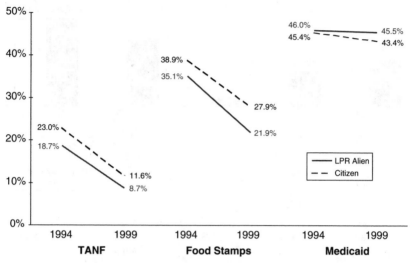

Source: Urban Institute tabulations from March 1995 and 2000 Current Population Surveys, with immigration status imputed with methods based on Passel and Clark (1998).

Note: Low-income is defined as family income, excluding welfare income, below 200 percent of federal poverty guidelines.

LPR = legal permanent resident.

demographically important group. About 1 in 10 American children live in a household where one or more of the parents is a noncitizen and one or more of the children is a citizen (Fix and Passel 1999); about three-quarters of all children living in immigrant-headed households are U.S. citizens (Fix and Zimmermann 2001). By law, children born in the United States to immigrant parents (even undocumented immigrants) qualify for public benefits on the same terms as children of native-born citizens. Yet this analysis shows that U.S.-born children of immigrants are much less likely than children of native-born citizens to participate in public benefits programs.

Among low-income immigrant[17] families with children who are U.S. citizens, 7.8 percent received TANF benefits in 1999, compared with 11.6 percent of low-income citizen families with children. Similarly, these immigrant families were considerably less likely than citizen families to receive food stamps—19.8 percent versus 27.9 percent. For both programs, participation of mixed-status families declined significantly from 1994 to 1999, with drops that were as steep as those for families of noncitizens. Medicaid, again, is an exception: Mixed-status, low-income families did not experience usage declines, and their participation was essentially equal to that of citizen families (42.7 percent versus 43.4 percent in 1999).

Refugee Families

Sharp declines in the use of public benefits were also apparent among low-income refugee families.[18] Usage decreased dramatically between 1994 and 1999: Food stamp use fell 53 percent for low-income refugee families with children; TANF participation dropped 78 percent; and Medicaid usage dropped 36 percent. Before PRWORA, participation rates for low-income refugee families with children were much higher than the rates for either citizens or legal permanent-resident families. For some programs, refugee participation rates were more than double those for legal permanent-resident families. By 1999, the rates for refugee families had fallen to roughly the same level as those of citizens for TANF, food stamps, and Medicaid. These results are especially striking because refugees are exempt from PRWORA's immigrant restrictions for their first five to seven years of residency in the United States.

TANF Caseloads and the Recipient Population

In addition to changes in usage rates, both the number and the distribution of families remaining on TANF is important. These remaining families may prove to be difficult to move off TANF, especially if they face barriers to work, such as limited English-language ability or low educational levels (Zimmermann and Tumlin 1999).

According to CPS data, the total number of families receiving TANF benefits shrank 55 percent, from 4.0 million to 1.8 million, between 1994 and 1999 (table 10-1). Legal permanent-resident families receiving TANF fell by 216,000, or 62 percent, and refugee recipients fell by 97,000 families, or 76 percent. At the same time, the number of naturalized citizen families participating in TANF increased by 24,000, or 45 percent. The number of participating undocumented families was essentially unchanged.

Table 10-1. *Number of Families Receiving TANF, by Citizenship of Head and Spouse, 1994 and 1999*

| | Families | | | Distribution (%) | | | |
| | | | | All Families | | Foreign-Born | |
Status of Family Head/Spouse	1994 (in Thousands)	1999 (in Thousands)	Change (%)	1994	1999	1994	1999
Citizen	3,502	1,607	-54	87	88	N/A	N/A
U.S.-born	3,450	1,531	-56	85	83	N/A	N/A
Naturalized	52	76	45	1	4	9	25
Noncitizen	411	197	-52	10	11	70	65
Legal	347	132	-62	9	7	59	43
Undocumented	63	66	4	2	4	11	22
Refugee alien	127	30	-76	3	2	21	10
Total	4,041	1,835	-55	100	100	100	100

Source: Urban Institute tabulations from March 1995 and 2000 Current Population Surveys, with immigration status imputed with methods based on Passel and Clark (1998).

Note: "Refugee alien" represents persons admitted as refugees since 1980 and who have not become naturalized citizens, regardless of current status. "Legal" includes all persons who are not citizens and who were admitted as legal permanent residents (LPR), except those admitted as refugees. "Legal nonimmigrants" or "legal temporary residents" are persons with valid entry visas who are considered U.S. residents, such as foreign students, intracompany transfers, or H-1 B "hi-tech" guest workers; to the extent that such persons are in the CPS, they appear in the totals but are not shown separately.

N/A = not applicable.

As a result of these shifts, the composition of the immigrant population remaining on TANF has been substantially altered since welfare reform. In 1994, naturalized citizens accounted for 9 percent of foreign-born recipient families, compared with 25 percent in 1999 (table 10-1). The share of immigrant TANF recipients in legal permanent-resident and refugee alien families dropped from 80 percent to 53 percent. As a share of *all* recipient families, these two groups dropped from 12 percent to 9 percent. PRWORA appears to have succeeded in reducing both the number of legal immigrants on welfare and their share of the recipient population.

Shifts in the composition of immigrant TANF recipients reflect both underlying changes in the immigrant population and changes in usage rates. It is particularly noteworthy that the reductions in immigrant recipients occurred even among immigrant populations whose numbers were increasing significantly. Overall, the foreign-born population grew 16 percent—from 24.5 million in the 1995 CPS to 28.4 million in the 2000 CPS[19]—but the growth differed substantially across categories of legal status. The number of naturalized citizen families increased by 28 percent, from 5.2 million to 6.7 million, and represents over one-third of all immigrant families.

Medicaid Use and Health Insurance

Changes in Medicaid and SCHIP[20] participation follow quite different trajectories from other programs. Overall decreases in family Medicaid/SCHIP participation were smaller than for the other programs. More-over, among low-income families with children, Medicaid usage between 1994 and 1999 hardly changed for either citizens or legal permanent-resident aliens. In addition, Medicaid/SCHIP usage among low-income legal permanent-resident and refugee families with children was virtually identical to the rates for citizen families.

The relatively stable level of Medicaid/SCHIP across groups and over time suggests that different attitudes and practices prevail in these programs. For health care, expanded services for immigrants in many states and SCHIP's provision of insurance for children have kept participation rates high. Moreover, in the case of Medicaid, the providers (doctors, hospitals, and clinics) have incentives to keep both immigrants and native-born citizens enrolled.

Individual Medicaid Participation and Lack of Health Insurance

The benefit extended by the Medicaid/SCHIP program—health insurance—is qualitatively different from the benefits provided by TANF, SSI, and food stamps. Health insurance can be used only by the individual beneficiary; cash and food stamps are fungible and can provide a benefit for the whole family. Thus, this Medicaid/SCHIP analysis focuses on individuals, examining use patterns among low-income working-age individuals (18 to 64 years old) and children (under 18 years) to get a clearer picture of welfare reform's overall effect on immigrants' benefit usage.

Among these low-income working-age individuals, Medicaid use declined significantly for both citizens and noncitizens between 1994 and 1999: from 18.4 to 16.9 percent for citizens; from 20.3 to 15.6 percent for legal permanent-resident aliens; and from 51.3 to 21.5 percent for refugee aliens (table 10-2). Unlike the pattern found for families, the decreases in Medicaid use among low-income legal permanent resident and refugee adults of working age were greater than those for citizens.

These Medicaid declines did not result from former recipients acquiring other forms of health insurance. In fact, the share of working-age adults without health insurance increased by 1.1 percentage points for citizens; 4.5 percentage points for legal permanent residents; and 16.2 percentage points for refugees. Furthermore, despite high rates of Medicaid participation among immigrants, low-income, working-age adult immigrants were more likely to be uninsured in 1999 than were U.S. citizens. Among U.S. citizens, 31.6 percent of working-age adults were uninsured in 1999, compared with 56.3 percent of legal permanent residents, 68.0 percent of undocumented immigrants, and 44.6 percent of refugees.

Children in low-income families have much higher rates of Medicaid participation than low-income, working-age adults. Forty-two percent of children in low-income U.S. citizen families participated in Medicaid in 1999, down slightly from 43 percent in 1994 (table 10-2). Children in low-income, legal permanent-resident families showed no significant decrease from 1994 to 1999, participating at about the same level as children in citizen families, regardless of their own citizenship status (45.2 percent for U.S. citizen children of noncitizens and 41.6 percent for noncitizen children). Children of refugees, however, experienced a large decrease in Medicaid participation over the period, falling from 69 percent in 1994, well above the children of citizens, to 39 percent in 1999, or about the same level as citizens.

Table 10-2. *Percentage Participating in Medicaid for Low-Income Adults and Children, by Nativity and Legal Status, 1994 and 1999*

Category	1994	1999	Percent Decrease (If Significant)
Adults			
Citizens	18.4	16.9	−8
Legal permanent residents	20.3	15.6	−23
Undocumented immigrants	7.9	6.6	—
Refugees	51.3	21.5	−58
Children			
Citizen parents	43.3	42.1	−3
Legal permanent-resident parents			
Citizen children	47.4	45.2	—
Noncitizen children	40.6	41.6	—
Undocumented parents			
Citizen children	38.4	38.4	—
Noncitizen children	19.3	13.8	−28
Refugee parents	68.5	39.1	−43

Source: Urban Institute tabulations from March 1995 and 2000 Current Population Surveys, with immigration status imputed with methods based on Passel and Clark (1998).

Note: "Refugees" refers to persons admitted as refugees since 1980 who have not become natural-ized citizens, regardless of current status. "Legal permanent residents" includes all persons who are not citizens and who were admitted as legal permanent residents, except those admitted as refugees.

Not surprisingly, given the steady levels of Medicaid participation among children, uninsurance rates for low-income children changed lit-tle between 1994 and 1999. Still, the uninsurance levels are much higher for children of immigrants than for children of native-born citizens. Less than 20 percent of low-income children of U.S. citizens were uninsured in 1994 and 1999 (figure 10-4). In 1999, the citizen children of legal per-manent residents had uninsurance rates of 27.4 percent, while rates for the noncitizen children of legal immigrants were 38.7 percent.

State-Level Differences in Immigrant Benefit Use and the "Welfare Magnet"

The large declines in program use among legal immigrants and refugees occurred in virtually all parts of the country. TANF participation by low-

Figure 10-4. *Percentage of Low-Income Children (under 18) without Health Insurance, by Status of Parents and Children, 1999*

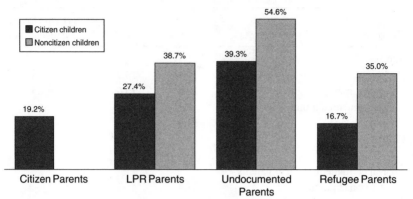

Source: Urban Institute tabulations from March 2000 Current Population Surveys, with immigration status imputed with methods based on Passel and Clark (1998).

Note: Low-income is defined as family income, excluding welfare income, below 200 percent of federal poverty guidelines.

LPR = legal permanent resident.

income, legal permanent-resident families with children dropped 73 percent in states identified by Urban Institute researchers as among the least generous in providing benefits to immigrants,[21] compared with a 45 percent decline in the other, more generous states. The larger drop occurred even though the 1994 TANF participation rate in the least generous states was only about half the initial rate in the most generous states—11.5 percent versus 23.1 percent. Thus, differences in immigrant benefit participation levels widened across states following welfare reform.

While rates of benefits use in these least generous states were declining sharply, their foreign-born populations were growing rapidly. Throughout the United States, the number of foreign-born families with children rose 15 percent between 1995 and 2000.[22] In the least generous states, the number of such families increased 31 percent, compared with a 7 percent increase in the relatively generous states. In California, a state offering one of the most generous packages of public benefits to legal immigrants, the number of foreign-born families grew only 2 percent from 1995 to 2000.

These differential growth patterns reflect two demographic trends. First, a greater number of immigrant families moved out of the most generous states into the least generous states. Second, the percentage of immigrants from abroad settling in the least generous states increased during the late 1990s, despite those states' more limited generosity. (See Passel and Zimmermann [2001] for an examination of these migration patterns.) These eligibility and migration trends call into question the theory underlying PRWORA's Title IV, that welfare benefits play a large role in determining where immigrants choose to live. The new settlement patterns raise concerns about the potential effects a recession and a tightening labor market could have on noncitizen families, many of whom may find themselves excluded from increasingly localized safety nets.

Naturalization Rates and Benefits Use

Because PRWORA made citizenship more central to benefit eligibility, it would be logical to expect an increase in the number of naturalized families receiving public assistance. While this analysis does reveal a rise in both the number and share of naturalized citizens receiving benefits, it also reveals that only a fraction of immigrants who naturalized after PRWORA sought benefits.

Between 1994 and 1999, the number of naturalized citizen families in the United States rose rapidly, in large part because the 2.7 million immigrants who acquired legal immigrant status under the 1986 Immigration Reform and Control Act became eligible for citizenship. New policies, including California's Proposition 187 (which barred illegal immigrants from public schools and other public benefits), and new limits on noncitizens' procedural rights incorporated in the 1996 illegal immigration reform law, as well as welfare reform's immigration restrictions, also drove increased naturalization.

The rise in naturalizations was accompanied by expanded use of some benefits by naturalized citizen families. For SSI, the number of naturalized citizen families receiving benefits increased from 133,000 in 1994 to 298,000 in 1999. The proportion of naturalized citizen families receiving SSI increased 75 percent (from 2.5 percent to 4.5 percent). The proportion receiving Medicaid increased a more modest 28 percent (from 8.1 percent to 10.4 percent). Naturalized citizens' participation rates in TANF and the food stamp program, however, did not register a statistically significant change.

Within the TANF program, naturalization apparently played only a minor role in decreased usage among legal immigrants. Although 480,000 families with children became naturalized between 1994 and 1999, the number of such families participating in TANF rose by only 16,000.[23] In contrast, the number of legal immigrant families with children receiving TANF dropped by 480,000.[24]

Although the benefit usage of naturalized citizen families has increased, the share of the total naturalized population receiving benefits remains relatively modest. Moreover, the increase in usage among naturalized citizen families offsets only a fraction of the reduced usage among legal noncitizens. CPS data show that while the number of families containing a naturalized citizen grew by 1.5 million between 1994 and 1999, the number of such families participating in welfare rose by only 170,000.

Similar patterns were evident in California, where naturalizations increased particularly sharply. The CPS data show that the number of California families with a naturalized citizen adult rose by more than 60 percent (from 1.2 million to 1.9 million) from 1994 to 1999—more than three times the national rate. Participation rates among California's naturalized citizen families were not significantly different in 1999 than in 1994. Moreover, the increase in naturalized citizen families receiving welfare (72,000) is much smaller than the declines in legal noncitizen families' participation (238,000).

These trends in California and the United States suggest that, while an interest in retaining access to public benefits may have played a role in some naturalizations, their dramatic increase was not broadly driven by the goal of retaining benefits. Moreover, the results indicate that increased naturalization rates did not vitiate the substantial declines in immigrants' benefit use that occurred in the wake of PRWORA, as some commentators have claimed (Borjas 2001).

Policy Implications

Welfare reform's devolution of immigrant policy to the states has led to a widening divide across states in both the generosity of benefits and immigrants' participation levels in safety net programs. The new divisions emerge at a time of rapid migration to states with the least, rather than the most, generous safety nets. These migration patterns raise doubts about the continuing power of the welfare magnet—the theory on which PRWORA's immigrant restrictions were at least partially based, and upon which they have been defended in the courts as elements of the nation's *immigration,* not *welfare,* policies. The patterns also raise concerns that many immigrants will find themselves in places with extremely porous local safety nets during an economic downturn.

If the upcoming reauthorization of welfare reform directly addresses the law's impacts on immigrant populations, it seems likely that the debate will begin by revisiting the restoration of benefits to both pre- and post-enactment immigrants. Proposals that continue to await action include the following:

Restoring food stamps to working-age adults who were in the United States at the time of the law's enactment and to the families of post-enactment immigrants. Legal working-age immigrants who entered the United States before PRWORA remain barred from receiving food stamps. These individuals had no notice of the exclusion when they became legal permanent residents. As a result of the restrictions, immigrant use of food stamps has declined dramatically. Our analyses indicate that increases in income generally cannot account for these declines (Fix and Passel 2001). The effects of this restriction, as with other benefit programs, have been felt by refugees and by citizen children—populations largely protected by the law. The restrictions remain in place despite comparatively high levels of food-related disadvantage among the children of immigrants.

Granting states authorization to provide post-enactment immigrants with Medicaid and SCHIP, as states are permitted to do for pre-enactment immigrants. Welfare reform's restrictions on Medicaid and SCHIP represented a particularly sharp departure from previous policy. Unlike other means-tested federal programs, Medicaid was extended to eligible legal immigrants from the date of their receipt of legal status, whereas food stamps, TANF, and SSI were deemed for three to five years, essentially requiring immigrants to wait that long after admission to receive benefits. Individual-level analysis of immigrants' use of Medicaid benefits in the wake of welfare reform indicates that noncitizens' use declined faster than citizens', and that noncitizen use rates in 1999 were lower than citizens'. We also find that immigrants who left Medicaid did not do so because they found private insurance. Rather, they became uninsured once they lost coverage.

Again, these developments raise important safety-net concerns for vulnerable immigrant populations. According to the NSAF, 22 percent of immigrants' children are uninsured, versus 10 percent of native children (Capps 2001). The impact of uninsurance on children, including fewer doctor visits and greater use of high-cost emergency health care, can lead to long-term health problems for individuals and greater burdens for communities.

Making immigrants who entered the United States after 1996 eligible to receive SSI, in the event that they become disabled after entry. Proponents of expanded SSI eligibility argue that individuals whose disabling conditions were clearly unanticipated at the time of entry, and who will likely find it difficult to naturalize, should be granted SSI eligibility. Proposals advanced at the close of the Clinton administration would have extended SSI benefits to post-enactment immigrants who had lived in the United States for five years.

Each of these proposals raises fundamental policy design issues. One is the merits of using citizenship rather than legal residence to qualify for public benefits.[25] It could be argued that legal immigrants, like citizens, are compelled to pay taxes, serve in the military in dangerous times, must obey all laws, and are subject to the vicissitudes of the market. Making safety net and work-support services contingent on naturalization creates incentives to naturalize that depart from loyalty and other nation-building goals. Further, to the extent that benefit restrictions are intended to affect the flow of incoming legal immigrants, it is arguably more efficient to introduce the desired criteria directly into admissions standards.

Second, proposals to restore benefits to noncitizen families raise the important, if difficult, issue of how immigrant support obligations should be shared between sponsors and the government. The current system shifts the full burden onto sponsors. This shift raises two issues: whether sponsorship should be limited to a specific number of years, and whether sponsor deeming should be extended beyond cash transfer programs to health insurance. With regard to the former, it could be argued that current law effectively extends the sponsor's support obligation until citizenship, creating a potentially open-ended liability for the sponsor. With regard to the second issue, it should be noted that Australia and Britain introduced new sponsor deeming requirements at the same time as the United States, but excluded health insurance from sponsor obligations (Fix and Laglagaron 2001).

Third, welfare reform has gone some distance toward remaking the welfare system into an engine of mobility rather than an agent of dependence. Yet working, low-income noncitizens are excluded, both from the safety net and from such work supports as health insurance, job training, and transportation subsidies. The successful adaptation of immigrants and the integration of immigrants and their children into American society are cherished American ideals and, arguably, are or should be the goals of immigrant and immigration policy. The exclusion of legal immigrant families from the reformed welfare system runs directly counter to this desired outcome.

NOTES

The authors would like to acknowledge the expert research assistance of Chris Henrichson and the support of the Ford Foundation.

1. 8 U.S.C. Section 1601(1) (Supp. V 1999).

2. The proposal was to extend the deeming period, during which a sponsor's income is ascribed to the immigrant, from three to five years.

3. Among immigrants, 65 percent of low-income families with children were two-parent families in the 1996 CPS, versus only 40 percent of native-born families. About 80 percent of working-age immigrant males in low-income families were in the labor force, versus less than 70 percent of working-age males in native-born families.

4. Federal public benefits include any retirement, welfare, health, disability, public or assisted housing, post-secondary education, food assistance, unemployment, or any similar benefits under which payment or assistance is provided to an individual, household, or family eligibility unit by an agency of the United States using appropriated funds of the United States (PL 104-193, Section 401c).

5. Benefit claimants must be able to prove that they, their spouses, or their parents have collectively worked 40 quarters (10 years) in the United States.

6. The Balanced Budget Act of 1997, PL 105-33.

7. The Agriculture, Research, Extension and Education Reform Act, PL 105-185 (1998).

8. The poverty guidelines are defined, in part, on the basis of family size. For assessing the sponsorship criteria, the guideline is based on the numbers of adults and children in the *combined* families of the sponsored immigrant and the sponsor, thus increasing the sponsor's required amount of income.

9. The new conditions include deeming and residency requirements, shorter time limits for receipt, and mandates that claimants pursue naturalization.

10. By this definition, "chilling effects" simply connotes steep benefit declines among an eligible population that cannot be explained by income gains.

11. Compared with administrative data on caseloads, the March supplements to the Current Population Survey understate usage. Further, coverage appears to have deteriorated somewhat in recent years (Wheaton and Giannarelli 2000). Nonetheless, the CPS data track overall trends in participation fairly well (O'Neill and Hill 2001). In general, our work compares usage among immigrants with that of native-born citizens, so that only differential changes in coverage would affect our conclusions. Work on participation of immigrants in the CPS suggests that this group is much *better* covered in the March 2000 CPS than in earlier years (Passel 2001b). Consequently, CPS undercoverage of program participation should not affect the conclusions we reach based on CPS analyses of immigrant-native trends and differentials.

12. The Current Population Survey reports population numbers for the year of the survey, but asks about benefit use for the year preceding the survey. Hence, the population and participation figures are for different years.

13. We use the terms "participation rate," "usage rate," and "use rate" interchangeably to describe the number of program participants divided by the population at issue. The terms are not meant to denote eligibility.

14. The analyses employ Urban Institute–generated data sets that correct for overreporting of naturalized citizens and identify four groups of noncitizens: refugee entrants, based on country of birth and year of entry; legal nonimmigrants (i.e., temporary residents), based on occupation, year of entry, and other characteristics; likely undocumented immigrants, based on occupation, country of birth, year of entry, age, and state; and legal permanent residents. (See Passel and Clark 1998 for a description of the assignment methods.) Families are classified according to the head and spouse (if present) as undocumented, refugee alien, legal permanent-resident alien, naturalized citizen, native, and legal nonimmigrant. All data from the March 1995 CPS use weights that have been corrected for errors in the original weights.

15. For the first time, the federal government released guidance clarifying how noncitizen use of public benefits affects the definition of becoming a "public charge" (i.e., an immigrant who is dependent on public benefits and is therefore ineligible to receive a green card). According to the published guidance, public charge issues would not be taken into account when noncitizens apply to naturalize, and would rarely be grounds for deportation. The guidance also established that, in general, only long-term dependence on cash assistance would raise public charge issues; the receipt of food stamps, Medicaid, or SCHIP would not. Further, use of benefits by the green card applicant's family members would not raise public charge issues. (See 8 CFR Parts 212, 237, P.28676 [1999].)

16. For individuals, however, Medicaid participation rates declined more for *individual* noncitizens than for citizens. See *Individual Medicaid Participation and Lack of Health Insurance* (in this chapter) for further discussion.

17. We include here legal permanent resident aliens and undocumented aliens because the parental status does not affect eligibility of their U.S.-born children.

18. We use the term "refugees" to refer to noncitizens who were admitted as refugees (in 1980 or later), without regard to their current immigration status or eligibility status. Almost all of the refugees adjust their legal status to legal permanent-resident alien after one or two years in the country; however, they retain their special access to benefits for five to seven years.

19. The results of the 2000 Census have created considerable uncertainty about the size of the foreign-born population and, more specifically, the undocumented immigrant population. The March 2000 CPS, which shows 28.4 million immigrants, is based on the 1990 Census. The total population from the 2000 Census, 281.4 million, exceeded pre-Census estimates by 5 to 7 million, with much of the excess thought to be unmeasured immigration (Passel 2001a). When the March 2000 CPS is reweighted to agree with the results of the 2000 Census, the reported foreign-born population is 30.1 million. The Census 2000 Supplementary Survey, administered in 2000 with a sample size 14 times larger than the March 2000 CPS, showed an even larger foreign-born population, 30.5 million people. Almost all of the difference in the various measures of the foreign-born population

can be attributed to the number of undocumented immigrants estimated to be represented in the different surveys (Passel 2001b).

20. The CPS data on Medicaid are based mainly on individual responses to questions on health insurance, but also include imputations based on other items (e.g., TANF recipients are assigned to Medicaid). In part because of the data collection methods, the CPS groups Medicaid, emergency Medicaid, state Medicaid-like programs and supplemental programs, and SCHIP together. The data reported in the paper thus cover Medicaid, emergency Medicaid, and SCHIP.

21. Zimmerman and Tumlin (1999), in their analysis of state policies determining immigrant eligibility for public benefits, group the 50 states into four categories: those where benefits are "most available," "somewhat available," "less available," and "least available." For our purposes, the least generous states are those that fall into the "less available" and "least available" categories; the most generous states are those where benefits are "most available" or "somewhat available."

22. The program participation rates are based on information collected for the year prior to the CPS, but the population figures are for the year the data were actually collected.

23. An alternative assumption might be that the use rate among naturalized citizen families decreased at the same rate as that among native-born or noncitizen families. Compared with this alternative, the "additional" participation by naturalized citizen families in 1999 would be 40,000—still well below the drop in TANF participation among legal noncitizen families.

24. Because the naturalized citizen population includes both refugee and legal permanent-resident entrants, the legal noncitizen population for the comparisons here combines the two groups.

25. A recent Urban Institute study of eight industrialized countries reveals that only Austria and the United States made benefits conditional on citizenship (Fix and Laglagaron 2001).

REFERENCES

Borjas, George J. 2001. "Welfare Reform and Immigration." In *The New World of Welfare*, edited by Rebecca Blank and Ron Haskins. Washington, D.C.: Brookings Institution Press.

Borjas, George J., and Lynette Hilton. 1995. *Immigration and the Welfare State: Immigrant Participation in Means Tested Entitlement Programs*. Cambridge, Mass.: National Bureau of Economic Research.

Capps, Randy. 2001. "Hardship among Children of Immigrants: Findings from the 1999 National Survey of America's Families." Washington, D.C.: The Urban Institute. *Assessing the New Federalism* Policy Brief B-29.

Duleep, Harriet Orcutt, and Mark Regets. 1994. *The Elusive Concept of Immigrant Quality*. Washington, D.C.: The Urban Institute. Discussion Paper PRIP-UI-28, Program for Research on Immigration Policy.

Fix, Michael, and Laureen Laglagaron. 2001. "Report of the Working Group on Social Rights and Citizenship." In *Citizenship Policies for an Age of Migration*, edited by

T. Alexander Alienikoff and Douglas Klusmeyer. Washington, D.C.: The Carnegie Endowment for International Peace.

Fix, Michael, and Jeffrey S. Passel. 1994. *Immigration and Immigrants: Setting the Record Straight.* Washington, D.C.: Urban Institute Press.

———. 1999. "Trends in Citizens' and Noncitizens' Use of Public Benefits Following Welfare Reform, 1994–1997." Washington, D.C.: The Urban Institute.

———. 2001. "The Scope and Impact of Welfare Reform's Immigrant Provisions." Washington, D.C.: The Urban Institute.

Fix, Michael, and Wendy Zimmermann. 2001. "All Under One Roof: Mixed-Status Families in an Era of Reform." *International Migration Review* 35 (134, Summer).

Genser, Jenny. 1998. "Who Is Leaving the Food Stamp Program: An Analysis of Caseload Changes from 1994 to 1997." Washington, D.C.: Office of Analysis, Nutrition and Evaluation, Food and Nutrition Service, U.S. Department of Agriculture.

Gillespie, Ed, and Bob Schellhas. 1994. *Contract with America.* New York: Random House.

O'Neill, June E., and M. Anne Hill. 2001. "Gaining Ground? Measuring the Impact of Welfare Reform on Welfare and Work." New York: Center for Civic Innovation, Manhattan Institute for Policy Research. Civic Report No. 17.

Passel, Jeffrey S. 2001a. "An Evaluation of Demographic Analysis in Census 2000." In *Final Report of the Census 2000 Monitoring Board, Presidential Members.* Washington, D.C.

———. 2001b. "Estimates of Undocumented Immigrants Living in the United States." Washington, D.C.: The Urban Institute.

Passel, Jeffrey S., and Rebecca L. Clark. 1998. "Immigrants in New York: Their Legal Status, Incomes, and Taxes." Washington, D.C.: The Urban Institute.

Passel, Jeffrey S., and Wendy Zimmermann. 2001. "Are Immigrants Leaving California? Settlement Patterns of Immigrants in the Late 1990s." Washington, D.C.: The Urban Institute.

Van Hook, Jennifer, Jennifer E. Glick, and Frank D. Bean. 1999. "Public Assistance Receipt among Immigrants and Natives: How the Unit of Analysis Affects Research Findings." *Demography* 36(1): 111–20.

Wheaton, Laura, and Linda Giannarelli. 2000. "Coverage of Social Benefit Programs in the Current Population Survey." Paper presented at the annual meeting of the American Statistical Association.

Zimmermann, Wendy, and Michael Fix. 1998. "Declining Immigrant Applications for Medi-Cal and Welfare Benefits in Los Angeles County." Washington, D.C.: The Urban Institute.

Zimmermann, Wendy, and Karen C. Tumlin. 1999. *Patchwork Policies: State Assistance for Immigrants under Welfare Reform.* Washington, D.C.: The Urban Institute. *Assessing the New Federalism* Occasional Paper No. 24.

11

Race, Ethnicity, and Welfare Reform

Kenneth Finegold and Sarah Staveteig

Any change in policy—particularly one as sweeping as welfare reform—is likely to affect various groups of the population differently. While welfare recipients may be grouped by any number of characteristics, race and ethnicity warrant particular attention because of their central role in the historical development of social policy in the United States (Quadagno 1994). Recent evidence (Gilens 1999; Soss et al. 2001) indicates that race and ethnicity continue to be significant factors in social policy.

This chapter focuses on the disparate effects of welfare reform on racial and ethnic groups. It examines evidence of these differences from several perspectives, discusses possible reasons for them, and lays out the policy implications of the findings. These disparities do not necessarily indicate intentional discrimination, but the data presented here suggest that welfare policies and practices deserve further examination.

Gauging differential effects of welfare reform is important for several reasons. First, TANF's stated objective is to change behavior—specifically, to move people into jobs, encourage marriage, and reduce births to unmarried women—and it presumes that people will respond to policy changes in certain ways. However, responses may vary among racial and ethnic groups because of differences in quality or amount of education, community and family resources, or language. Responses may also differ depending on welfare recipients' attitudes toward government, work, and marriage, and on the attitudes of employers and welfare office personnel toward various types of recipients.

Second, an assistance policy that supports blacks or Hispanics less well than whites, regardless of the reasons, will not meet the needs of a large segment of the welfare population, greatly reducing the effectiveness of welfare reform.

Third, examination of disparities may point to the need for additional policies or programs to achieve the law's objectives. For example, Hispanics who leave welfare for work are more likely than their white counterparts to have jobs that do not offer health insurance. This suggests that other sources of coverage are necessary to support Hispanics as they move to work.

Fourth, along with their responsibility for moving welfare recipients into jobs, states have been granted authority to determine support policies, services, and exemptions. In turn, many states have delegated responsibility and authority to localities and caseworkers. Thus, by increasing discretion, welfare reform has also increased the potential that policies and practices will reflect regional or individual biases against specific groups of applicants and recipients.

Existing Evidence and Its Limitations

Evidence of racial and ethnic disparities in the effects of welfare reform is limited. Many of the most provocative findings apply to a particular state or locality or are based on nonrandom samples (see Gordon 2001; Bell and Strege-Flora 2000; Gooden 1998); nevertheless, these studies suggest hypotheses that deserve further testing. Even national surveys based on random samples can pose problems, because race and ethnicity are intertwined with geographic patterns of residence and with differences in education, family structure, income, and well-being, making it difficult to isolate the impact of race and ethnicity per se.

Despite using relatively large samples, broad population surveys are also unable to detect what may be significant differences within the heterogeneous black and Hispanic populations. Moreover, the small sample sizes for Native Americans and Asian Americans in these surveys make it difficult to say much about these groups.[1] This chapter therefore focuses on comparisons among non-Hispanic whites, non-Hispanic blacks, and Hispanics of all races. For simplicity, these racial and ethnic groups are referred to as whites, blacks, and Hispanics.

The next four sections review findings on racial and ethnic differences in the characteristics of current and former welfare recipients and in patterns of work supports and overall well-being among low-income families.

Current Welfare Recipients

The most obvious measure of differences among racial and ethnic groups under TANF is the composition of the welfare caseload (figure 11-1). Much attention has been given to recent growth in the minority share of the caseload (e.g., DeParle 1998), but the white share of the caseload was declining even before welfare reform, and the black share of the caseload remains within historical levels.

Caseload proportions reflect demographic shifts in the race and ethnicity of the welfare-eligible population, as well as differential rates of applying for benefits and leaving welfare. A more accurate way of assessing changes since welfare reform is to ask what percentage of low-income families in each racial and ethnic group receives public assis-

Figure 11-1. *Welfare Caseload, by Race and Ethnicity of Parent,*[a] *1985–1999*

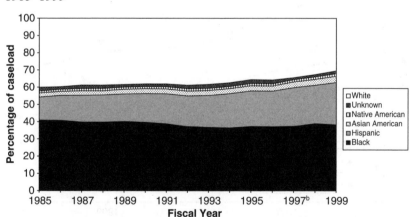

Source: Lower-Basch (2000), table 2.

[a] By race and ethnicity of youngest child in child-only cases.

[b] 1997 data are for October 1996–June 1997 only, due to the transition from AFDC to TANF.

tance.[2] Figure 11-2 shows that receipt of benefits by black families nationwide has fallen as rapidly as, or more rapidly than, receipt of benefits by white families. The pattern for Hispanic families generally tracks that for all racial and ethnic groups. Thus, since the decline in receipt of benefits under TANF has been similar among blacks, whites, and Hispanics, it appears that much of the increase in the minority share of the welfare caseload has indeed been driven by population shifts.

Lack of change in caseload patterns does not rule out the possibility of racial and ethnic disparities, for two reasons. First, national data may blur regional and local trends. Second, some of the factors that produce disparities in receipt of benefits under TANF have offsetting effects on caseload. For example, if persons of color are deterred from applying for benefits, or believe that they will not be eligible for welfare because of their immigration status, the percentage of minorities on welfare would *decrease;* other factors, such as discrimination in the labor market and lower use of child care and other work supports, might *increase* the percentage of minorities on welfare.

Figure 11-2. *Low-Income Families with Children Receiving Public Assistance*[a] *in the Past Year, by Race and Ethnicity of Parent, 1996–2000*

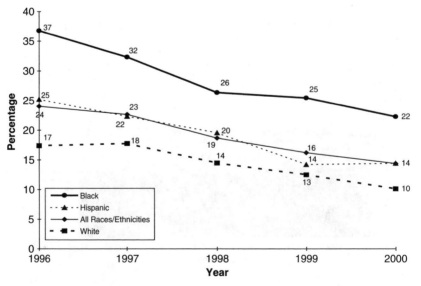

Source: Analysis by authors of March CPS data.
[a] Public assistance refers to cash payments from AFDC, TANF, or general assistance.

Clearly, any examination of the differential effects of welfare reform on racial and ethnic minorities must look beyond data on caseloads. The following sections take a broader look at patterns of benefit receipt under TANF, beginning with families who have recently left the program.

Former Welfare Recipients

Several issues are particularly useful in examining disparities among former welfare recipients by race and ethnicity: their reasons for leaving welfare, receipt of government supports after leaving, employment status, current hardship, and the effects of time limits. Data from the NSAF point to two important trends: Whites are less likely than other former recipients to leave the program for administrative reasons, and whites are more likely to receive help with expenses when they leave.[3]

Former recipients cited several reasons for leaving welfare: an increase in earnings or a new job, income from other sources, change in family situation, not wanting or needing welfare, not following program rules, an administrative problem or mix-up, or reaching time limits on benefits (table 11-1). Although none of these reasons alone differed significantly by race and ethnicity, a striking pattern emerged when the three administrative reasons were tabulated. Blacks reported leaving welfare because of administrative problems, time limits, or not following program rules much more frequently than did whites or all races, while whites reported leaving welfare for administrative reasons far less often than other recipients.

Government supports, including health insurance, job training, and help with expenses, are often given to welfare recipients upon their departure in order to ease the transition to work. The vast majority of former recipients reported receiving some type of government assistance in the first three months after leaving the welfare rolls. However, whites are significantly more likely to report getting help with expenses than other recipients, and blacks are significantly less likely to do so. This is consistent with the finding that white recipients in two Virginia counties were more likely to receive discretionary supports from their caseworkers than were black recipients (Gooden 1998).

Over half of all former welfare recipients were working at the time they were interviewed for the NSAF. The median hourly wage[4] for whites was $7.31; for blacks, $6.88; and for Hispanics, $6.71. The wage gap

Table 11-1. *Self-Reported Characteristics of Former Welfare Recipients by Race and Ethnicity, 1995–1999*[a]

	White (%)	Hispanic (%)	Black (%)	All Races/ Ethnicities (%)
Reason for leaving welfare				
Earnings increased, got a new job	63	59	68	63
Income from other sources	9	5	6	7
Did not want or need	10	12	7	10
Change in family situation	6	5	4	5
Administrative reasons[b]	**8**	14	**14**	10
Receipt of government supports in the first three months after leaving welfare				
Health insurance	62	57	65	61
Help with expenses	**12**	9	**7**	10
Job training	16	16	19	17
Any government program	71	63	73	69
Current employment				
Currently employed	60	62	67	62
Professional or technical occupation	19	17	**11**	16
Service occupation	34	**54**	35	36
Current well-being				
Uninsured	41	43	37	41
Food hardship in past year	67	67	64	66
Housing hardship in past year	**46**	**33**	38	42

[a] Based on the 1997 and 1999 National Surveys of America's Families. Includes only persons who left welfare in the two years prior to the survey and who had not returned to welfare at the time of the survey.

[b] Administrative reasons include not following program rules, an administrative problem or mix-up, or reaching time limits on benefits.

Numbers in bold are significantly different from all races/ethnicities at the .10 level.

between white and black former recipients is statistically significant, as is the gap between white and Hispanic former recipients. These differences may be related to occupation: 16 percent of all employed former recipients work in managerial, professional, or technical occupations, compared with only 11 percent of black former recipients. More than half of those in the Hispanic group work in service occupations, compared with slightly over one-third of all employed former recipients. Other possible reasons for this wage differential, such as education, work experience, and employer discrimination, are discussed later.

The well-being of former recipients and their families are measured in the NSAF by whether they have experienced food or housing hardship in the past year and whether they have health insurance.[5] Despite higher wages and more frequent receipt of help with expenses, whites are significantly more likely to have experienced housing hardship than other groups. Hispanics are less likely to have experienced housing hardship than other groups, but more likely to be uninsured.

It is not clear whether time limits on benefits will have disparate impacts by race and ethnicity. One study found that black women were 55 percent more likely, and Hispanic women 90 percent more likely, than white or other women to spend at least five years on welfare (Pavetti 1994). Another suggests that blacks will be disproportionately represented among recipients who reach the time limits (Duncan, Harris, and Boisjoly 2000). Evidence from most states has not come in yet, but a study of one county in Florida found that blacks constituted 52 percent of recipients, 70 percent of recipients who reached the time limits, and 63 percent of recipients receiving exemptions from work requirements (Bloom et al. 2000).[6] Data from Massachusetts (Massachusetts Department of Transitional Assistance 2000) and Virginia (Gordon et al. 1999) do not indicate racial and ethnic disparities in the operation of time limits.

Work Supports

Chapter 4 discusses the availability of work supports for low-income families, regardless of whether they have ever received welfare. It shows that for many people who earn low wages and do not receive employer-sponsored health insurance, supports such as Medicaid, SCHIP, EITC, child care subsidies, and child support are crucial to their family's well-being. How does receipt of work supports differ by race and ethnicity?

EITC

Low-income Hispanic parents are less likely to report having received the EITC than their non-Hispanic counterparts (Ross Phillips 2001). The main reason for the difference appears to be knowledge. Non-Hispanic parents reported having heard of the EITC more frequently than Hispanic parents, but of those who had heard about the tax credit, roughly the same proportion of Hispanic and non-Hispanic parents received it. NSAF respondents who requested a Spanish-language interview and respondents who were not U.S. citizens were less likely to have heard about or received the EITC than other low-income parents.[7]

Health Insurance

Low-income Hispanics, both adults and children, are less likely to have health insurance coverage than low-income whites or blacks (Staveteig and Wigton 2000b; Almeida and Kenney 2000; Holahan and Brennan 2000), in large part because low-income Hispanics are significantly less likely to work for employers that offer a health plan (Garrett, Nichols, and Greenman 2001). Among workers whose firms do sponsor a health plan, rates of eligibility and usage are virtually identical across racial and ethnic groups. Low-income Hispanics are more likely than low-income people from other groups to receive public coverage under Medicaid, SCHIP, and other programs, but this coverage is not enough to close the insurance gap. Public coverage of Hispanic children has fallen by 5 percentage points under welfare reform (Staveteig and Wigton 2000b). Although low-income black children are less likely to receive health insurance coverage through an employer than are other low-income children, a comparatively high rate of coverage under the public programs boosted the insurance rate of black children above the average for all low-income children in 1999 (ibid.).

Food Stamps

Welfare reform reduced food stamp benefits and income limits, and added restrictions on benefits for immigrants and able-bodied adults without dependents. These changes, combined with a strong economy and the tendency of those who left welfare to leave the Food Stamp program also (Zedlewski and Brauner 1999; Zedlewski and Gruber 2001), have reduced receipt of this benefit across the board.

Both the proportion of each racial and ethnic group eligible for food stamps and their rates of participation dropped between 1994 and 1998 (Castner 2000). Recent declines in food stamp eligibility and participation have been greater for Hispanics than for whites, and greater for whites than for blacks.[8] These figures, however, do not include state programs designed to restore benefits to immigrants, and may therefore overstate the extent to which Hispanics have actually lost access to food stamps.

Child Support

According to 1997 NSAF data, slightly over half of all children with a nonresident parent received child support. White children (58 percent) were more likely to receive support than black (48 percent) or Hispanic (40 percent) children (Staveteig and Wigton 2000a). Since nonresident fathers generally have the same racial and ethnic characteristics as the mothers, these findings may indicate racial and ethnic disparities in fathers' ability, rather than willingness, to pay child support (Sorensen and Zibman 2000).

Well-Being

Because current welfare recipients or recent welfare leavers represent small proportions of the total low-income population in the United States, it is difficult to draw conclusions about welfare reform from the racial and ethnic patterns observed within these groups. An examination of the well-being of all low-income Americans provides a broader view of racial and ethnic disparities among welfare recipients.

Data from the 1999 NSAF reveal a fairly consistent picture. Compared to the overall U.S. population, white families are less likely to be low-income. Those white families that are low-income are less likely than other low-income families to experience food and housing hardship. Low-income white parents are more likely to be employed than other low-income parents. Compared to other U.S. children, white children are more likely to live in two-parent families, and low-income white children are more likely than other low-income children to be covered by health insurance.

Compared to all U.S. families, Hispanic families are the most likely to be low-income, followed by black families. Black children are less likely than other children to live with two married parents. Among low-income families, Hispanics have lower rates of parental employment, higher rates of food hardship, and the lowest rates of insurance coverage for children. Black low-income families are more likely than other low-income families to experience food and housing hardship, but children in these families are also more likely to have insurance coverage.

Many of these disparities and their sources predate welfare reform, but some significant changes occurred between the 1997 and 1999 surveys. For whites and for the low-income population as a whole, there have been improvements in family income, decreases in food hardship, and increases in the percentage of two-parent families. Hispanics have also seen a rise in family income. For blacks, however, there have been no significant improvements in these measures, despite extremely positive overall economic conditions.[9]

Possible Causes of Racial and Ethnic Disparities

Some of the disparities that have emerged since welfare reform may be more closely related to broad economic and social conditions than to changes in welfare policies. What follows is a partial list of such factors.

Labor Market

Welfare reform emphasizes moving recipients into work. It imposes time limits on benefits, provides work supports for welfare recipients, and in several states requires recipients to conduct a job search before they are even eligible for benefits.[10] Lack of education and job skills, limited access to transportation and child care, high rates of incarceration, and employer discrimination all make finding and keeping a job difficult for low-income blacks and Hispanics (Holzer 2000; Holzer, Stoll, and Wissoker 2001), and may contribute to other disparities in the effects of welfare reform.

In one study, employers reported that the black welfare recipients they have hired are less likely than their white or Hispanic counterparts to have acquired the "soft skills" needed to get or keep a job, such as getting along with coworkers or arriving at work on time (Holzer et al. 2001). As the authors note, however, employers' assessments of workers' ability to get along with their peers are subjective, and problems with child care or transportation may contribute to lateness.

Employer demand for minority workers, welfare recipients, and minority workers among welfare recipients is particularly sensitive to variations in the job vacancy rate, which in turn is related to macroeconomic conditions (Holzer and Stoll 2001). In this respect, economic conditions between 1996 and 2000 may have represented a best-case scenario for welfare reform, with racial and ethnic disparities in employment or earnings muted in comparison to what might be expected during a recession.

Even in a favorable economy, however, employer discrimination adversely affects hiring. One study finds that small establishments and suburban employers are less likely than other employers to hire black or Hispanic welfare recipients, and retail stores are less likely to hire blacks than other welfare recipients (Holzer and Stoll 2001). Using interview length as an indicator of disparate treatment, another study found that 55 percent of black welfare recipients were interviewed for 5 minutes or less, whereas all white welfare recipients were interviewed for at least 10 minutes, even though the black respondents had more education than the whites (Gooden 1999, 2000). A test of temporary employment agencies in Wisconsin found extensive evidence of racial discrimination in hiring for entry-level jobs (National Association of Working Women 2001).

Geography

Labor market disparities are exacerbated by racial and ethnic residential patterns. Although racial segregation in the United States continues to decline (Glaeser and Vigdor 2001), most major cities remain segregated by race and ethnicity. Geographic location profoundly affects transportation, education, and availability of child care—and thus a person's job prospects. For example, the Gautreaux program in Chicago has shown that inner-city minority residents who are relocated to wealthier neighborhoods leave public assistance in greater numbers than those who remain in the old neighborhood (Rosenbaum and DeLuca 2000). Welfare recipients who are not located near their employer tend to rely on public transit, which can be unreliable and time-consuming.

State Policies

Distinct patterns also exist in the distribution of minorities across the United States. Compared to all Americans, blacks are more likely to live in the South, and Hispanics in the Southwest. Similar patterns can be seen in the distribution of welfare recipients.

Soss et al. (2001) conclude that these differences influenced state policy choices under TANF. States with higher percentages of blacks and Hispanics on welfare at the time of reform were more likely to adopt shorter time limits and a family cap on benefits than states with lower percentages of these minorities. States with larger shares of black recipients at the time TANF was enacted were also more likely to adopt stronger sanctions against recipients who broke program rules. However, the racial and ethnic composition of a state's welfare caseload did not significantly affect the adoption of stricter work requirements, which was more closely tied to labor market variables.

The result of these patterns, as shown in table 11-2, is that blacks are more likely than all Americans to live in states that have made restrictive state policy choices under TANF, and thus are more likely to be subject to these restrictions. The states that adopted strong sanctions, for example, are home to 33 percent of blacks, compared with 26 percent of the total population. In each of the other three categories studied by Soss et al. (2001), the percentage of blacks in states adopting restrictive policies is higher than the percentage for the total population. Hispanics are more likely than the total population to live in states with family caps or with any of the restrictive policies, but less likely to live in states with strong sanctions, stricter work requirements, or time limits.

These findings that blacks and Hispanics are more likely than other Americans to be subject to restrictions on welfare benefits are particularly striking in light of Quadagno's discussion (1994) of the history of local welfare policy and race. During the creation of AFDC in the 1930s,

Table 11-2. *Percentage of Each Racial and Ethnic Group Residing in States with Restrictive Welfare Policies*

State Policy Type	White (%)	Hispanic (%)	Black (%)	All Races/ Ethnicities (%)
Strong sanctions	25	12	33	26
Strict work requirements	57	55	57	56
Short time limits	47	45	54	47
Family cap	50	59	57	51
Any restrictive policy	*85*	*95*	*88*	*86*

Sources: Calculated by authors from TANF state policy measures in Soss et al. (2001), Rector and Youssef (1999), American Public Welfare Association (1997), and July 1, 1999, population data from U.S. Census Bureau (2000). Data include the 50 states and the District of Columbia.

Southern planters, fearing that standardized federal social assistance would undermine the available supply of black sharecroppers, insisted that welfare standards and benefits be determined by states and localities. Until the civil rights movement in the 1960s, state and local officials were able to use their administrative flexibility to establish low benefits in areas with a high concentration of minorities.

Caseworker Implementation

Implementation of welfare reform has given caseworkers more discretion in deciding such critical matters as which recipients will receive work supports and which will be sanctioned. Bias in the use of this discretion, whether intentional or unintentional, can result in racial and ethnic disparities in the receipt of benefits. One study in two Virginia counties found that 41 percent of the white recipients—but none of the black recipients—reported that their caseworker encouraged or supported increased education. Similarly, 47 percent of white recipients and no black recipients reported assistance with transportation beyond the gas vouchers available to all recipients (Gooden 1998). Sample sizes in this study were small, but the results are stark enough to suggest the need for further investigations along these lines.

Language Barriers

Limited knowledge of English significantly reduces the probability of working[11] (Zedlewski 1999) and can prevent low-income families from getting needed benefits or services from government. Welfare recipients who are not fluent in English also report problems getting information about benefits in a language they can understand (Ng 1999; Rodriguez and Kirk 2000). Ethnic groups with low literacy in their native language, such as the Hmong (Moore and Selkowe 1999) and Haitians (Dunn, Kretsedemas, and Beneckson 2001), are particularly hard to serve. Failure to receive work supports because of limited English skills further compounds the need for assistance: Recipients who do not receive appropriate work and literacy training services, for example, are unlikely to be able to find the jobs they need to leave welfare.

In 1999, a group of advocacy organizations filed a complaint with the Department of Health and Human Services, claiming that Spanish-speaking immigrants were being discriminated against because welfare offices failed to provide translators. The Office of Civil Rights found that these practices had the effect of discriminating on the basis of national origin (DHHS 1999), and a memorandum reminding all state agencies of TANF's nondiscrimination policy has since been released (DHHS 2000). Similar lawsuits in Minnesota and California have required local agencies to take corrective action, and two others are pending (Frye 2001).

Restrictions on Benefits for Noncitizens

Twenty-nine percent of Hispanics in the United States are noncitizen immigrants, in contrast to 3 percent of blacks and 1 percent of whites.[12] Therefore, TANF's restrictions on benefits to noncitizen immigrants, discussed in chapter 10, are likely to hit Hispanic families especially hard. State policies regarding noncitizen immigrants do not seem to be related to the size of a state's noncitizen population. Wealthier states, states with traditionally generous social policies, and states with strong advocacy coalitions have been more likely to continue assistance to immigrants (Zimmermann and Tumlin 1999).

Family Structure

Differences in family structure by race and ethnicity complicate discussions of welfare reform, because these differences may be both causes and effects of other disparities. Indeed, one study suggests that racial and ethnic differences in marriage patterns and family size contribute to differences in the well-being of former welfare recipients (Lower-Basch 2000). White women who left welfare were at least twice as likely to marry or cohabit as black women who left welfare, and white former recipients were also more likely to receive child support than their black counterparts. These findings may help explain why white women return to welfare at lower rates than black women. Furthermore, since parents with larger families need to earn more, and Hispanic and black families tend to be larger than average, Hispanic and black parents may have to stay on welfare longer before finding a job that pays enough to support their family (ibid.).

Differences in Attitudes

Differences in attitudes toward welfare and working mothers—among potential recipients as well as among caseworkers and employers, as mentioned earlier—may contribute to some of the disparate effects of welfare reform. Evidence from NSAF interviews with mothers suggests that Hispanic women in particular hold distinctly negative views about working mothers: 60 percent of Hispanic mothers, 50 percent of white mothers, and 35 percent of black mothers agreed that "mothers with small children should not work outside the home" (Wertheimer, Long, and Vandivere 2001). Such attitudes may inhibit the movement of women from welfare to work, which is exactly what TANF requires. Hispanic mothers were also less likely than black or white mothers to say that "a working mother can establish a secure relationship with her child."

Survey responses also suggest that black mothers view welfare less harshly than white mothers do, and that blacks and Hispanics are more accepting of childbirth outside of marriage than whites are (Wertheimer et al. 2001; Brown 2001). These findings seem to be related to racial and ethnic differences in welfare receipt and family structure, but sorting out cause and effect is difficult. Are black mothers more likely to apply for welfare than white mothers because they attach less stigma to welfare receipt, or do they attach less stigma to welfare receipt because it is more common among their relatives, friends, and neighbors? Similarly, are rates of childbirth outside of marriage higher for black and Hispanic women because they are less likely to view such childbirth as shameful, or are black and Hispanic women less likely to view childbirth outside of marriage as shameful because it is more common in their communities?

Policy Implications

The policy changes embodied in PRWORA are not explicitly based on race or ethnicity.[13] Yet even welfare reform laws that are neutral in this sense may produce disparities, whether because race and ethnicity are correlated with other variables, or because discrimination exists in the implementation of policies and in the labor market. Given what research has revealed about the existence and possible sources of racial and ethnic disparities under welfare reform, what changes should be part of TANF reauthorization or future welfare policy?

Sufficient funding to provide child care, assistance with education and transportation, and job training (both in job-specific and in more general work-related skills) to all low-income families would address some of the barriers that limit employment opportunities for minorities. Internally standardized, and better publicized, state or local rules for determining who gets these supports might help prevent discrimination; however, these rules must be flexible enough to match benefits and services to each family's needs. Multilingual services and outreach can help low-income people who do not speak English receive the government assistance for which they qualify and could help them improve their prospects for work. Other means of avoiding discrimination might include stronger enforcement of applicable federal and state civil rights laws, improved training for caseworkers and other agency staff, and expanded outreach to employers (Frye 2001).

New provisions enabling states to exempt more than 20 percent of their caseload from time limits on benefits, or basing the number of exemptions on individual cases rather than uniform standards (see chapter 2), might improve states' ability to respond to any racial and ethnic disparities stemming from time limits. Exemptions, however, should not be used as an excuse for denying particular groups of welfare recipients the chance to develop the skills they need to become more self-sufficient and escape permanently from poverty.

Finally, legislation should require and fund the collection and dissemination of administrative data by race and ethnicity at the national, state, and local levels. These data should be published in standardized form so they can be compared across jurisdictions, and they should be available to the public. It would be useful, for example, to have standard measures on the racial and ethnic composition of recipients denied benefits because of time limits or sanctions and recipients exempted from work requirements.

Some data are already collected by race and ethnicity, and some are made available to the public—but because these data are not used to determine programmatic eligibility, they may not be reliable (National Research Council 2001). Better administrative data on low-income Native Americans and Asian Americans are particularly important. Because the samples of these groups in national surveys are very small, survey data cannot be used to compensate for the limitations of current administrative data, as they sometimes can for the larger white, black, and Hispanic populations.

Failure to collect reliable administrative data by race and ethnicity, or to collect it without standardizing it or making it available to the public, is in essence a decision to remain ignorant about possible disparities caused by welfare reform. Remaining ignorant about disparities makes it

impossible to address inequities at the state, regional, or national level—
or to learn from those states that have excelled in implementing TANF to
benefit low-income families of all racial and ethnic backgrounds.

NOTES

We thank Jocelyn Frye, Eric Rodriguez, Margaret Simms, Matthew Stagner, and Alan
Weil for the extraordinarily helpful and timely feedback they gave us on earlier drafts;
Donald Alderson, Sarah Brauner, Brett Brown, Melissa Long, Pam Loprest, and LaDonna
Pavetti for patiently sharing and clarifying aspects of their previous work; Gina Adams,
Fritz Scheuren, Rebecca Steinbach, and Kevin Wang for their expert NSAF data advice;
Anjali Thakur for her accurate and responsive help with locating source materials; and
Sarah Hicks for answering our questions about Native Americans and TANF.

1. Targeted studies are more likely to address questions about these groups, such
as the impact of devolving authority for TANF to tribal governments (Pandey et al. 1999,
2000) or the specific barriers that limit employment opportunities of Hmong refugees
(Moore and Selkowe 1999).

2. Data are derived from the Current Population Survey (CPS), which uses a
"public assistance" variable that includes both welfare and general assistance cash benefits (see http://www.bls.census.gov/cps/ads/1995/sglosary.htm). Since general assistance
is a small program relative to TANF and AFDC, and since CPS indicates that "public
assistance" is interchangeable with "welfare payments," the public assistance variable is
used to determine welfare receipt in this section.

3. The combined sample of welfare leavers from the 1997 and 1999 NSAF contains adults who left welfare in the two years prior to the survey and who have not
returned to welfare (Loprest 1999). The pooled sample size is 2,276 leavers: 1,146 are
white, 704 are black, 325 are Hispanic, and 101 are other race or ethnicity. Evidence comparing the two leaver samples indicates that they are very similar (Loprest 2000). The
combined sample represents 2.7 million leavers who left AFDC or TANF between 1995
and 1999 and who were surveyed within two years of exiting the rolls. Whites compose
51 percent of these leavers, blacks 30 percent, and Hispanics 13 percent; 6 percent are
other race or ethnicity.

4. Wages adjusted to 1999 dollars using CPI-U.

5. Housing hardship means that the adult respondent reported having problems
paying mortgage, rent, or utility bills in the past year. Food hardship means that in the
past year the adult respondent or their family worried that food would run out before
they got money to buy more, the food they bought did run out, or one or more adults
ate less or skipped meals because there was not enough money for food.

6. Bloom et al. (2000) do not include a separate breakdown for the county's small
Hispanic population.

7. A complicating factor is that low-income families who use paid tax preparers
may get EITC benefits yet report that they have not received it or heard about it. However, geographic analysis of actual tax returns, which would not be affected by this survey response problem, also suggest that EITC receipt is disproportionately low among

Hispanics. An analysis of 27 metropolitan areas found disproportionately low rates of EITC receipt in Miami and San Antonio, the two central cities studied that had Hispanic majorities (Center on Urban and Metropolitan Policy 2001).

8. Calculated from administrative data on recipients and CPS data on eligibility, in Castner (2000).

9. Dupree and Primus (2001) report CPS data showing a significant increase in two-parent families among black children from 1995 to 2000. NSAF data suggest that changes from 1997 to 1999 were in the opposite direction but not significant. Similarly, Haskins, Sawhill, and Weaver (2001) report CPS data suggesting that poverty among black children declined from 1997 to 1999, whereas NSAF data do not suggest a significant change during this period. These differences between NSAF and CPS findings might be due to differences in the samples or, for the family structure data, to differences in the years compared.

10. Fifteen states and the District of Columbia had this requirement in 1999 (Rowe 2000).

11. NSAF data may understate the impact of language barriers on ethnic groups other than Hispanics, since respondents who do not speak English or Spanish cannot be interviewed unless someone else in the household can act as translator (Zedlewski 1999; Vaden-Kiernan et al. 1999).

12. Calculated from 1999 NSAF data on persons under age 65. Hispanic/white and Hispanic/black differences are significant at the .01 level. Similarly, Urban Institute calculations from the March 1999 CPS suggest that 28 percent of Hispanics under age 65 are not citizens, compared to 2 percent of whites and 3 percent of blacks.

13. The exceptions are the provisions that pertain specifically to Native Americans.

REFERENCES

Almeida, Ruth, and Genevieve Kenney. 2000. *Gaps in Insurance Coverage for Children: A Pre-CHIP Baseline.* Washington, D.C.: The Urban Institute. *Assessing the New Federalism* Policy Brief B-19.

American Public Welfare Association. 1997. *State-by-State Welfare Reform Policy Decisions: From the Survey of the Status of States' Implementation of Welfare Reform.* Washington, D.C.: Welfare Reform Information Center.

Bell, Lissa, and Carson Strege-Flora. 2000. *Access Denied: Federal Neglect Gives Rise to State Lawlessness; Families Denied Access to Medicaid, Food Stamps, CHIP, and Child Care.* Seattle: Northwest Federation of Community Organizations and National Campaign for Jobs and Income Support (National Campaign).

Bloom, Dan, James J. Kemple, Pamela Morris, Susan Scrivener, Nandita Verma, and Richard Hendra, with Diana Adams-Ciardullo, David Seith, and Johanna Walter. 2000. *The Family Transition Program: Final Report on Florida's Time-Limited Welfare Program.* New York: Manpower Demonstration Research Corporation.

Brown, Brett V. 2001. *Youth Attitudes on Family, Work, and Community Service: Implications for Welfare Reform.* Washington, D.C.: The Urban Institute. *Assessing the New Federalism* Policy Brief A-47.

Castner, Laura. 2000. *Trends in FSP Participation Rates: Focus on 1994 to 1998.* Alexandria, Va.: U.S. Department of Agriculture, Food and Nutrition Service.

Center on Urban and Metropolitan Policy. 2001. *Rewarding Work: The Impact of the Earned Income Tax Credit in Greater Miami.* Washington, D.C.: Brookings Institution.

DeParle, Jason. 1998. "Shrinking Welfare Rolls Leave Record High Share of Minorities." *New York Times.* July 27, A-1.

DHHS. *See* U.S. Department of Health and Human Services.

Duncan, Greg J., Kathleen Mullan Harris, and Johanne Boisjoly. 2000. "Time Limits and Welfare Reform: New Estimates of the Number and Characteristics of Affected Families." *Social Science Review* 74 (1): 55–75.

Dunn, Marvin, Phillip Kretsedemas, and Robert E. Beneckson. 2001. *Haitian-Americans in Miami-Dade County and the Welfare System.* Miami: Florida Atlantic University. W.K. Kellogg Devolution Initiative, Scholar-Practitioner Program.

Dupree, Alan, and Wendell Primus. 2001. *Declining Share of Children Lived with Single Mothers in the Late 1990s.* Washington, D.C.: Center on Budget and Policy Priorities.

Frye, Jocelyn. 2001. *The Forgotten Question: Exploring the Impact of Welfare Reform on Civil Rights.* Working Paper. Washington, D.C.: National Partnership for Women and Families.

Garrett, Bowen, Len M. Nichols, and Emily K. Greenman. 2001. *Workers without Health Insurance: Who Are They and How Can Policy Reach Them?* Washington, D.C.: The Urban Institute.

Gilens, Martin. 1999. *Why Americans Hate Welfare: Race, Media, and the Politics of Antipoverty Policy.* Chicago: University of Chicago Press.

Glaeser, Edward, and Jacob Vigdor. 2001. *Racial Segregation in the 2000 Census: Promising News.* Washington, D.C.: Brookings Institution Center on Urban and Metropolitan Policy.

Gooden, Susan T. 1998. "All Things Not Being Equal: Differences in Caseworker Support toward Black and White Welfare Clients." *Harvard Journal of African American Public Policy* 4: 23–33.

———. 1999. "The Hidden Third Party: Welfare Recipients' Experiences with Employers." *Journal of Public Management and Social Policy* 5 (1): 69–83.

———. 2000. "Race and Welfare: Examining Employment Outcomes of White and Black Welfare Recipients." *Journal of Poverty* 4 (3): 21–41.

Gordon, Anne, Carole Kuhns, Renee Loeffler, and Roberto Agodini. 1999. *Experiences of Virginia Time Limit Families in the Six Months after Case Closure: Results for an Early Cohort.* Richmond, Va.: Virginia Department of Social Services.

Gordon, Rebecca. 2001. *Cruel and Usual: How Welfare "Reform" Punishes Poor People.* Oakland, Calif.: Applied Research Center.

Haskins, Ron, Isabel Sawhill, and Kent Weaver. 2001. *Welfare Reform: An Overview of Effects to Date.* Washington, D.C.: Brookings Institution. *Welfare Reform and Beyond* Brief No. 1.

Holahan, John, and Niall Brennan. 2000. "Who Are the Adult Uninsured?" Washington, D.C.: The Urban Institute. *Assessing the New Federalism* Policy Brief B-14.

Holzer, Harry J. 2000. *Career Advancement Prospects and Strategies for Low-Wage Minority Workers.* Washington, D.C.: The Urban Institute.

Holzer, Harry J., and Michael A. Stoll. 2001. *Employer Demand for Welfare Recipients by Race.* Washington, D.C.: The Urban Institute. *Assessing the New Federalism* Discussion Paper 01-07.

Holzer, Harry J., Michael A. Stoll, and Douglas Wissoker. 2001. *Job Performance and Retention among Welfare Recipients.* Chicago: Joint Center for Poverty Research. Working Paper 231.

Loprest, Pamela. 1999. *Families Who Left Welfare: Who Are They and How Are They Doing?* Washington, D.C.: The Urban Institute. *Assessing the New Federalism* Discussion Paper 99-02.

———. 2000. "How Are Families Who Left Welfare Doing Over Time?: A Comparison of Two Cohorts of Welfare Leavers." Results from the National Survey of America's Families. Paper prepared for "Welfare Reform Four Years Later: Progress and Prospects." Federal Reserve Bank of New York. December 8.

Lower-Basch, Elizabeth. 2000. *"Leavers" and Diversion Studies: Preliminary Analysis of Racial Differences in Caseload Trends and Leaver Outcomes.* Washington, D.C.: Department of Health and Human Services, Office of the Assistant Secretary for Planning and Evaluation.

Massachusetts Department of Transitional Assistance. 2000. *After Time Limits: A Study of Households Leaving Welfare between December 1998 and April 1999.* Boston: Massachusetts Department of Transitional Assistance.

Moore, Thomas, and Vicky Selkowe. 1999. *The Impact of Welfare Reform on Wisconsin's Hmong Aid Recipients.* Milwaukee, Wisc.: Institute for Wisconsin's Future.

National Association of Working Women. 2001. *Report on Discriminatory Hiring Practices in Temporary Employment Agencies.* http://www.9to5.org/temp.html. (Accessed December 18, 2001.)

National Research Council. 2001. *Evaluating Welfare Reform in an Era of Transition.* Washington, D.C.: National Academy Press. Panel on Data and Methods for Measuring the Effects of Changes in Social Welfare Programs. Robert A. Moffitt and Michele Ver Ploeg, editors. Committee on National Statistics, Division of Behavioral and Social Sciences and Education.

Ng, Doris. 1999. *From the War on Poverty to War on Welfare: The Impact of Welfare Reform on Lives of Immigrant Women.* San Francisco: Equal Rights Advocates.

Pandey, Shanta, Eddie F. Brown, Leslie Scheuler-Whitaker, Bethney Gundersen, and Karin Eyrich. 1999. "Promise of Welfare Reform through Devolution on Indian Reservations." *Journal of Poverty* 3 (4): 37–61.

Pandey, Shanta, Min Zhan, Shannon Collier-Tenison, and Kathryn Hui. 2000. "How Are Families on Reservations Faring under Welfare Reform?" St. Louis, Mo.: Kathryn M. Buder Center for American Studies, Washington University. Working Paper 2.

Pavetti, LaDonna. 1994. "Policies to Time-Limit AFDC Benefits: What Can We Learn from Welfare Dynamics?" Mimeo. Presented at Institute for Social and Policy Studies, Yale University, November 30.

Quadagno, Jill. 1994. *The Color of Welfare: How Racism Undermined the War on Poverty.* New York: Oxford University Press.

Rector, Robert E., and Sarah E. Youssef. 1999. *The Determinants of Welfare Caseload Decline.* Washington, D.C.: Heritage Foundation.

Rodriguez, Eric, and Kaydee Kirk. 2000. "Welfare Reform, TANF Caseload Changes, and Latinos: A Preliminary Assessment." Washington, D.C.: National Council of La Raza. Issue Brief No. 3.

Rosenbaum, James E., and Stefanie DeLuca. 2000. *Is Housing Mobility the Key to Welfare Reform?: Lessons from Chicago's Gautreaux Program.* Washington, D.C.: Brookings Institution.

Ross Phillips, Katherin. 2001. "Who Knows about the Earned Income Tax Credit?" Washington, D.C.: The Urban Institute. *Assessing the New Federalism* Policy Brief B-27.

Rowe, Gretchen. 2000. *Welfare Rules Databook: State TANF Policies as of July 1999.* Washington, D.C.: The Urban Institute. *Assessing the New Federalism.*

Sorensen, Elaine, and Chava Zibman. 2000. *A Look at Poor Dads Who Don't Pay Child Support.* Washington, D.C.: The Urban Institute. *Assessing the New Federalism* Discussion Paper 00-07.

Soss, Joe, Sanford F. Schram, Thomas P. Vartanian, and Erin O'Brien. 2001. "Setting the Terms of Relief: Explaining State Policy Choices in the Devolution Revolution." *American Journal of Political Science* 45 (2): 378–95.

Staveteig, Sarah, and Alyssa Wigton. 2000a. "Racial and Ethnic Disparities: Key Findings from the National Survey of America's Families." Washington, D.C.: The Urban Institute. *Assessing the New Federalism* Policy Brief B-5.

———. 2000b. *Key Findings by Race and Ethnicity (Findings from the 1999 National Survey of America's Families).* Washington, D.C.: The Urban Institute.

U.S. Census Bureau. 2000. *Population Estimates for States by Race and Hispanic Origin: July 1, 1999.* ST-99-32. Washington, D.C.: Population Estimates Program, Population Division.

U.S. Department of Health and Human Services, Office for Civil Rights. 1999. *New York Human Resources Administration Letter of Findings.* Washington, D.C.: U.S. Government Printing Office. Docket Number 02-99-3130.

———. 2000. *Summary of Policy Guidance: Prohibition Against Discrimination on the Basis of Disability in the Administration of TANF.* Washington, D.C.: U.S. Government Printing Office.

Vaden-Kiernan, Nancy, David Cantor, Pat Cunningham, Sarah Dipko, Karen Molloy, and Patricia Warren. 1999. *1997 NSAF Telephone Methods.* Washington, D.C.: The Urban Institute. NSAF Methodology Reports No. 9.

Wertheimer, Richard, Melissa Long, and Sharon Vandivere. 2001. "Welfare Recipients' Attitudes toward Welfare, Nonmarital Childbearing, and Work: Implications for Reform?" Washington, D.C.: The Urban Institute. *Assessing the New Federalism* Policy Brief B-37.

Zedlewski, Sheila R. 1999. *Work-Related Activities and Limitations of Current Welfare Recipients.* Washington, D.C.: The Urban Institute. *Assessing the New Federalism* Discussion Paper 99-06.

Zedlewski, Sheila R., and Sarah Brauner. 1999. *Declines in Food Stamp and Welfare Participation: Is There a Connection?* Washington, D.C.: The Urban Institute. *Assessing the New Federalism* Discussion Paper 99-13.

Zedlewski, Sheila R., with Amelia Gruber. 2001. *Former Welfare Families Continue to Leave the Food Stamp Program.* Washington, D.C.: The Urban Institute. *Assessing the New Federalism* Discussion Paper 01-05.

Zimmermann, Wendy, and Karen Tumlin. 1999. *Patchwork Policies: State Assistance for Immigrants under Welfare Reform.* Washington, D.C.: The Urban Institute. *Assessing the New Federalism* Occasional Paper No. 24.

12

TANF Funding and Spending across the States

Sheila R. Zedlewski, David Merriman,
Sarah Staveteig, and Kenneth Finegold

When welfare reform legislation changed the method of financing benefits from an open-ended entitlement to a series of fixed block grants, it transformed the face of welfare in the United States. The new law used pre-1996 welfare spending to fix the amount of federal spending available for TANF and to set a floor on states' spending. As the number of people on welfare plummeted in the years after reform was enacted, federal and state TANF monies came to far exceed the amount required to maintain benefits at earlier levels. These excess funds, plus considerable flexibility in spending them, enabled states to expand services for welfare families and to assist low-income working families with children that are not on welfare.

The move to block-grant financing generated considerable debate. Most states welcomed the opportunity to devote monies to areas of greatest need for low-income families, but some states worried about their heightened financial risk during recession, when the number of people on welfare would be likely to increase. Many analysts worried that there would be a "race to the bottom" as the states, wanting to save money and avoid becoming "welfare magnets," reduced spending on low-income families (Brueckner 1999). Some also argued that states would use TANF dollars to supplant other spending rather than to expand services for low-income families. Others argued that basing

TANF allocations on pre-PRWORA funding would lock in existing inequities in spending and benefits across the states.

This chapter examines states' TANF allocations and spending in 2000 and compares them to AFDC allocations and spending in 1996, the last full fiscal year before reform.[1] The comparisons highlight the differences in funds available per welfare family and in how states have spent their funds. The chapter also examines the difference between actual TANF spending and hypothetical spending if the AFDC funding structure had continued but the number of welfare recipients had dropped as it did under TANF. The results shed light on issues such as the race to the bottom, supplantation, and TANF funding during a recession. The final section of the chapter examines the implications of the current funding structure for TANF reauthorization.

TANF Funding Structure

The basic premise that states' funding allocations should depend primarily on historical expenditures emerged early in the TANF political debate (Merriman and Staveteig 2000). Although Congress considered several different formulas for allocation, the only exception to basic block grants that won passage was an adjustment mechanism that provided $800 million over the course of the first four years of TANF to states with high population growth or historically low spending on welfare. This supplemental spending expired on September 30, 2001.

Congress based the annual TANF block grant on combined federal contributions to the three programs that TANF replaced: AFDC, Emergency Assistance, and Job Opportunities and Basic Skills Training (JOBS) (box 12-1). Funding, totaling almost $17 billion annually, was based on a state's maximum spending in one of three base periods.[2] To receive their block grant, states must meet or exceed a maintenance-of-effort spending requirement. The maintenance-of-effort requirement is 80 percent of the amount a state spent on the three pre-TANF programs, plus welfare-related child care programs, during the base period. States that meet their work participation targets are subject to a lower standard, 75 percent of base-period spending.[3]

The amount of a state's block grant is also affected by performance bonuses and penalties. The federal government distributes an additional $200 million per year among states whose current and former welfare

Box 12-1. Highlights of the Current TANF Block Grant Allocation Formula

The Personal Responsibility and Work Opportunity Reconciliation Act of 1996 (PRWORA)[a] established the following rules for distributing welfare block grants among the states. States that meet the requirements receive a fixed block grant each year from fiscal year (FY) 1997 through 2002.

Each state is awarded a fixed block grant equal to the *maximum* of the following:[b]

- The average amount owed to the state for Aid to Families with Dependent Children (AFDC), Emergency Assistance, and JOBS programs during FY 1992 through FY 1994 (excluding funds for child care);
- The total amount owed to the state for FY 1994 AFDC, Emergency Assistance, and JOBS programs (excluding child care) plus 85 percent of any additional Emergency Assistance funds approved by the Secretary of Health and Human Services from FY 1994 to FY 1995 intended for family preservation; or
- The total amount owed to the state for AFDC, Emergency Assistance, and JOBS programs for the first three-quarters of FY 1995 (prorated to an annual amount, excluding child care) plus the total amount owed to the state under the JOBS program for FY 1995.

Requirements

- States must maintain spending on welfare at a minimum of 80 percent of their 1994 level (75 percent if work participation rates are high enough).
- States must submit a plan to the federal government, follow federal rules on many topics (time limits, child support, etc.), and meet federal goals for work participation.

(*continued*)

Box 12-1. Highlights of the Current TANF Block Grant Allocation Formula (*Continued*)

Bonuses

- States with high population growth or below-average historical spending on welfare benefits may qualify for a 2.5 percent grant increase.
- The five states with the largest reductions in births outside of marriage (without an increase in abortions) receive a total of $100 million in bonuses each year.
- The top 10 states in each of four job performance categories (job placement, job success,[c] improvement in job placement, and improvement in job success) receive a total of $200 million in bonuses each year.

Penalties

States can be penalized for rule violations, including failure to
- Meet work requirements;
- Reduce grants to individual recipients for refusing to participate in work activities without good cause;
- Maintain assistance when parents cannot find child care for a child under age 6;
- Comply with paternity establishment and child support enforcement requirements.

States must use their own funds to replace funds lost through federal penalties. States can seek exceptions under limited circumstances, and may develop a corrective compliance plan before being penalized. The total penalty assessed in a given year may not exceed 25 percent of a state's block grant allotment.

[a]U.S. Congress (1996).
[b]National Conference of State Legislatures (1999).
[c]Job success is a combined measure based on job retention and increases in earnings.

recipients have the greatest job market success, and gives out $100 million per year among states with the largest reduction in births outside of marriage without an increase in abortions. States are subject to penalties for failing to meet TANF work participation requirements, noncompliance with child support enforcement rules, and other causes.

To date, 98 percent of federal TANF funds have been allocated on the basis of historical expenditures.[4] Only 1 percent has been based on performance, and 1 percent was based on recent state need, allocated from the supplemental grants that expired at the end of 2001.

To create the political consensus necessary to pass PRWORA, Congress had to base state TANF allocations primarily on pre-1996 spending, a formula that effectively locked in wide disparities among the states (Zedlewski and Giannarelli 1997). AFDC funding had been based on a federal matching rate and state discretion about benefits and coverage. Since the matching rate was higher for poorer states, which spent less on welfare, the federal government contributed (and continues to contribute) a greater share of money to support low-income families in those states. However, total spending per low-income family under TANF continues to be generally lower in poor states because of their historically lower benefits and spending.

Relative Shares of Funding

The federal share of welfare funding has increased relative to the state share because TANF block grants were set at 100 percent of prior funding, whereas states were required to maintain only 75 or 80 percent of their prior spending. Federal appropriations also increased because of the supplements and bonuses mentioned above. In 1996, states spent over $32 billion (in 2000 dollars) on the programs replaced by TANF, with federal and state governments providing nearly equal shares (figure 12-1). By 2000, total spending for TANF had dropped to just over $26 billion, adjusted for inflation. Approximately 58 percent of this spending came from federal revenues, with states accounting for the remaining 42 percent.

The state spending shown in figure 12-1 includes all state-reported maintenance-of-effort money. Most states need only spend 75 percent of their base period amount, because most have met TANF's work participation requirements. However, 23 states reported spending 80 percent or more of their base period amount (including 8 states that were required

Figure 12-1. *Federal and State Shares of Total Welfare Spending, 1996 and 2000 (in 2000 dollars)*

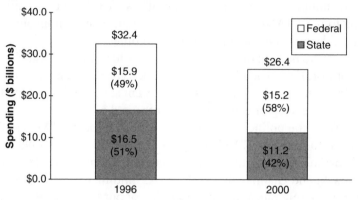

Source: 1996 data collected from federal sources on individual spending on programs replaced by TANF; 2000 data from the ACF (2000c).

to do so). Some states may actually spend more on TANF than they report as maintenance-of-effort to the federal government. There is no evidence that this has happened, but if it has, total TANF-related spending is likely to have been underestimated here. The analysis in this chapter is limited to states' TANF-related spending—that is, federal block-grant monies and states' self-reported maintenance-of-effort spending. It excludes state spending on other non-TANF programs that support low-income families.[5]

Funds Available per Welfare Family

Because of the large decline in the number of welfare recipients since 1996, every state had more funds available per welfare family under TANF in 2000 than under AFDC in 1996. However, because the system for allocating TANF grants reflects historical funding rather than current conditions, there is wide variation in the increase in real funds per family on welfare (table 12-1). For example, available resources per family more than tripled in 12 states, but increased by less than half in Delaware, Hawaii, Nebraska, and Rhode Island. As a result, states differ in their ability to broaden TANF-related services to families not receiving welfare and in their ability to deliver intensive services to families remaining on welfare.

Table 12-1. *Real Increase in Available TANF Funds per Family on Welfare, 1996–2000*[a]

Increase per Family (%)	States in Category
0–50	Delaware, Hawaii, Nebraska, Rhode Island
50–100	*Alaska*, California, Connecticut, Illinois, Iowa, Kansas, **Kentucky**, Maine, *Massachusetts*, Missouri, *New Hampshire*, New Mexico, *New York, North Dakota, Oregon, Pennsylvania, Vermont*, Virginia, *Washington*
100–150	Arizona, District of Columbia, *Minnesota*, Nevada, New Jersey, **Tennessee, Texas**, Utah (U.S. average = 118%)
150–200	**Alabama, Georgia**, Maryland, Michigan, Montana, North Carolina, **South Carolina**, South Dakota
200+	**Arkansas**, Colorado, Florida, Idaho, Indiana, **Louisiana, Mississippi**, Ohio, Oklahoma, **West Virginia**, Wisconsin, Wyoming

Source: Calculated from financial data from the ACF (2000b, 2000c).
Note: States in *italics* were approximately in the top quintile in 1996 spending (more than $8,500 per family on welfare); states in **bold** were in the bottom quintile (less than $4,800 per family).
[a]Includes federal allocation combined with states' maintenance-of-effort (MOE) monies.

Changes in available TANF dollars per family indicate that the states that spent the least under AFDC tended to experience the fastest percentage growth in dollars per family under TANF. For example, 7 of the 10 states in the lowest quintile of spending per family in 1996 had increases of 150 percent or more between 1996 and 2000 (table 12-1). In contrast, spending per family increased by less than 100 percent for most states in the top quintile of spending in 1996.

The changes in available funds also reflect the uneven decline in welfare caseloads across states. In general, high-benefit states had smaller declines than low-benefit states. One reason is that families receiving lower cash benefits are more likely than families receiving higher cash benefits to be able to leave welfare and replace its support with their earnings and with work supports, such as the EITC.[6] Other TANF policies may affect how quickly families leave welfare. For example, only one-third of high-benefit states (those with monthly maximum benefits of $550 or more for a family of three) employed full family sanctions in 2000, compared to almost two-thirds of states in the nation as a whole. (Under full family sanctions, a recipient's entire family may lose all assistance if the recipient does not comply with program regulations.)

TANF Spending and Saving

Spending rules under federal block grants give states enormous flexibility. Federal funds can be used to provide families on welfare with several types of assistance—that is, payments directed at ongoing, basic needs—including cash, child care, job training, education, subsidized work programs, and job placement. Federal funds may not be used for families with an adult who has received cash welfare payments for more than five years unless they fall into the exempt 20 percent of a state's caseload, or for recipients under age 19 unless they are attending school or have obtained a high school degree or general equivalency diploma. States can transfer a total of 30 percent of their federal allotment to the Social Services Block Grant and the Child Care and Development Fund, provided that no more than 10 percent of the federal allotment goes to the Social Services Block Grant.[7] States can also use federal TANF funds to support low-income families with children that do not receive cash assistance, provided those families include an employed adult. These supports can include child care, transportation, diversion (or emergency assistance), the refundable portion of states' earned income tax credits, and contributions to individual development accounts.

States can set aside federal TANF funds for future use by leaving unobligated funds or unliquidated obligations in the federal treasury until needed.[8] Technically, unliquidated obligations are funds committed to a specific purpose, such as payments to a private contractor that provides services to welfare recipients or to a county for expenses incurred in administering a welfare program. In contrast, unobligated funds represent rainy-day funds or funds for which the state has made no specific plans in future years. The GAO finds that there is often little difference between these two types of funds (GAO 2001). Some states report having specific plans for unobligated balances, and unliquidated obligations often entail only very loose commitments.

States have even more freedom in meeting their required maintenance-of-effort spending. For example, they can set up state-only programs that provide benefits and services to recipients who are excluded from federal TANF assistance or who face federal time limits on benefits. State funds designated as a TANF rainy-day account do not count toward the spending requirement at the time they are deposited, but if they are withdrawn later and spent on an allowable activity, they do count toward the requirement.

Changes in TANF-Related Spending between 1996 and 2000

If the same decline in welfare families since 1996 had occurred under AFDC, federal and state spending would have dropped dramatically, and funds per family would not have increased. Assuming that average cash assistance per welfare family remained constant between 1996 and 2000 (i.e., with no adjustment for inflation) and that states retained all emergency and JOBS assistance,[9] spending would have declined from $32 billion in 1996 to $17 billion in 2000. Instead, TANF expenditures in 2000 were $26 billion.

The focus of TANF-related spending also shifted considerably between 1996 and 2000 (figure 12-2). Cash assistance, consistently the largest category, accounted for over three-quarters of expenditures in 1996, but less than half of expenditures in 2000. Child care replaced administrative costs as the second-largest category, accounting for about one-fifth of TANF spending in 2000, or $5.3 billion.[10] Spending on work activities nearly doubled, and administrative costs declined.

While nearly half of the "other" TANF spending was unspecified, the details that were reported show that some states are setting off in new directions (figure 12-2). Most states transferred some TANF funds into their Social Services Block Grant and spent money on transportation assistance. Fewer states devoted TANF funds to family formation and out-of-wedlock pregnancy prevention, and only six states supported refundable tax credits. Finally, 32 states had separate state programs, which often provide cash assistance to families that the states wish to keep off the federal TANF rolls, such as two-parent families that face a 90 percent work participation requirement.[11]

The decline in cash spending reflects primarily the 50 percent decline in the number of welfare families,[12] not the race to the bottom that some analysts predicted when TANF passed. In fact, many states have increased TANF benefits since 1996. For example, a majority of states have increased the amount of earnings a recipient can keep and still receive some cash assistance, and a majority have adopted more liberal asset tests (Rowe and Roberts forthcoming). Twenty states increased the maximum TANF benefit, including seven whose increases exceeded the rate of inflation.[13] As was true under AFDC, the majority of states simply left their benefits unchanged, allowing inflation to gradually erode the benefits' value. Three states and the District of Columbia reduced their maximum TANF benefit between 1996 and 2000.

Figure 12-2. *Distribution of Federal and State Welfare Spending, 1996 and 2000 (in 2000 dollars)*

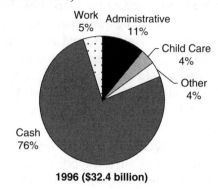

1996 ($32.4 billion)

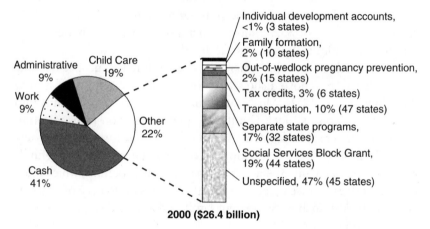

2000 ($26.4 billion)

Source: 1996 data collected from federal sources on individual spending on programs replaced by TANF; 2000 data from the ACF (2000c).

Because of wide variations in caseload decline and benefit policies, the share of TANF funds that states devoted to cash assistance varied considerably across the country (table 12-2). Only three states devoted more than half of their TANF expenditures to cash assistance in 2000. Two of these states increased maximum TANF benefits between 1996 and 2000, while one (Hawaii) decreased benefits substantially (from $712 to $570 for a family of three). At the other end of the spectrum, nine states spent less than one-quarter of TANF funds on cash assistance. With one exception, all of these states had had relatively large declines in the number of welfare

Table 12-2. *Share of TANF Funds Spent on Cash Assistance, 2000*[a]

TANF Funds for Cash Assistance (%)	States in Category
Less than 25	Colorado, Florida, Idaho, Indiana, Kansas, **Mississippi**, **South Carolina**, *Wisconsin*, Wyoming
25 to 35	**Alabama**, Arizona, **Arkansas**, Delaware, **Georgia**, Illinois, Massachusetts, Michigan, Nevada, **North Carolina**, Ohio, Oregon, **Texas**
35 to 45	Connecticut, District of Columbia, Iowa, **Kentucky**, **Louisiana**, Maryland, Missouri, Montana, *New Hampshire*, North Dakota, Oklahoma, South Dakota, **Tennessee**, Utah, Virginia, West Virginia (U.S. average = 41%)
45 to 55	*Alaska*, Maine, *Minnesota*, *Nebraska*, New Jersey, *New York*, Pennsylvania, *Rhode Island*, *Vermont*, Washington
55+	*California*, *Hawaii*, New Mexico

Source: Calculated from financial data from the ACF (2000b, 2000c).

Note: States in *italics* were in the top quintile for maximum monthly TANF benefits paid to a family of three in 2000 ($532 and above); states in **bold** were in the bottom quintile ($280 and below).

[a] Includes federal and state spending.

families since 1996, and had low demand for cash assistance. Only three of these nine states increased maximum benefits between 1996 and 2000.

Savings between 1996 and 2000

By the end of 2000, states had set aside $8.5 billion, or almost one-quarter of TANF dollars available for spending in 2000. (Available dollars included the federal TANF block grant for 2000, states' reported maintenance-of-effort spending for 2000, and accumulated unspent TANF funds from prior years.) States designated $5.3 billion of the unspent funds as unliquidated obligations and $3.2 billion as unobligated funds.

The size of these unspent TANF balances has occasioned considerable controversy. Some analysts argue that unspent balances provide evidence that states do not need all of their federal TANF allocations. Others point out that states need time to put programs in place and that some funds should be set aside for an economic downturn and an increase in the number of families needing assistance. Examination of the data suggests that states' TANF spending has evolved between 1996 and 2000. A large share of the unspent balances accumulated early in the program, but as time went by, states spent a larger fraction of each new year's allocation.[14]

Some states had spent all or most of their TANF funds by the end of 2000, whereas others had significant unspent balances (table 12-3). In general, states with relatively small unspent balances also had smaller-than-average increases in TANF funds per welfare family between 1996 and 2000 (table 12-1). While the relationship was not as clear-cut, states with large unspent balances tended to have average or large increases in TANF funds available per welfare family (table 12-1). That is, states with relatively more TANF funds available per welfare family tended to have more unspent funds. Relative spending on cash assistance also provides clues as to states' propensity to spend TANF dollars. States with low percentages of TANF funds spent on cash benefits (table 12-2) tended to have high levels of unspent funds. However, some states spent an above-average share of their TANF funds, yet devoted only a small share of those dollars to cash assistance, indicating a relative propensity to spend TANF dollars on new types of supports for low-income families (examples include Delaware, Kansas, Illinois, and Oregon). These relationships

Table 12-3. *Unspent Share of Total Available TANF Funds for 2000*[a]

Unspent TANF Funds (%)	States in Category
Less than 10	**Connecticut, Delaware, Illinois, Kansas, Kentucky, Maine**, Oregon, Rhode Island
10 to 20	Alaska, Hawaii, Massachusetts, Michigan, New Hampshire, Texas, Vermont, Virginia
20 to 30	Arizona, **California, Colorado**, Indiana, Iowa, Maryland, Missouri, New Mexico, New York, North Carolina, **South Carolina**, Tennessee, Washington (U.S. average = 24%)
30 to 40	Alabama, Arkansas, District of Columbia, **Florida**, Georgia, Idaho, Montana, Nebraska, North Dakota, Ohio, Oklahoma, **Pennsylvania**, South Dakota, Utah, Wisconsin
40+	Louisiana, Minnesota, Mississippi, **Nevada, New Jersey**, West Virginia, Wyoming

Source: Calculated from financial data from the ACF (2000b, 2000c).

Note: States in **bold** have no unobligated TANF funds.

[a] Available funds include the 2000 federal block grant and state maintenance-of-effort funds plus accumulated balances from prior years.

are very complex, however, and there are many exceptions to these general patterns.

Do States Spend TANF Funds for Other Purposes?

At the time of welfare reform, many analysts feared that the wide range of allowable expenditures under TANF would result in states using federal funds to supplant their own spending on low-income families. Supplantation is difficult to identify because it entails comparing observed state spending to the state spending that would have occurred if federal funding were unavailable. To investigate the question of supplantation, the GAO conducted a detailed analysis of pre- and post-TANF spending on low-income people in 10 states (GAO 2001). It concluded that supplantation occurred in 9 of the 10 states, but that most of the supplanted monies were used to increase funds for other types of programs that support low-income persons. For instance, although Michigan used federal TANF funds to finance a low-income homestead credit that had previously been financed with state funds, it used state funds to pay for child welfare activities that were not eligible for federal TANF funds. Connecticut directed $40 million of federal TANF monies to replace state expenditures on child welfare and early childhood development programs, arguing that the federal funds compensated the state for earlier state expenditures in these programs. Several other states increased funding of the State Children's Health Insurance Program.

With the evidence available, it is not possible to determine whether supplantation is widespread. While the GAO (2001) reports that only 2 states (New York and Wisconsin) of the 10 it studied decreased overall spending on programs for low-income people from 1995 to 2000, experience with other intergovernmental programs suggests that careful monitoring is needed. The GAO (1996) estimated that, on average, each dollar of federal revenue transferred to states results in only 40 cents of additional services; the other 60 cents supplant funds that would otherwise have been spent by the state.

TANF-related spending per low-income family declined by 12 percent, on average, between 1996 and 2000.[15] One factor in this decline, noted earlier, is that states are required to contribute only 75 to 80 percent of their prior spending. Another factor is the reduced buying power of federal and state TANF grants because of inflation. In addition, many states reserved some of the funds available for TANF.

This picture varies tremendously across states. Spending per low-income family increased by more than the rate of inflation in 16 states (table 12-4). In fact, spending increased by 15 percent or more in six states and the District of Columbia. Seventeen states fell at the other end of the spectrum, with spending declines of 15 percent or more; seven of these states had declines of 30 percent or more.

A number of factors influence states' spending per low-income family, including the desire to conserve funds rather than set up new programs. For example, all but one of the states (North Carolina) with the largest decline in spending per low-income family also fell into the highest categories of states having the most unspent funds (table 12-3), and many of these states, as noted earlier, had the highest increases in available resources per family under TANF (table 12-1). In other words, many states with large increases in resources per welfare family chose to save some of the additional money rather than shift all of it to new kinds of supports for low-income families. Some other states that did not have a large increase

Table 12-4. *Change in Real TANF-Related Spending per Low-Income Family, 1996–2000*

Change in Spending (%)	States in Category
+15 or more	Arkansas, Connecticut, District of Columbia, Indiana, Maryland, Rhode Island, Wisconsin
+1 to +15	Florida, Kansas, Kentucky, Michigan, Minnesota, Mississippi, Oklahoma, Tennessee, Virginia
0 to −15	Alabama, Arizona, Colorado, Delaware, Idaho, Iowa, Louisiana, Maine, Massachusetts, Montana, New Mexico, New York, Ohio, South Carolina, Texas, Vermont, Washington, West Virginia (U.S. average = −12%)
−15 to −30	Alaska, California, Georgia, Hawaii, Illinois, Missouri, New Hampshire, Oregon, South Dakota, Utah
−30 or more	Nebraska, Nevada, New Jersey, North Carolina, North Dakota, Pennsylvania, Wyoming

Sources: Calculated from financial data from the ACF (2000b, 2000c) and from authors' tabulations of the Current Population Surveys.

Note: Calculated as total federal and state TANF-related spending in the state in 1996 (adjusted to 2000 dollars) and in 2000, divided by the number of low-income families in each state (based on two-year average counts of low-income families from the 1995, 1996, 1998, and 1999 Current Population Surveys).

in resources per family also had relatively large declines in spending per low-income family, perhaps indicating a stronger desire to conserve funds than to begin new low-income programs. Pennsylvania is a particularly interesting example. It fell into the highest quintile of pre-TANF spending (table 12-1) and had a below-average increase in resources per welfare family, yet was among the states with the highest amounts of unspent funds and largest decreases in spending per low-income family. These shifts suggest a change in Pennsylvania's philosophy toward spending on low-income families relative to the pre-TANF era.

It is important to remember that low-income families in all states are receiving more support under TANF than they would have received under AFDC, assuming the same decline in caseloads. Spending on low-income families declined by 12 percent under the TANF block grant, but it would have declined by 42 percent from 1996 to 2000 under AFDC. While it is probably unrealistic to assume that welfare caseloads would have declined as quickly if AFDC had remained in place, this hypothetical situation does demonstrate that a drop-off in the number of people on welfare under AFDC would likely have resulted in a larger drop in federal and state spending than it did under TANF.

What Will Happen in a Recession?

The TANF spending picture to date reflects states' decisions during a period of national economic prosperity, when there was low unemployment, rapid economic growth, and low inflation. However, a recession began even before the terrorist attacks of September 11, 2001, and economic conditions worsened thereafter. States may face great pressure to redirect TANF funds in this environment.

In the past, increases in unemployment have been followed by increases in the number of welfare recipients, albeit with a lag time because potential recipients exhaust other means of support before resorting to welfare. A study based on AFDC-era data estimates that one year of a typical recession increases welfare expenditures by between $2.5 billion and $3.2 billion (roughly 9 to 12 percent of combined federal and state TANF spending in 2000) (Boyd and Davis 1998).[16]

Whether welfare spending will be more sensitive or less sensitive to macroeconomic conditions under TANF is not clear. Welfare reform's emphasis on work could increase the sensitivity of welfare costs to the business cycle, since more current and former recipients are working now than under AFDC (see chapter 2). Also, because TANF does not provide a federal match for states' expenditures, states have stronger incentives to cut the program as costs rise. However, because former recipients tend to work in the historically recession-resistant service sector, and because more former recipients may qualify for unemployment insurance, a post-TANF recession may not increase welfare rolls as much as predicted (Holzer 2000). Furthermore, because welfare reform placed lifetime limits on benefits, some potential claimants will not be eligible to return to TANF, and others may avoid returning in order to preserve their eligibility.

Possible State Strategies for Dealing with a Recession

Most states appear not to have done any formal contingency planning for economic downturns (GAO 2001). Currently, states have two options for dealing with a recession: drawing upon additional resources, or decreasing spending on welfare. Two alternatives—the TANF federal contingency fund and TANF loan funds—were not included in the 2002 budget and thus expired on September 30, 2001.

OPTION 1: ADDITIONAL RESOURCES

Additional resources could come from a state's TANF funds reserved in the federal treasury or from state tax increases. Most unobligated balances ($3.2 billion at the end of 2000) will be available through 2002—longer, if existing balances are maintained when TANF is reauthorized. Some of the $5.3 billion designated as unliquidated obligations might also be available. Even if states can use unliquidated balances, some states will face severe fiscal constraints if welfare costs rise. Eight states have balances of less than 10 percent of available TANF funds.

States could raise taxes to fund some of the increased welfare spending. Historically, legislated state tax changes have partially offset revenue changes caused by business-cycle fluctuations (Merriman 2000). Also, Dye and McGuire (1999) found that tax revenues rose in most states between 1977 and 1995, even during periods when gross state product fell.

OPTION 2: REDUCED SPENDING

States could cope with increased welfare costs by reducing TANF benefits and services. States might consider reducing cash benefits in order to provide support for more families. States could also reduce noncash assistance, such as child care, which accounts for 19 percent of TANF dollars. Reducing the number of families that receive free or subsidized child care may be more palatable than cutting cash assistance.

States could also protect TANF from cuts during a recession by cutting spending in other areas of their budgets. Most states financed welfare during periods of recession between 1977 and 1995 without reducing nonwelfare spending (Dye and McGuire 1999). States may be less likely to favor welfare spending under TANF, because they bear sole responsibility for marginal expenditure increases.

Policy Implications

TANF has transformed the face of welfare in the United States. As plummeting caseloads reduced the demand for cash benefits, TANF's fixed block grant and state maintenance-of-effort requirements provided states with funds to expand services for welfare families and for low-income working families with children that are not on welfare. The race to the bottom that some analysts feared has not materialized. However, serious concerns remain about the increasing disparity in the level of support for low-income families across the states and about the effects of an economic downturn on states' TANF programs. Congress should consider a number of financing issues during TANF reauthorization and future welfare policy deliberations.

TANF Funds Should Be Adjusted to Account for Inflation

By the end of 2000, inflation had already eroded about 11 percent of the real value of the 1996 TANF block grant. If no allowance is made for inflation, monies available to support low-income families will buy less child care, transportation, and basic cash assistance over time. Experience suggests that states will not make up the difference. Congress should adjust the value of federal TANF block grants and state spending requirements to compensate for eroded buying power. Although this represents an increased obligation for states, it protects the purchasing power of low-income families.

Cross-State Allocations Should Be Reconsidered

Because it is based so heavily on past expenditures, the allocation formula for TANF does little to adjust for changes in need or state performance over time. Even if past expenditures remain the primary basis for allocating TANF funds, Congress should revise the distribution formula to gradually place more emphasis on current need and state performance.

- *Congress should reduce the weight given to pre-1996 expenditures in the TANF distribution formula, and increase the weight for the needs of a state's population.* Using expenditures from 1992 to 1995 to allocate TANF grants makes less and less sense as time goes by. Pre-TANF expenditures were determined primarily by the proportion of a state's population on welfare, benefit levels, and matching rules. Since 1996, the goals of welfare have changed, as have states' needs for assisting low-income families. Allocation of TANF funds on the basis of almost any reasonable measure of need (e.g., the number of children living in poverty or the poverty rate) would result in a dramatic shift of funds among states (Merriman and Staveteig 2000).[17] Failure to target TANF funds on the basis of need is unfair to states that have disproportionately large low-income populations and numbers of residents on welfare. At a minimum, Congress should restore the supplemental grants. Yet Congress should also be mindful that greater emphasis on equity carries the risk of creating perverse incentives: States that perform poorly may have increased needs, and hence may secure more funding in the future.
- *Congress should phase in an increased weight for states that achieve program goals.* Congress should expand state performance bonuses to reflect additional goals, such as increasing the number of former and current welfare recipients successfully participating in work activities and reducing poverty among children. Although appropriate outcome measures are sometimes difficult to construct, they can provide powerful incentives for states to implement effective welfare programs (Merriman and Staveteig 2000).

States Should Be Held More Accountable for Spending

States now spend TANF funds on a wide variety of services, including child care, transportation, and promoting family formation. The diversity in state patterns of spending demonstrates the potential for innovation but also for supplantation. Monitoring is difficult because there are significant gaps in information about states' use of TANF funds, especially funds not yet withdrawn from the federal treasury.

- *Congress should require states to make full, timely, and comparable disclosures of their expenditures of both state and federal funds under TANF.* Such information should include details of all spending and an accounting for unspent funds. This will enable Congress to modify TANF legislation when needed.

Adequate Resources Should Be Available during Economic Downturns

In a significant recession, financial pressures on states will build.

- *Congress should ensure that states have incentives to plan for funding TANF over the business cycle.* Federal authorities should make a political pledge to ensure that TANF accounts in the federal treasury will be used exclusively to support low-income families. Congress might also allow states to designate a portion of their TANF balances as rainy-day funds.[18] Each state could establish its own standards for withdrawal of funds.
- *Congress should reinstate a less restrictive TANF contingency fund.* The original contingency fund, which expired in 2001, made it difficult for states to qualify even in the event of significant economic distress; moreover, no state could be assured of access to the fund, because the total amount was fixed at $2 billion (Posner 2001). Congress should reauthorize a contingency fund, and include in it more realistic criteria for benefits and guaranteed access to every state that meets the criteria. This would shift financial risk from the states to the federal government, which is better able to manage it.

NOTES

We thank Ed Lazere, Zoë Neuberger, Paul Posner, Matthew Stagner, and Alan Weil for their comments on earlier drafts of this chapter, and Desiree Principe for her research assistance.

1. Throughout this chapter, references to years indicate federal fiscal years. Thus, for example, "2000" refers to the period from October 1, 1999, to September 30, 2000. Data for 2000 are those reported by the federal government as of June 29, 2001 (Department of Health and Human Services, Administration for Children and Families [ACF] 2000c).

2. For 24 states and the District of Columbia, funding was based on spending in fiscal year 1994, the year in which national spending was highest. Funding was based on fiscal year 1995 spending for 17 states, and on the average of 1992 to 1994 spending for the remaining 9.

3. PRWORA reduces the minimum work participation rate for states whose average monthly caseload was lower in the previous year than in 1995. While many states have met the participation targets without using their caseload reduction credits, others have benefited from this provision in the law. All states met the one-parent and all-family participation rates in 1999; however, eight states did not meet the 90 percent two-parent participation requirement, even with the caseload reduction credit. These states face potential financial penalties (ACF 2000a). As explained later in the text, many states maintained an 80 percent or higher maintenance-of-effort, even though their requirement was 75 percent.

4. Authors' calculations from data in U.S. House of Representatives, Committee on Ways and Means (2000), Lazere (2001), and ACF (2000c).

5. For example, state spending under the Child Care and Development Fund and Social Services Block Grant (SSBG) is excluded, because these grants do not count toward states' maintenance-of-effort spending. State spending for child care and social services under the SSBG predates TANF, and to the extent that it continues is not TANF spending. The federal government still provides states with separate monies for SSBG, but these dollars are not counted as federal TANF spending. Non-TANF health and child welfare spending are also excluded. In contrast, the U.S. General Accounting Office (GAO) took a much broader approach in its examination of supplantation (2001) by including, for example, state spending on children's health care.

6. A larger share of welfare recipients now combine paid work with cash benefits, because many states have increased the amount of earnings a recipient can keep and still receive some cash assistance. However, these so-called earned income disregards are much more effective work incentives in states that have relatively high benefits. In states with low cash benefits, the advantages of being on welfare phase out rapidly once recipients have some earned income.

7. The CCDF requires that families receiving assistance have children under age 13 and incomes below 85 percent of the state median. In addition, a large share of these funds must be earmarked to assist families trying to be independent of TANF cash assistance. The SSBG provides funds for services related to reducing dependency, maintaining self-sufficiency, and remedying neglect and inappropriate institutional care.

8. The federal government prohibits states from drawing down funds until those funds are expended.

9. Historically, states have not adjusted benefits to keep up with inflation (Zedlewski and Giannarelli 1997).

10. Total child care funds reported here differ from those in chapter 7 because this chapter includes state child care spending, while that chapter focuses on federal spending. Also, chapter 7 uses federal child care spending reported by the Center on Law and Social Policy, which shows an additional $400,000 in TANF transfers to the CCDF compared to data reported by the federal government.

11. Since some benefits paid through state-only programs are cash assistance, the total share spent on cash assistance reported earlier is somewhat understated. However, it is not possible to break out the spending on cash assistance in separate state programs.

12. Authors' calculations, based on average monthly families data from the U.S. House of Representatives' Committee on Ways and Means (2000) for 1996 through 1999, and from ACF (2000c) for 2000.

13. Calculated from Rowe and Roberts (forthcoming), p. 145, table L5.

14. Falk (2001) reports that the following totals have accumulated over time: $6.3 billion in unspent funds in 1998, of which $3.0 billion was unobligated; $6.9 billion in 1999, with $2.2 billion unobligated; and $8.6 billion in 2000, with $3.2 billion unobligated. In addition, because states have been spending at a higher rate than expected, both the Office of Management and Budget and the Congressional Budget Office increased expected outlays for TANF in their 2001 midyear reports.

15. Changes in spending per low-income family (under 200 percent of the federal poverty level, the income cutoff for assistance set by TANF) were calculated for 1996 and 2000 after adjusting for the effects of inflation. The calculations also take into account changes in the number of low-income families in each state between 1996 and 2000 (a decline of 7 percent, on average).

16. This estimate is based on the assumption of a 3.5 percent increase in welfare families for each 1 percent increase in unemployment. The caseload responds to many different factors, including states' economic environments and welfare policies, and it is difficult to predict change with precision. See, for example, Bell (2001) for a review of the recent literature explaining the recent decline in welfare caseloads.

17. The percentage of people who are on welfare (a determinant of funding under AFDC) is often not proportional to the percentage of people who are in poverty (a possible indicator of need) because states differ in the degree to which residents in poverty receive assistance.

18. Posner (2001) also suggests that states be allowed to draw down their entire grant at the beginning of the year to eliminate the risk that Congress will interpret state savings as unneeded funds that can be reallocated elsewhere.

REFERENCES

ACF. See U.S. Department of Health and Human Services, Administration for Children and Families.

Bell, Stephen H. 2001. *Why Are Caseloads Falling?* Washington, D.C.: The Urban Institute. *Assessing the New Federalism* Discussion Paper 01-02.

Boyd, Donald J., and Elizabeth Davis 1998. "Welfare Reform and Expenditure Pressures in the Next Recession." In *National Tax Association Proceedings—1997* (3–14). Washington, D.C.: National Tax Association.

Brueckner, Jan K. 1999. *Welfare Reform and Interstate Welfare Competition: Theory and Evidence*. Washington, D.C.: The Urban Institute. *Assessing the New Federalism* Occasional Paper No. 21.

Dye, Richard F., and Therese McGuire. 1999. *State Fiscal Systems and Business Cycles: Implications for Welfare Spending when the Next Recession Occurs*. Washington, D.C.: The Urban Institute. *Assessing the New Federalism* Discussion Paper 99-04.

Falk, Gene. 2001. *Welfare Reform: TANF Grants, Transfers, and Unspent Funds Through FY 2000*. Washington, D.C.: Congressional Research Service.

GAO. See U.S. General Accounting Office.

Holzer, Harry J. 2000. "Unemployment Insurance and Welfare Recipients: What Happens when the Recession Comes?" Washington, D.C.: The Urban Institute. *Assessing the New Federalism* Policy Brief A-46.

Lazere, Ed. 2001. *Unspent TANF Funds at the End of Federal Fiscal Year 2000*. Washington, D.C.: Center on Budget and Policy Priorities. http://www.cbpp.org/1-22-01sfp00sur-plus.pdf. (Accessed August 1, 2001.)

Merriman, David. 2000. "Economic Conditions and State Tax Policy: Experience over the Last Decade and Implications for the Future." Washington, D.C.: The Urban Institute. *Assessing the New Federalism* Policy Brief A-40.

Merriman, David, and Sarah Staveteig. July 2000. "How Should the Federal Government Distribute TANF Funds among States? Tools to Evaluate Current and Alternative Allocations." Washington, D.C.: The Urban Institute. Photocopy.

National Conference of State Legislatures. 1999. "Analysis of the Personal Responsibility and Work Opportunity Reconciliation Act of 1996." http://www.ncsl.org/statefed/hr3734.htm. (Accessed November 19, 2001.)

Posner, Paul. 2001. "Testimony before the Subcommittee on Human Resources of the House Committee on Ways and Means: Hearing on 'Rainy Day' and Other Special TANF Funds". April 26. http://waysandmeans.house.gov/humres/107cong/4-26-01/r-26posn.htm. (Accessed August 1, 2001.)

Rowe, Gretchen, and Tracy Roberts. Forthcoming. *Welfare Rules Databook: State TANF Policies as of July 2000*. Washington, D.C.: The Urban Institute. *Assessing the New Federalism*.

U.S. Congress. 1996. *Personal Responsibility and Work Opportunity Reconciliation Act* (Public Law 104-193). Washington, D.C.: Government Printing Office.

U.S. Department of Health and Human Services, Administration for Children and Families. 2000a. *Temporary Assistance for Needy Families Program: Third Annual Report to Congress*. Washington, D.C.: Government Printing Office. August.

———. 2000b. *4th-Quarter FY 1998 TANF Data*. http://www.acf.dhhs.gov/programs/ofs/data. (Accessed June 29, 2001.)

———. 2000c. *4th-Quarter FY 2000 TANF Data*. http://www.acf.dhhs.gov/programs/ofs/data. (Accessed June 29, 2001.)

U.S. General Accounting Office. 1996. *Federal Grants: Design Improvements Could Help Federal Resources Go Further*. Washington, D.C.: General Accounting Office.

———. 2001. *Challenges in Maintaining a Federal-State Fiscal Partnership*. Washington, D.C.: General Accounting Office.

U.S. House of Representatives, Committee on Ways and Means. 2000. *2000 Green Book*. Washington, D.C.: U.S. Government Printing Office.

Zedlewski, Sheila R., and Linda Giannarelli. 1997. "Diversity among State Welfare Programs: Implications for Reform." Washington, D.C.: The Urban Institute. *Assessing the New Federalism* Policy Brief A-1.

Table of Acronyms

ACF	Administration for Children and Families, DHHS
AFDC	Aid to Families with Dependent Children
ANF	*Assessing the New Federalism*
ASPE	Assistant Secretary for Planning and Evaluation, DHHS
CCDF	Child Care and Development Fund
CPS	Current Population Survey
DHHS	United States Department of Health and Human Services
EITC	Earned Income Tax Credit
FPL	Federal Poverty Level
FSA	Family Support Act of 1988
FY	Fiscal Year
GA	General Assistance
GAO	United States General Accounting Office
JOBS	Job Opportunities and Basic Skills Training Program
NSAF	National Survey of America's Families
PRWORA	Personal Responsibility and Work Opportunity Reconciliation Act of 1996
SCHIP	State Children's Health Insurance Program
SSI	Supplemental Security Income
TANF	Temporary Assistance for Needy Families
TRIM3	Transfer Income Model, Version 3
WIA	Workforce Investment Act of 1988
WRD	Welfare Rules Database
WtW	Welfare-to-Work Grants Program

Urban Institute Data Resources for Welfare Reform

Assessing the New Federalism (ANF) Case Studies

The explicit emphasis on devolution as a component of welfare reform makes it particularly necessary to study what is happening in the field. Even under AFDC, important aspects of welfare policy were determined state by state, county by county, or caseworker by caseworker; a researcher looking only at statutes and regulations might miss the variations in administrative practices that developed. In order to obtain better information on welfare administration, ANF conducted case studies of 17 sites in 13 states (table A-1).[1]

The first set of ANF case studies was conducted in 1996 and 1997 to provide a baseline for understanding whatever changes might emerge from welfare reform. A second set of case studies was completed in 1999 and 2000 to examine the changes that did occur.[2] Study teams visited each of the sites and conducted semi-structured interviews with staff responsible for TANF, workforce development, child care, and child welfare program administration and delivery. These interviews with staff were conducted from the state level to local offices. Discussions with advocates and other knowledgeable people in the community were used to supplement information from interviews with agency staff. The child care case studies also included focus groups with parents receiving child care subsidies.

Table A-1. *ANF Targeted States and Case Study Sites*

State	Site	County
Alabama	Birmingham	Jefferson
California	Los Angeles	Los Angeles
	Oakland	Alameda
	San Diego	San Diego
Colorado	Denver	Denver
Florida	Miami	Dade
	Tampa	Hillsborough
Massachusetts	Boston	Suffolk
Michigan	Detroit	Wayne
Minnesota	Minneapolis	Hennepin
Mississippi	Jackson	Hinds
New Jersey	Jersey City	Hudson
New York	Buffalo	Erie
Texas	El Paso	El Paso
	Houston	Harris
Washington	Seattle	King
Wisconsin	Milwaukee	Milwaukee

State updates based on the recent case studies are available at http://newfederalism.urban.org/html/state_focus.html, as are the baseline case studies.

National Survey of America's Families (NSAF)

The NSAF produces reliable state-specific and national estimates on a wide range of child, adult, and family well-being measures, with particularly precise estimates for people in families with incomes below 200 percent of the federal poverty threshold. The 13 targeted states (table A-1) account for about half of the total population of the United States, and represent a broad range of fiscal capacity, indicators of child well-being, and approaches to government programs. Interviews conducted in all other states and the District of Columbia allow for the production of reliable national estimates as well.

In order to produce estimates of change over time, the survey is conducted in multiple rounds. The first round was conducted in 1997 and the second in 1999, with a third round being conducted in 2002. In each round, data were collected on more than 100,000 people living in more than 42,000 households.

The NSAF sample includes households with and without telephones. A random-digit dialing (RDD) frame, or random sample of telephone numbers, is used to cover households with telephones. This sample is supplemented with an area sample of households without telephones. Interviews with nontelephone households were carried out using cellular phones carried by field staff.

Child Trends developed and analyzed the measures of child well-being used in the NSAF. Public use data and methodology reports can be obtained from http://newfederalism.urban.org/nsaf/index.htm.

Welfare Rules Database (WRD)

The WRD is a longitudinal database of state AFDC and TANF policies since 1996. Rules for all 50 states and the District of Columbia are included. The WRD organizes the detailed information on welfare rules across states, time, and geographic areas within states, and by different types of assistance units. Caseworker manuals and state regulations provide the data from 1997 to the present, while AFDC State Plans and Waiver Terms and Conditions provide the data for 1996.

Funding for the initial development of the WRD and for the coding of the rules through 1999 was provided by ANF. The Department of Health and Human Services' Administration for Children and Families (ACF) is now funding the continued development of the WRD and annual updates starting with the 2000 data.

The WRD can be accessed via an online point-and-click interface at http://anfdata.urban.org/wrd/WRDWelcome.CFM. Rowe and Roberts (forthcoming) provide an overview of the database, as well as tables summarizing TANF policies for each state as of July 2000. Longitudinal tables showing a subset of state policies from 1996 to 2000 are also included.

Transfer Income Model (TRIM3)

TRIM3 is a microsimulation model developed by the Urban Institute. The model calculates the effects of complex, large-scale governmental transfer, tax, and health programs at the individual, family, state, and national levels. Since the 1960s, analysts have used TRIM3 and its predecessors to understand the potential outcomes of public policy changes, such as welfare reform, tax reform, and national health care reform.

TRIM3 corrects for the underreporting of participation in transfer programs by identifying additional participants from among those simulated as eligible according to program rules. For each transfer program, the final simulated caseload reaches administrative totals. TRIM3 can be used for analysis across programs and for what-if experiments that simulate the effects of changes in program parameters. Input data come from the annual March Current Population Survey (CPS).

Recent work has made it possible to use NSAF data as input. The most important aspects of TRIM3 for the purposes of NSAF-TRIM work are the corrections for underreporting and the imputation of variables that are not directly available from NSAF, such as federal income tax liability and the actual or potential value of the EITC for a particular family.

Primary funding for the development of TRIM3 has come from the Department of Health and Human Services, Office of the Assistant Secretary for Planning and Evaluation (ASPE). Development of TRIM3 for NSAF data has been supported by ANF.

The public-use Web interface, at http://trim3.urban.org/T3Welcome. cfm, includes training materials, a data dictionary, rules for simulated programs, and microdata. Additional features are available to registered users.

NOTES

The editors thank Linda Giannarelli, Pamela A. Holcomb, Gretchen Rowe, and Kevin Wang for their suggestions.

1. Welfare reform has stimulated increased interest in the implementation of TANF and related programs and policies. For example, the Nelson A. Rockefeller Institute of Government at the State University of New York, Albany, is also examining local welfare implementation.

2. At the time of the second round, it was not possible to cover TANF and workforce development in New York City, or child care and child welfare in Jackson. All four topic areas were covered for both sites in the first round of case studies.

REFERENCES

Rowe, Gretchen, and Tracy Roberts. Forthcoming. *Welfare Rules Databook: State TANF Policies as of July 2000.* Washington, D.C.: The Urban Institute. *Assessing the New Federalism.*

About the Editors

Alan Weil is director of the Urban Institute's *Assessing the New Federalism* project. His research focuses on health policy, welfare policy, and federalism. He was the executive director of the Colorado Department of Health Care Policy and Financing. He received his J.D. from Harvard Law School and an M.P.P. from the John F. Kennedy School of Government.

Kenneth Finegold is a senior research associate with the Urban Institute's *Assessing the New Federalism* project. His research interests include the U.S. federal system, state policy, race and ethnicity, and fiscal issues. Dr. Finegold is the author of *Experts and Politicians: Reform Challenges to Machine Politics in New York, Cleveland, and Chicago* and, with Theda Skocpol, *State and Party in America's New Deal.* He received his Ph.D. in government from Harvard and his A.B. in government from Cornell.

About the Authors

Gina Adams is a senior research associate at the Urban Institute, where she codirects child care research. Her current research includes multistate studies on child care subsidy implementation, analyses of child care data from the National Survey of America's Families, research on child care providers and subsidy policies, and the National Head Start Impact Study. She was the assistant director of the Child Care and Development Division at the Children's Defense Fund. She was also a child care teacher, and has worked with low-income families. She has an M.A. in public policy from Duke University.

Martha R. Burt directs the Urban Institute's Social Services Research Program; her career has spanned many aspects of public policy relating to vulnerable populations. She participated in the first round of ANF case studies, and wrote the Minnesota state report and a brief analyzing linkages among safety net programs at the beginning of federal welfare reform. She directed the second round of income support and social services case studies, and orchestrated production of state updates and analytic papers based on case study findings. Dr. Burt received her Ph.D. in sociology from the University of Wisconsin-Madison in 1972.

Michael Fix is an attorney and principal research associate at the Urban Institute, where he directs the Immigration Studies Program. His previous publications include *Overlooked and Underserved: Immigrant Students in U.S. Secondary Schools* (with Jorge Ruiz-de-Velasco) and "All Under One Roof: Immigrant Families in an Era of Reform" (with Wendy Zimmermann).

John F. Holahan is director of the Urban Institute's Health Policy Research Center. Dr. Holahan has managed numerous health research projects in the last 25 years and authored many books and papers on health policy. Much of his work has focused on the Medicaid program, as well as state health policy more broadly, and issues of federalism and health. He has also published research on the reasons for the growth in the uninsured over the past decade and on the effects of proposals to expand health insurance coverage on the number of uninsured and the cost to federal and state governments.

Pamela A. Holcomb, a senior research associate, joined the Urban Institute in 1985. Her research has addressed a wide range of issues concerning poverty, welfare, employment, training, and social services. She has focused special attention on identifying factors that affect policy implementation and institutional performance, particularly in the area of welfare reform. She directed the second round of TANF case studies for ANF, and is currently engaged in several other implementation studies of welfare reform.

Robert I. Lerman, director of the Urban Institute's Labor and Social Policy Center, is a professor of economics at American University. He has written widely on welfare, income inequality, child support, youth employment, and fatherhood issues, and has worked on government efforts to reform welfare programs. Dr. Lerman's publications include the prize-winning essay "Separating Income Support from Income Supplementation" (Institute for Socioeconomic Studies, 1985), and "Retreat or Reform: New U.S. Strategies for Dealing with Poverty," in *Social Policy Review* (2000). Dr. Lerman earned his A.B. from Brandeis University and his Ph.D. in economics from the Massachusetts Institute of Technology.

Pamela J. Loprest is a labor economist and senior research associate at the Urban Institute. Dr. Loprest's research focuses on low-wage labor markets and barriers to work among disadvantaged populations. Her work includes study of the economic status and employment prospects of former welfare recipients, including how former welfare recipients transition into the labor market, how welfare agencies serve recipients with disabilities, and the impact of disability among welfare recipients on work. Dr. Loprest has a Ph.D. in economics from the Massachusetts Institute of Technology and has been at the Urban Institute since 1991.

Karin Martinson is a consultant to the Urban Institute. She has over 15 years of experience as both a researcher and a policy analyst on a range of issues related to low-income families, including welfare reform, employment and training programs, child support, and child care. She has extensive experience designing and conducting implementation and process research. She was a senior policy analyst at the Office of the Assistant Secretary for Planning and Evaluation at DHHS and a researcher at the Manpower Demonstration Research Corporation (MDRC).

David Merriman is a professor of economics at Loyola University Chicago. He spent the 1999–2000 academic year as a senior research associate in the Urban Institute's *Assessing the New Federalism* project. He specializes in state and local public finance. Professor Merriman's past research has included studies of the distributional effects of state income and sales taxes, differing rates of health care expenditure growth across states, and the impact of cigarette tax increases on state revenues. He received a Ph.D. in economics from the University of Wisconsin-Madison in 1983.

Kristin Anderson Moore, a social psychologist, is president and senior scholar of Child Trends. She studies trends in child and family well-being, the effects of family structure and social change on children, positive development, the determinants and consequences of adolescent parenthood, and the effects of welfare and welfare reform on children. She is a member of the Family and Child Well-Being Research Network, which examines factors enhancing children's development and well-being. She also serves on the Advisory Council for the National Institute of Child Health and Human Development. In 1999, Dr. Moore received the Foundation for Child Development Centennial Award for linking research on children's development to policies that serve the public interest.

Demetra Smith Nightingale is a principal research associate in the Urban Institute's Labor and Social Policy Center, where she is director of the Welfare and Training Research Program. She is an expert in social policy, and for over 25 years has conducted research on employment, welfare, and poverty. Her recent books include *The Low-Wage Labor Market: Challenges and Opportunities for Economic Self-Sufficiency*, coedited with Kelleen Kaye, and *The Government We Deserve: Responsive Democracy and Changing Expectations*, coauthored with C. Eugene Steuerle, Edward Gramlich, and Hugh Heclo. She holds a Ph.D. in public policy from the George Washington University.

Jeffrey S. Passel is a principal research associate at the Urban Institute, where he has focused on the impacts and integration of immigrants on American society, and the demography of immigration. Prior to joining the Urban Institute in 1989, Dr. Passel directed the Census Bureau's program of population estimates and projections and its research on demographic methods for measuring census undercount. Dr. Passel is a Fellow of the American Association for the Advancement of Science. He has a Ph.D. in social relations from the Johns Hopkins University, an M.A. in sociology from the University of Texas at Austin, and a B.S. in mathematics from the Massachusetts Institute of Technology.

Monica Rohacek is a research associate at the Urban Institute, where she conducts research on child care and early education. Her main areas of interest include the supply, demand, and costs of child care; child care workforce issues; the child care subsidy system; and related national, state, and local policies. She is currently working on the National Head Start Impact Study, on a study about child care providers and subsidy policies, and on a project examining the availability and use of child care policy variables for research.

Juliet P. Scarpa is a senior research assistant at Child Trends; she has a background in sociology, and particular interest in criminology, deviance, and community ecology. Ms. Scarpa has provided analytical and programming support, as well as synthesizing research materials for literature reviews, for multiple Child Trends projects. In addition, she has provided support for many *Assessing the New Federalism* papers and briefs using NSAF data.

Sarah Staveteig is a research associate with the Urban Institute's *Assessing the New Federalism* project, where she has participated in research on topics relating to the devolution of social policy. She has analyzed quantitative data from the NSAF, and has published papers on racial and ethnic inequalities in the United States and on marginal tax rates facing low-income families. She helped manage social impact surveys in southern Africa. She earned a B.A. in sociology from Grinnell College.

Kathryn Tout is a senior research associate at Child Trends. She is a developmental psychologist with a background in the study of children's socioemotional development, early childhood care and education, and welfare policy. As part of the *Assessing the New Federalism* project, Dr. Tout has used the NSAF to analyze variations in child care patterns for children of different ages and with different family characteristics. She also participated in case studies investigating state child care policies and practices under welfare reform.

Sharon Vandivere is a senior research analyst at Child Trends. She is interested in adolescent risk-taking behaviors, the well-being of children in poverty, and child abuse and neglect. She has coauthored a number of briefs through the *Assessing the New Federalism* project. In addition, she coedits *The Child Indicator,* a quarterly newsletter focusing on social indicators.

Martha Zaslow is a developmental psychologist and a senior scholar at Child Trends. She also serves as director of the Content Areas on Welfare and Poverty and Early Childhood Development at Child Trends. Her work focuses on the development of children in poverty. In particular, she has studied the implications of the family, child care, and policy contexts on the development of young children and adolescents.

Sheila R. Zedlewski is the director of the Urban Institute's Income and Benefits Policy Center. Ms. Zedlewski's research deals with welfare reform, participation in safety net programs, and poverty. She is also an expert on the development and use of microsimulation models to address the effects of taxes and spending programs on the distribution of income. Her recently published articles examine the relationship between welfare reform and Food Stamp program participation and the changing characteristics of families in cash assistance programs, including levels of disadvantage among those who have remained on welfare.

Index